lip Kerr & Ceri Jones

Str   /ard

dent's Book

MACMILLAN

Contents

		Reading & Listening	Speaking	Writing	
				Student's Book	**Workbook**
7A	R	*ecochat*	Persuading others to make lifestyle changes	An email to a friend p132	Writing to a friend (1): opening & closing emails, inviting, register
7B	L	Conversation about home improvements	Judging a green lifestyle competition		
7C	R	*Close up: life coaching*	Roleplay: life-coaching session		
7D	L	Three experts' future predictions	*Did you know?* Martha Stewart		
8A	R	*How to ... have a heavy cold*	Talking about ill health Roleplay: health problems		Writing to a friend (2): short notes & messages
8B	L	Radio programme about health insurance	*Did you know?* Australia's flying doctors		
8C	R	*The Office Doctors: an alternative approach to fighting stress*	Discussing creating a healthy environment		
8D	L	Five conversations about back pain	Discussing lifestyle changes		
9A	R	*Celebrity Worship Syndrome*	Talking about role models	A story p134	Writing a story (1): avoiding repetition, punctuating direct speech
9B	L	Two radio news items about Monkey Man	Inventing a superhero *Did you know?* Wonder Woman		
9C	R	*Win 100 DVDs*	Talking about screen villains		
9D	L	Radio programme about a job survey	Discussing annoying situations		
10A	R	*Why are humans good?*	Talking about altruism		Writing a story (2): a story with a twist in the tale
10B	L	Conversation about a charity shop	Deciding on a course of action *Did you know?* Charity-giving in the UK		
10C	R	*A day in the life of ...*	Describing job responsibilities		
10D	L	Job interview	Job interview: advising a friend Roleplay: a job interview		
11A	R	*1421: The Year China Discovered America?*	Talking about an itinerary for a cruise	A report p136	Writing a report (1): beginning and ending a report, describing a place, linking words
11B	L	Conversation about a map	Choosing five important places		
11C	R	Happiness throughout the world	Ranking happiness factors		
11D	L	Interview with a location scout	*Did you know?* Universal Studios		
12A	R	*Cocos Island*	Discussing pirate films		Writing a report (2): a report about a meeting
12B	L	Radio programme about Domino Harvey	Reporting a news story		
12C	R	Article about scam-baiting	Talking about personal experiences		
12D	L	Radio programme about the dollar bill	Discussing money *Did you know?* The history of credit cards		

1A | Consuming passions

SPEAKING & VOCABULARY: leisure interests

1 Work in pairs. Look at the photos A–D and answer the questions.

- What are the hobbies of the people in the photos?
- Do you think these are strange or normal hobbies?
- What do you think they do on a typical day devoted to their hobby?

2 Read the texts. Match the descriptions 1–4 to the photos A–D.

1

Matthew Gibbon has been a supporter of the Scottish national rugby team for as long as he can remember. As a schoolboy, he was crazy about the sport, but he became more and more obsessed with it. He now reckons that he devotes about 30 hours a week to training, playing or watching games.

2

It was a colleague at work who first suggested that Charlotte Pullman should give paintballing a try. Charlotte quickly got a taste for it and now spends every weekend running around with a paint gun in her hand. 'It's a great way of meeting people,' she says, 'and it also takes my mind off work.'

3

As a teenager Greg Schutz and his friends were all big fans of *Star Trek*, but Greg's interest turned into a passion. Greg got the 'Trekkie' bug in a big way and became a real aficionado, setting up his own website and organizing annual conventions.

4

Tony O'Neill was always keen on ghost stories, but decided to take up ghost hunting after watching a TV documentary about it. 'Once you're into it, there's no turning back,' says Tony, who has spent over £30,000 on the specialized equipment he needs. 'I wouldn't call it a hobby,' he says, 'it's more a way of life.'

3 Work in pairs. Look at the highlighted words and phrases in the descriptions 1–4 in exercise 2 and put them into three groups of meaning. Use a dictionary if necessary.

4 Think of two people that you know and talk about their interests using the phrases in exercise 3.

READING

1 Read the article and choose the best title 1–3.

1 Great ways to lose your job
2 The truth can be dangerous
3 What not to put on your CV

People write such strange things on their CVs that it's tempting to believe that they don't want the job at all. What, for example, was going through the mind of the applicant who wrote
5 that his previous contract had been terminated because 'they insisted that we get to work by 8.45 every morning and I couldn't work under those conditions'? Or the candidate who described himself as 'married, eight children,
10 would prefer frequent travel'. And let's not forget the typos – people who are proud of their 'rabid typing' or who announce that they were responsible for 'ruining their company's sales department'.

15 But the most revealing part of a CV is often the 'personal interests' section. Job seekers need to make their application stand out, so there's little point in saying that you're into pop music, that you like going to the cinema or that you've
20 been a supporter of your local football club for ten years. And if you're thinking of putting down something more original, think carefully. The fact that you have a passion for rock climbing and have been training for the World
25 Championships may be of central importance in your life, but prospective employers are more likely to think 'Uh-oh, dangerous, injuries, absences ...' Most bosses would rather their employees didn't risk their lives every weekend.

30 A recent survey has shown that one in four CVs contain a lie of some kind, but resist the temptation to
35 invent an interesting background for yourself. If, at the interview, you <u>are asked</u> questions
40 about your voluntary work with those with special needs, you could find yourself in deep water if you made it all up. Even the truth, however well-meaning, can be dangerous. One
45 job applicant who <u>was obviously trying</u> to make a good impression wrote that she had taken up blood-donating (fourteen gallons so far!). Weird.

The simple rule to remember is that you are applying for a job, so only include personal interests that are
50 relevant to the application. Do your research carefully and identify what personal qualities <u>are being looked for</u>. Only decide what to write when you <u>have found out</u> what the job involves. And if you can think of nothing relevant to say, just say nothing at all!

"Well I don't think much of your CV, but your paper clip is the smartest I've ever seen."

2 Read the article again and find examples of ...

1 an unfortunate typing mistake.
2 dishonest information.
3 completely uninteresting information.
4 information which says too much about the candidate's personal life.
5 information which shows that the candidate is not a reliable employee.
6 information which will worry an employer.

In your opinion, which was the most foolish thing to include on a CV?

3 What would you put in the personal interests section on your own CV? Compare your answer with other students.

GRAMMAR: verb forms review

1 Match the underlined verbs in the text to the labels in the box.

present simple   present continuous
present perfect   present perfect continuous
past simple   past continuous   past perfect

Which verbs are a) active b) passive?

2 Complete the question tags with the auxiliary verbs in the box.

are (x2)   do   have   were   did

1 You don't have any strange hobbies, _____ you?
2 You've never been obsessed with anything, _____ you?
3 You're not thinking of taking up a new sport, _____ you?
4 You're not a football supporter, _____ you?
5 As a child, you weren't a fan of Britney Spears, _____ you?
6 You never got into stamp collecting, _____ you?

3 Work in pairs. Discuss the questions in exercise 2.

Simple tenses: present and past
Simple tenses do not normally have an auxiliary in affirmative sentences.

	simple verb form	
People He	*write* *became*	*such strange things.* *more and more obsessed.*

Use *do/does/did* if an auxiliary is needed.
I had a great time. Did you?

Perfect verb forms
Make perfect verb forms with *have* + past participle.

	have	**past participle**	
She Tony	*had* *has*	*taken* *spent*	*up blood-donating.* *over £30,000.*

Continuous verb forms
Make continuous verb forms with *be* + verb + *-ing*.

	be	**verb + -ing**	
She	*was*	*trying*	*to make a good impression.*
You	*have been*	*training*	*for the World Championships.*

Passive verb forms
Make passive verbs with *be* + past participle.

	be	*past participle*
His contract	*had been*	*terminated.*

▶ SEE LANGUAGE REFERENCE PAGE 14

1B | Paintballing

LISTENING

1 Look at the poster and answer the questions below.

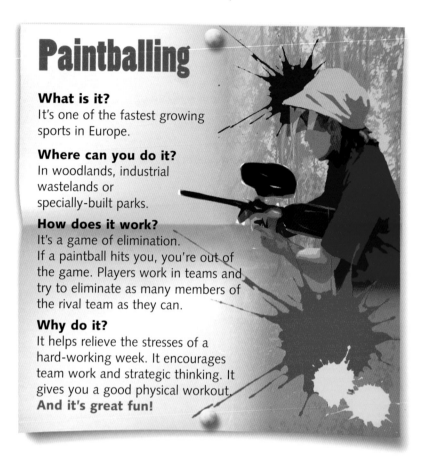

Paintballing

What is it?
It's one of the fastest growing sports in Europe.

Where can you do it?
In woodlands, industrial wastelands or specially-built parks.

How does it work?
It's a game of elimination. If a paintball hits you, you're out of the game. Players work in teams and try to eliminate as many members of the rival team as they can.

Why do it?
It helps relieve the stresses of a hard-working week. It encourages team work and strategic thinking. It gives you a good physical workout. **And it's great fun!**

- Is paintballing popular in your country?
- Have you ever tried it? If not, would you like to? Why or why not?

2 🔘 1.1 Listen to three workmates (Dave, Jayne and Harry) discussing paintballing and decide if the sentences below are true or false.

1 Dave knows a lot about paintballing.
2 Jayne thinks paintballing is dangerous but would be happy to try it.
3 Harry tries to keep the peace between Jayne and Dave.

3 🔘 1.1 Listen again and complete the information.

1 Dave has won _____ paintballing championships.
2 Jayne calls paintballing a type of _____ game.
3 Dave compares paintballing to _____.
4 Jayne says paintballing was designed to be used for _____.
5 According to Dave its original use was for _____.
6 Jayne says that paint guns are _____.
7 Dave suggests that _____ bats can also be used to hurt people.
8 Harry suggests that Jayne should _____.

4 Do you think that paintballing should be banned?

GRAMMAR: negatives & questions

1 Make the verbs in bold negative.

1 Jayne**'s** a big fan of paintballing.
2 Dave**'s been training** very hard recently.
3 Harry **knows** a lot about the sport.
4 Jayne**'d like** to see paintballing banned.
5 Dave**'d heard** people criticizing paintballing before.
6 Jayne**'ll be going** paintballing with Dave some time soon.

2 Complete the questions with the correct form of the auxiliary verbs in the box. Leave a blank if an auxiliary is not needed.

be do have

1 When _____ you going? Tomorrow, isn't it?
2 National champion? How long _____ you been doing that, then?
3 _____ I touched a raw nerve there?
4 Who _____ started it off? _____ n't it designed for training soldiers?
5 What _____ happened? _____ anyone get hurt?
6 What _____ you saying? _____ you suggesting the sport should be banned?

3 Check your answers in tapescript 1.1 on page 150. Why do two questions not need an auxiliary?

4 Write questions from the prompts.

1 How long / do it?
2 When / usually do it?
3 Who / with?
4 How / get into it?
5 Who / start you off?
6 What aspect / interest you / the most?
7 What / best way / to get started?
8 You / recommend it to a friend?

5 Work in pairs. Use the questions in exercise 4 to interview your partner about one of his/her hobbies.

Questions & negatives

The word order in normal statements is ...

subject	(auxiliary verb) verb	object
Everybody	*has*	*the same reaction.*

Make negatives by putting *not* after the first auxiliary verb.

*I **haven't** been doing it for that long.*

If there is no auxiliary verb (ie present simple and past simple) add *do/does/did*.

*I **didn't** know such a thing existed.*

Make questions by putting the subject between the auxiliary verb and the main verb.

	(auxiliary verb)	subject	verb
What	*was*	*it*	*used for in the first place?*

If there is no auxiliary verb (ie present simple and past simple) add *do/does/did*.

***Did** he hurt anybody?*

In questions with *be* put the subject after the verb.

***Are you** a bit sensitive about it?*

If the question word *who* is the subject of the verb, do not use *do/does/did* with the present or past simple. Put the verb after the subject as in a normal statement.

***What happens** if someone gets killed one day?*

❯ SEE LANGUAGE REFERENCE PAGE 14

FUNCTIONAL LANGUAGE: saying *no*

1 Choose the correct phrase to complete the responses.

1 **A:** Are you coming tonight?
   B: *Not really / I'm afraid not / You must be joking.* I'd love to, but I can't, it's my turn to babysit!

2 **A:** Is there something special you'd like to do for your birthday?
   B: *Not to my knowledge / Certainly not / Not really,* I'd be happy to stay at home.

3 **A:** So, your brother's a chess champion, is he?
   B: *Not exactly / No way / Possibly not,* I mean, he's won a few matches, but I wouldn't describe him as a champion yet!

4 **A:** Do you think you'll pass?
   B: *Not to my knowledge / Possibly not / Not exactly,* but I'm going to try my best.

5 **A:** Has Mr Smith checked out of his hotel yet?
   B: *Not to my knowledge / Not really / Not exactly,* but you'd better check with reception.

6 **A:** Can I stay up and watch the film?
   B: *Possibly not / Certainly not / Not really,* it's time you were in bed, you've got to go to school tomorrow.

7 **A:** Are you going to apologize to them?
   B: *Not exactly / Not really / No way!* I don't see why I should, it's all their fault.

8 **A:** Are you coming up the mountain with us then?
   B: *You must be joking / Not to my knowledge / I'm afraid not!* You lot are mad. I'm not climbing up there today.

🔊 **1.2** Listen and check.

2 Match the expressions a–h to the correct answers in exercise 1. More than one answer is possible.

a Are you kidding?   e Not likely!
b Definitely not!   f Not quite.
c I wish I could!   g Not that I know.
d Not especially.   h Probably not.

3 Work in pairs, A and B. Prepare eight *yes/no* questions which ask for personal information.

Do you live near here?
Have you ever been to New York?

A: Ask Student B *yes/no* questions. Stop your partner if you think he/she is not telling the truth.
B: Answer Student A's questions. You must always answer in the negative, no matter what the true answer is!
Exchange roles and repeat.

SPEAKING

1 Work in pairs. Discuss these questions.

● Do you enjoy playing video games?
● If yes, what kind of games do you enjoy most? What do you like about them? If not, why not?

2 Work in two groups, A and B.

Group A: Your teenage son/daughter wants to buy a violent video game. Think of three reasons you could give for not buying the game.
Group B: Your parents don't want you to buy a video game that they think is violent. Think of three reasons you could give in defence of the game.

3 Work in pairs, one student from Group A and one student from Group B. Compare your lists of reasons and discuss these questions.

● Who do you think has the strongest case?
● Do you think video games encourage violence?

1c | Autograph hunters

Speaking

1 Work in pairs. Show your partner your signature.

- Turn to page 138 and give your partner an analysis of her/his signature.
- How accurate is your partner's analysis of your signature?

2 Look at the autographs. What can you say about the writers' personalities?

3 Discuss these questions.

- Have you ever got the autograph of someone famous? If so, who and how?
- Whose autograph would you like to have? Why?
- Why do so many people want the autographs of famous people?
- If you were famous, would you be happy to sign your autograph for fans?

Reading

1 Read the article about someone who buys and sells autographs. Match the questions 1–5 to the answers A–E.

1 What's the attraction? Why are people so keen to pay money for a simple signature?
2 How do you work out the prices?
3 How did you start out, James?
4 What's the most valuable autograph you've handled?
5 What kind of autographs do you collect?

2 Read the article again and put the phrases 1–7 in the gaps a–g.

1 It took some finding –
2 He had a really rough time making the film
3 like all the other autograph hunters
4 with all the other fans
5 He's famous for being a non-signer and
6 she kept coming back for more
7 (especially in her later years)

3 Work in pairs. Discuss these questions.

- What kinds of jobs are connected to your interests or hobbies?
- Would you like to do one of these jobs?

The Autograph Man

James Morton is an autograph dealer who runs his own agency, The Hall of Fame, and makes more than £50,000 a year indulging himself in what was once his favourite hobby.

A Well, initially I was just an autograph hunter (a) _____. I went backstage at concerts to get my tour T-shirt signed like everybody else. I used to go to movie premieres too and queue in the rain (b) _____. Until one day someone tapped me on the shoulder and asked if he could buy the photo that Sean Connery had just signed for me. At first, I said no, but then he offered me ten pounds, then twenty-five, and finally fifty. It was my first deal, but later on, I found out that it was worth five times what he'd paid for it!

B I don't collect anymore. At the beginning, I found it really difficult to draw a line between collecting and trading. I found it hard to decide between keeping an autograph I liked or selling it for a lot of money. But after a while I realized that you can't mix up your job with your personal interests. The autographs I trade are still the same kind of thing – mainly current TV, film and music stars – but if someone asks me to track down one of the old names I'm quite happy to do it. Once, a woman asked me to get a John Wayne autograph for her father's 70th birthday. She wanted a signed photo from his favourite film, *True Grit*. (c) _____ I had to use contacts in the US to help me, but I got it in the end. She was so pleased (d) _____ – now she's hooked and she's started her own collection.

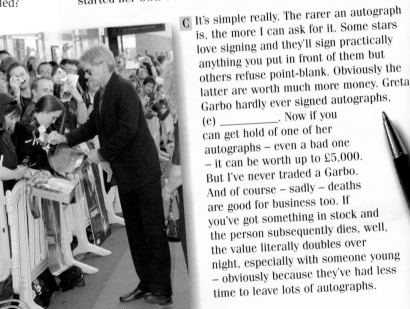

C It's simple really. The rarer an autograph is, the more I can ask for it. Some stars love signing and they'll sign practically anything you put in front of them but others refuse point-blank. Obviously the latter are worth much more money. Greta Garbo hardly ever signed autographs, (e) _____. Now if you can get hold of one of her autographs – even a bad one – it can be worth up to £5,000. But I've never traded a Garbo. And of course – sadly – deaths are good for business too. If you've got something in stock and the person subsequently dies, well, the value literally doubles over night, especially with someone young – obviously because they've had less time to leave lots of autographs.

D Probably a Harrison Ford – and not only for financial reasons. He's one of my favourites from when I used to collect. (f) _____ to begin with, I thought I'd never get it. But I followed him for months and eventually he signed a photo for me. It's valuable because it's a picture from the film *Blade Runner*. (g) _____ so he won't usually sign *Blade Runner* memorabilia. But before you ask how much I got for it, I'll have to confess that I made an exception with this one – it's not for sale! It's up on the wall in my office and it's staying there – no matter how much they offer me for it!

E I don't know really. It's like you're buying a part of the person I suppose. A tiny piece of fame, a share of the glamour. You know that that person touched that piece of paper, took the time, however short, to dedicate themselves to that particular task and now you can own the result. I don't know. I suppose it sounds a bit crazy, but then why does anyone collect anything? To own it, I suppose. It's a basic human instinct. And you can always sell it afterwards.

VOCABULARY: time adverbials

1 Complete the table with the time adverbials in the box to show how they are used.

| eventually finally initially subsequently |
| afterwards after a while at first at the beginning |
| in the end later on to begin with |

to show the first in a series of actions	to show that one action happens after another	to show the last in a series of actions
_____	_____	_____
_____	_____	_____
_____	_____	_____
_____		

2 In which position, A, B or C in the sentence below can you place the words and phrases in exercise 1? Look at the highlighted words in the article to help you.

I said no.
↑ ↑ ↑
A B C

What do you notice about the words *eventually*, *finally*, *initially* and *subsequently*?

3 Choose the best time adverbials to complete the text.

We arrived outside the cinema two hours before the stars were due to arrive. (1) *At the beginning / Eventually,* there were only about a hundred other fans, but (2) *at first / later on* hundreds of others began arriving. (3) *Subsequently / To begin with,* the atmosphere was calm and friendly, but (4) *afterwards / to begin with,* people began to push and shout. It became quite scary and we (5) *after a while / subsequently* learnt that there were more than six thousand people. (6) *At the beginning / Finally,* the first limousine pulled up. (7) *Afterwards / Initially,* we thought it was Penelope Cruz, but nobody seemed very excited, so we (8) *eventually / in the end* decided that we had been mistaken. But soon we began to recognize some famous faces. Some of the stars signed a few autographs but (9) *after a while / at the beginning* it became too dangerous for them. The crowd was getting out of control and, (10) *at first / in the end,* the police pushed everybody back.

4 Work in pairs. Choose a famous film, music or sports personality. Imagine that you have four weeks to obtain this person's autograph. How will you do it?

Brainstorm as many ideas as possible. Then decide on the order in which you will attempt them.

Report your ideas to the class using the time adverbials in exercise 1.

1D | Collectors

SPEAKING

1 Work in pairs. Match the phrases 1–10 to the photos A–J.

1 Barbie dolls
2 button badges
3 garden gnomes
4 model frogs
5 Panini stickers
6 postage stamps
7 model cars
8 dead butterflies
9 movie memorabilia
10 antique postcards

- How many more things can you think of that people collect?
- What kind of things are the most interesting to collect? Why?

2 Discuss these questions.

- Do you know anyone who has a collection? What do they collect?
- Do you (or have you ever) collected anything?
- Do you have any things at home that a collector would be interested in?

LISTENING

1 🔘 1.3–1.7 Listen to five people talking about their collections. Match each speaker 1–5 to one of the photos A–J.

2 🔘 1.3–1.7 Listen again. Which speaker 1–5 …

a began their collection at university?
b connects their career to their collection?
c has a thousand items in their collection?
d is proud of their collection?
e started collecting as a joke?
f talks about good places to add to their collection?
g talks about the cost of adding to their collection?
h thinks that their children will find their collection interesting?

3 Work in pairs. Discuss the questions.

- Why do so many people enjoy collecting things?
- Why do you think that collectors are more often men than women?

GRAMMAR: *what* clauses

> We can make statements more emphatic by beginning with a *what* clause.
> *I wanted something to liven up the garden.*
> ***What** I wanted was something to liven up the garden.*
>
> *I prefer stuff from the 1970s.*
> ***What** I prefer is stuff from the 1970s.*

> ⟩ SEE LANGUAGE REFERENCE PAGE 14

1 Look at tapescripts 1.3–1.7 on page 150 and find five more examples of this kind of sentence.

2 Rewrite the sentences beginning with *what*.

1 I would never sell my wedding ring.
2 I love the way that you sign your name.
3 I can't understand why adults enjoy collecting things.
4 I think that some people never grow up.
5 I haven't forgotten the wonderful day we spent together.
6 I really want to get a better-paid job.

3 Rearrange the words to make *what* clauses.

1 What   anything   else   enjoy   I   more   than …
2 What   gets   my   nerves   on   really …
3 What   about   classes   English   I   like   my …
4 What   difficult   find   I   to   understand …
5 What   do   I   love   next   to   would   year …
6 What   about   best   childhood   I   my   remember …

4 How many different ways can you complete the sentences in exercise 3? Compare your ideas with a partner.

VOCABULARY: expressions with *thing*

1 Choose the best word or phrase to complete the sentences.

1 *A / One* thing led to another.
2 I've always had *a / the* thing about football.
3 I don't know why really, it's just *one of those things / one thing*.
4 It's *a / the* good thing we've got quite a big house.
5 It's *a / one* thing of the past.
6 Bratz are *one / the* in-thing these days.
7 They're just plain ugly, for *a / one* thing.

Check your answers in tapescripts 1.3–1.7 on page 150.

2 Match the expressions with *thing* 1–7 in exercise 1 to the definitions a–g.

a be very interested in
b events happened, but I won't explain why
c fashionable or popular
d I can't explain
e it no longer exists
f it's fortunate
g this is one reason

3 Complete the sentences with one of the expressions from exercise 1.

1 It's _____ I can take time off work because it means I can travel to away matches.
2 I really don't like travelling by train. There's no real reason, I guess it's just _____.
3 To start with I just worked 9 to 5, but then _____ and now I'm doing more than ten hours overtime a week.
4 I really can't understand how 1970s fashion got to be _____ again. It's horrible!
5 I never go jogging. I think it's really boring, _____, and it's supposed to be really bad for your knees.
6 I've always _____ butterflies – I've loved them since I was a child.
7 When I was younger I used to love rugby, but I completely lost interest and now it's _____.

PRONUNCIATION: emphatic stress

1 Read the sentences and mark the words which are heavily stressed.

1 I can understand why people collect books. But stamps?
2 I wouldn't call it a hobby. It's more of an obsession.
3 He doesn't do it for fun. He does it to make money.
4 I don't think his collection is interesting. I think it's sad.
5 She talks about it all the time. In fact, she talks about nothing else.
6 What the attraction is for adults is beyond me. Children maybe.

🔊 **1.8** Listen to the recording to check your answers.

2 Correct the factual mistakes in the sentences.

A: A gnome is the spirit of a dead person.
B: It's a **ghost**, not a gnome.

1 An automobile is the signature of a famous person.
2 A hobbit is something we do in our spare time.
3 *Blade Runner* was a film that starred Michael Douglas.
4 Kermit was a pig in *The Muppet Show*.
5 Giorgio Armani is a famous Japanese designer.

DID YOU KNOW?

1 Work in pairs. Read the text and discuss these questions.

ONE OF THE MOST POPULAR WEEKEND leisure activities in Britain is attending car boot sales. Hundreds of people park their cars in fields or large car parks. They set up tables at the back of their car to display the items they want to trade. Anything and everything is bought and sold, from unwanted household items to collectable items to stolen goods. Most of it is junk, but people occasionally find incredible bargains.

• Where do people buy and sell second-hand goods in your town?
• Are there any special areas or markets for collectors?
• Do you enjoy going to places like these? Why or why not?

GRAMMAR
Verb forms

A Simple tenses

1 Present simple (see units 2 & 7)

Affirmative	I write/She writes
Negative	I don't write/She doesn't write
Question	Do you write?/Does she write?

2 Past simple (see units 2 & 5)

Affirmative	I wrote/She wrote
Negative	I/She didn't write
Question	Did you/she write?

B Perfect verb forms

We make perfect verb forms with subject + *have* + past participle.

3 Present perfect (see unit 4)

Affirmative	I have/She has written
Negative	I haven't/She hasn't written
Question	Have you/Has she written?

4 Past perfect (see units 5 & 6)

Affirmative	I/She had written
Negative	I/She hadn't written
Question	Had she/you written?

5 Future perfect (see unit 7)

Affirmative	I/She will have written
Negative	I/She won't have written
Question	Will she/you have written?

C Continuous (progressive) verb forms

We make continuous verb forms with subject + *be* + verb + *-ing*.

6 Present continuous (see units 2 & 7)

Affirmative	I am/She is writing
Negative	I am not/She isn't writing
Question	Are you/Is she writing?

7 Present perfect continuous (see unit 4)

Affirmative	I have/She has been writing
Negative	I haven't/She hasn't been writing
Question	Have you/Has she been writing?

8 Past continuous (see unit 5)

Affirmative	I/She was writing
Negative	I/She wasn't writing
Question	Were you/Was she writing?

9 Past perfect continuous (see unit 5)

Affirmative	I/She had been writing
Negative	I/She hadn't been writing
Question	Had you/she been writing?

10 Future continuous (see unit 7)

Affirmative	I/She will be writing
Negative	I/She won't be writing
Question	Will you/she be writing?

D Passive verb forms (see unit 12)

We make passive verbs with *be* + past participle.

	is		here.
	is being		now.
It	was	written	ages ago.
	hasn't been		yet.
	will be		soon.

E Modal verbs (see units 2, 6, 7 & 8)

There are nine modal auxiliaries (*will, would, can, could, shall, should, may, might, must*). They are followed by an infinitive without *to*. In addition, some other verbs (semi-modals) work in a similar way to these modal verbs. These include: *have to, need to, ought to*.

Subject questions

We make **questions** by putting the subject between the auxiliary verb and the main verb:

(auxiliary verb)	subject	verb
Have	*you*	*finished?*

If there is no auxiliary verb in the affirmative (ie present simple and past simple) add *do/does/did*.
   Do you drive?
We put the subject after the verb in questions with *be*.
   Are you sure?

If the question word (*who, what* or *which*) is the subject of the verb, we put the verb after the subject, as in a normal statement. We do not use *do /does/did* with the present simple or past simple.
   Who gave you that?
   What happened to you?

What clauses

We can make statements more emphatic by beginning with a *what* clause.

> *I don't understand why they do it.*
> ***What*** *I don't understand* ***is*** *why they do it.*

FUNCTIONAL LANGUAGE

Saying *no*

I'm afraid not
= A polite way of saying *no*.
Not really
= You don't care very much about something.
I don't think so/Not as far as I know/Not to my knowledge/Possibly not/Probably not
= You think you know something but are not completely sure.
Certainly not/Definitely not
= To emphasize that your answer to a question or request is definitely *no*.
Of course not
= You think an idea is stupid or insulting.
No way/Not likely
= Informal: very definite way of saying *no*.
You must be joking/Are you kidding?
= Shows that you think somebody's suggestion or request is crazy.
Not exactly/Not quite
= You think that something is almost (but not) correct or true.
I wish I could
= Used to express regret that something is not possible.
Not especially/Not very (much)
= Used to say *no* to a question about your opinion of something.

WORD LIST

Leisure interests

aficionado *n C*	/ə,fɪʃiə'nɑːdəʊ/
be crazy about	/bi 'kreɪzi ə,baʊt/
fan *n C* **	/fæn/
get a taste for	/get ə 'teɪst fə/
get the bug for	/get ðə 'bʌg fə/
give (sth) a try	/gɪv ə 'traɪ/
be into	/bi 'ɪntə/
be keen on	/bi 'kiːn ɒn/

be obsessed with	/bi əb'sest wɪð/
passion *n C* **	/'pæʃ(ə)n/
supporter *n C* ***	/sə'pɔː(r)tə(r)/
take (sth) up	/teɪk 'ʌp/

Time adverbials

after a while	/,ɑːftə(r)ə'waɪl/
afterwards ***	/'ɑːftə(r)wə(r)dz/
at first	/ət 'fɜː(r)st/
at the beginning	/ət ðə bɪ'gɪnɪŋ/
eventually ***	/ɪ'ventʃuəli/
finally ***	/'faɪn(ə)li/
in the end	/,ɪn ðiː 'end/
initially ***	/ɪ'nɪʃ(ə)li/
later on	/,leɪtə(r) 'ɒn/
subsequently **	/'sʌbsɪkwəntli/
to begin with	/tə bɪ'gɪn wɪð/

Expressions with *thing*

in-thing	/,ɪn'θɪŋ/
it's just one of those things	/ɪts dʒʌst ,wʌn əv ðəʊz 'θɪŋz/
one thing led to another	/,wʌn θɪŋ led tu ə'nʌðə(r)/
the good thing is	/ðə 'gʊd θɪŋ ɪz/
the thing about	/ðə 'θɪŋ ə,baʊt/

Other words & phrases

antique *adj* *	/æn'tiːk/
attend *v* ***	/ə'tend/
autograph *n C*	/'ɔːtə,grɑːf/
babysit *v* *	/'beɪbi,sɪt/
background *n C* ***	/'bæk,graʊnd/
backstage *adv*	/,bæk'steɪdʒ/
badge *n C* *	/bædʒ/
bargain *n C* *	/'bɑː(r)gɪn/
bat *n C* **	/bæt/
bear (sth) *v* ***	/beə(r)/
bloke *n C* **	/bləʊk/
blood-crazed *adj*	/'blʌd,kreɪzd/
blood-donating *n U*	/'blʌddəʊ,neɪtɪŋ/
brand *v*	/'brænd/
bulging *adj*	/,bʌldʒɪŋ/
car boot sale *n C*	/,kɑː(r) 'buːt ,seɪl/
cattle *n pl*	/'kæt(ə)l/
chess *n U* *	/tʃes/
clay *adj* **	/kleɪ/
collectable *adj*	/kə'lektəb(ə)l/
convention *n C*	/kən'venʃ(ə)n/
dark horse *n C*	/,dɑː(r)k 'hɔː(r)s/
deal *v/n C* ***	/diːl/
dedicate *v* **	/'dedɪ,keɪt/
defensive *adj* **	/dɪ'fensɪv/
devote *v* **	/dɪ'vəʊt/
draughts *n pl*	/drɑːfts/
draw a line between	/drɔː ə 'laɪn bɪ,twiːn/
dress up *v*	/dres 'ʌp/
eliminate *v* **	/ɪ'lɪmɪneɪt/
enamel *n C/U*	/ɪ'næm(ə)l/
exception *n C* ***	/ɪk'sepʃ(ə)n/

get carried away *v*	/get ,kærɪd ə'weɪ/
get hold of *v*	/get 'həʊld əv/
glamour *n U*	/'glæmə(r)/
glorify *v*	/'glɔːrɪfaɪ/
gnome *n C*	/nəʊm/
goods *n pl* ***	/gʊdz/
handle *v* ***	/'hænd(ə)l/
hang around *v*	/,hæŋ ə'raʊnd/
have a tendency to	/,hæv ə 'tendənsi ,tə/
household *adj/n C*	/'haʊs,həʊld/
hunter *n C* *	/'hʌntə(r)/
impatient *adj* *	/ɪm'peɪʃ(ə)nt/
in deep water	/ɪn ,diːp 'wɔːtə(r)/
instinct *n C* **	/'ɪnstɪŋkt/
in stock	/ɪn 'stɒk/
introverted *adj*	/'ɪntrəʊ,vɜː(r)tɪd/
job seeker *n C*	/dʒɒb ,siːkə(r)/
junk *n C* *	/dʒʌŋk/
kid *n C* ***	/kɪd/
lacking *adj* **	/'lækɪŋ/
latter *adj* ***	/'lætə(r)/
lawn *n C* **	/lɔːn/
let off steam	/,let ɒf 'stiːm/
liven up *v*	/,laɪv(ə)n 'ʌp/
looped *adj*	/luːpt/
make (sth) up *v*	/,meɪk 'ʌp/
maniac *n C*	/'meɪni,æk/
memorabilia *n pl*	/,mem(ə)rə'bɪliə/
nasty *adj*	/'nɑːsti/
nutter *n C*	/'nʌtə(r)/
outgoing *adj*	/'aʊt,gəʊɪŋ/
overreact *v*	/,əʊvəri'ækt/
paintball *n C*	/'peɪnt,bɔːl/
paintballing *n U*	/'peɪnt,bɔːlɪŋ/
pellet *n C*	/'pelɪt/
point-blank *adv*	/,pɔɪnt'blæŋk/
prospective *adj* **	/prə'spektɪv/
rabid *adj*	/'ræbɪd/
re-enact *v*	/,riːɪn'ækt/
relieve *v* **	/rɪ'liːv/
resist *v* ***	/rɪ'zɪst/
reveal *v* ***	/rɪ'viːl/
rival *adj* **	/'raɪv(ə)l/
ruin *v* **/*n C* *	/'ruːɪn/
selfish *adj* *	/'selfɪʃ/
set up *v*	/,set 'ʌp/
stall *n C* **	/stɔːl/
stand out *v*	/,stænd 'aʊt/
sticker *n C*	/'stɪkə(r)/
strategy *n C* ***	/'strætədʒi/
survey *n C* ***	/'sɜː(r)veɪ/
swap *v* *	/swɒp/
swap *n C*	/swɒp/
tempt *v* **	/tempt/
terminate *v*	/'tɜː(r)mɪneɪt/
trade *v/n U* ***	/treɪd/
typo *n C*	/'taɪpəʊ/
voluntary *adj* **	/'vɒlənt(ə)ri/
weapon *n C* ***	/'wepən/
weird *adj* *	/wɪə(r)d/
workout *n C*	/'wɜː(r)kaʊt/

2A | Wildlife

SPEAKING & VOCABULARY: adjectives (character)

1 Underline the word that does not belong in each group. If necessary, use a dictionary to help you.

1 inquisitive   cuddly   cute   lovely
2 aggressive   ferocious   playful   vicious
3 cold-blooded   docile   obedient   tame

2 Match the adjectives in exercise 1 to the animals 1–10. More than one answer is possible.

1 crocodile   6 pony
2 eagle   7 shark
3 fox   8 snake
4 kitten   9 tiger
5 ape   10 tortoise

3 🔊 1.9–1.10 Listen to two people, each describing an animal from exercise 2, and answer the questions.

1 Which animals are they talking about?
2 Which adjectives do they use to describe the animals?

4 Work in pairs. Discuss these questions.

- Think of five well-known people and an animal that could represent each of them. Give your reasons.
- Which animal would you be? Why?

READING

1 Work in pairs and discuss the question.

What adjectives would you use to describe the dolphin in the photo?

2 Read the newspaper article. How does its description of dolphins differ from yours?

3 Read the article again and underline all the accusations it makes against dolphins.

4 Read the letter that was written in response to the article. How many of the accusations does it answer?

5 Work in pairs. Discuss these questions.

- Do you think that people should be stopped from swimming with dolphins? Why or why not?
- Do you agree with the letter-writer that animals have a right to privacy? Why or why not?

GRAMMAR: present habits

> Use present simple + adverb of frequency to talk about habits.
> Use *will/won't* + infinitive to talk about predictable behaviour (eg habits, tendencies).
> They **will look** after injured dolphins.
> Dolphins **will** not normally **attack** humans.
> Use *keep* + verb + *-ing* to talk about repeated behaviour.
> Your newspaper **keeps publishing** this type of sensationalist journalism.
> Use present continuous + *forever/always/constantly* to talk about annoying habits.
> They **are forever scaring** them with their engines.

> ➤ SEE LANGUAGE REFERENCE PAGE 24

1 Tick the sentences 1–5 which describe a habit.

1 I will not buy any more copies in the foreseeable future.
2 Dolphins will attack to protect their young.
3 People keep swimming out to him despite the warnings.
4 The popular press is constantly filling its pages with sensationalist stories.
5 The number of these operators is increasing year by year.

2 Rewrite the sentences using the word in brackets.

1 Popular newspapers invent stories all the time. (*constantly*)
2 They don't worry about the accuracy of their facts. (*won't*)
3 They refer to anonymous 'experts' who don't actually exist. (*will*)
4 They regularly print apologies for giving incorrect information. (*forever*)
5 They get into trouble for invading people's privacy all the time. (*always*)
6 Unfortunately, millions of people continue to buy these papers. (*keep*)

3 Write the names of three people who annoy you in some way. They can be people you know personally or famous people.

Work in pairs. Tell your partner about the habits of the three people.

Cold-Blooded Killers?

A girl of thirteen years old was in hospital last night after surviving a terrifying ordeal while playing in the sea near Sarasota in Florida.

Holidaymakers looked on in horror early yesterday afternoon when they heard screams coming from the waves. Terrified sunbathers thought the girl was being attacked by a shark, but a spokesman for the paramedics later confirmed
5   that the aggressor was actually a bottlenose dolphin.
    The victim had been playing with friends in the sea when they spotted the dolphin a short distance from them. The children swam out to get a closer look, but were horrified when the dolphin viciously turned on them, biting the girl on the arm.

10 The incident comes only months after a similar attack on a French tourist in the same area. On the Dorset coast in Britain, a well-known dolphin called Georges has hurt several people who have tried to play with him. The local authorities have had to close two beaches to bathers because
15 people keep swimming out to him despite the warnings.
    Experts say dolphins will not normally go out of their way to attack humans, but they insist that they are not the cute, cuddly animals of popular imagination.
    Like any other wild animal, dolphins will attack to protect
20 their territory or their young. And when they are faced with food shortages, they can become very aggressive. Off the coast of Scotland, food shortages have led to a number of attacks on porpoises (their smaller, more docile cousins).
    Malcolm Hunter, an Inverness resident, who witnessed
25 an attack on a porpoise, said he was horrified by the viciousness of the assault. 'At first, they just looked like they were having fun,' he said, 'but then I realized that the dolphins were battering the porpoise to death. It was horrific.' Recent research shows that dolphins will also kill
30 their own young. It is believed that a number of dead dolphin calves washed up on British beaches were killed by adults of their own species. Far from being the cuddly animals of our imagination, dolphins can actually be cold-blooded killers.

---

* Dear Sirs,
I was shocked and sickened to read your article *Cold-blooded-killers*. It is yet another example of how the popular press is forever filling its pages with sensationalist stories in the belief that this is going
5   to help them sell more newspapers. And the article in question is not only insensitive, it is inaccurate. Dolphins are neither dangerous nor ferocious. They are inquisitive and playful and anyone who has seen documentaries of young dolphins playing together will
10 understand that playful bites and gentle nose butts are just part of the game. The dolphin in Florida was probably more scared than the girl who was injured and it certainly wouldn't have meant to harm her. The real problem is the tourist operators who offer
15 the chance to swim with wild dolphins. The number of these operators is increasing year by year, and many of them do not know how to approach these animals. They are forever scaring them with their loud engines, or worse still, attempting to play with the youngest
20 dolphins. Then they complain when they are attacked by an anxious mother. It is common sense to observe wild animals at a distance and we should respect their privacy and natural habitat.

For every story of a dolphin attack, there are hundreds
25 of stories of how these intelligent, sensitive creatures have helped and worked with people across the ages. Far from being the cold-blooded killers the article suggests, they are actually very caring of their fellow dolphins. They will look after injured dolphins,
30 bringing them fish to eat and holding them afloat on the surface of the water until they recover. It is this side of their character, sociable, loyal and gentle, that makes them ideal playmates for autistic children. Is the writer of the article aware of the work
35 of dolphins and their volunteer handlers in helping disabled children overcome their fears and handicaps? This would make an excellent topic for a second article on dolphins; one to right the wrongs of the first article with its deliberate misinformation.
40 But somehow I doubt this article will ever appear on your pages and while your newspaper keeps publishing this type of sensationalist journalism, you will continue to lose loyal readers. I myself will not buy any more copies in the foreseeable future.
Yours disappointedly,
Wayne Preston

2B | Animal rights

LISTENING

1 Work in small groups. Do you know any stories or legends about foxes?

2 Read the newspaper article and answer the question.

What were the two groups of people protesting about?

Urban fox lovers arrested in town hall clash

Four animal rights protesters were arrested yesterday following a violent exchange on the steps of the town hall. Angry residents clashed with the protesters as they presented a petition to the mayor calling for urgent measures to be taken to reduce the number of foxes living in our town. They claim they are a pest and a health hazard, as well as being a potential danger to pets and children. The four protesters, dressed in fox suits, attacked the residents, throwing rubbish at them. A fight broke out and one of the residents was taken to hospital with a broken nose. The four protesters were later released with no charges.

3 🔘 **1.11** Listen to a radio debate between a member of the residents' association and a member of the Urban Fox Lovers movement. Put the points below in the order in which you hear them.

☐ Foxes cause a mess by turning over rubbish bins.

☐ Foxes control their own numbers, so there's no point killing them.

☐ Foxes dig holes in gardens to bury their food.

☐ Foxes reduce the number of pests by killing rats and mice.

☐ Foxes are responsible for a number of attacks on domestic animals.

☐ Many people like having foxes in their gardens. Other animals, like cats and dogs, cause more problems than foxes.

☐ There are other ways to discourage foxes besides killing them.

4 🔘 **1.11** Listen again. What are the speakers referring to when they use the following words?

1	unfortunate	4	not difficult
2	unhygienic	5	totally absurd
3	ridiculous	6	cruel and pointless

5 Work in pairs. Discuss these questions.

- Which of the two speakers is better at putting their point across? Why?
- Which speaker do you sympathize with more?

PRONUNCIATION: sounding angry

1 🔘 **1.12** Listen to a caller who joins the debate on fox culling. Is he for or against the cull?

2 🔘 **1.12** Look at the transcript of the call. Listen and underline the words that he stresses.

Frankly, it's about time Tom faced facts. Urban foxes are not only a nuisance – they're a real menace! The authorities need to do something now, before homeowners start taking the law into their own hands!

3 Turn to tapescript 1.12 on page 151 to check your answer. Then listen again and read the transcript aloud at the same time.

VOCABULARY: verb idioms

1 Replace the phrases in italics with verb idioms from the box.

> add up   butt in   clear up
> draw a line   face   miss the point

1 Could I just *explain* one thing before we start?
2 But in any case, you *misunderstand* completely.
3 Let's *accept* it, they are a serious nuisance.
4 I'm sorry, but I really must *interrupt* here.
5 Jean's marvellous plan to kill all the foxes just doesn't *make sense.*
6 We have to *say stop* somewhere, we can't just allow their numbers to keep on growing.

Check your answers in tapescript 1.11 on page 151.

2 Complete the sentences with the correct form of the verb idioms from exercise 1.

1 He lives in a real dream world, he needs to learn to _____ facts.
2 She can be really annoying, she's forever _____ to other people's conversations.
3 His ideas on how to manage the problem just don't _____.
4 She's always playing practical jokes, but she doesn't know where to _____ and she often ends up offending people.
5 He always seems to be listening to you, but it's amazing how often he _____ of what you're saying.
6 She always tries her best to _____ any misunderstandings.

Do you know anyone who fits the descriptions above? Tell your partner about them.

FUNCTIONAL LANGUAGE: expressing opinions

1 Look at the extracts below. Who is speaking, (J) Jean, (T) Tom or (P) the presenter?

1 **Personally**, this is what upsets me.
2 **Frankly**, this is absolutely ridiculous.
3 **As far as I'm concerned** there is no problem.
4 **We are absolutely convinced** that measures need to be taken to control all fox numbers.
5 **But if you ask me**, what we need to do now is put it behind us.
6 **I really don't think** everyone agrees with you there, Tom.
7 **I may be wrong**, but not everyone actually wants foxes in their gardens.
8 **To be perfectly honest**, we think it's about time we did something to control their numbers.
9 **I don't believe for a minute** that foxes will attack children.

2 🔘 **1.13** Listen to the recording and mark the main stress in the phrases in bold. Then work in pairs and read the sentences in exercise 1 aloud to each other.

3 Work in pairs. Take it in turns to react to the statements below. Use the phrases from exercise 1.

1 Zoos are cruel and unnecessary. They should be closed down and the animals returned to the wild.
2 All children should have a pet. Caring for an animal helps them learn to be more responsible.
3 People shouldn't be allowed to have dogs if they live in a small flat.
4 Animals have exactly the same rights as human beings.
5 There are more important things in the world to worry about than cruelty to animals.
6 Hunting animals is a crime.

SPEAKING

1 Work in pairs. Read the list of activities that animal rights movements campaign against. Then discuss the questions below.

- testing cosmetics and cleaning products on live animals
- testing new drugs, vaccines and surgical techniques on live animals
- farming animals to make fur coats
- using intensive farming techniques to obtain cheaper meat products
- transporting live animals thousands of miles before slaughtering them
- selling exotic animals as pets

1 Can you think of any other activities that animal rights activists find unacceptable?
2 Which of these activities do you think are (a) acceptable and necessary (b) acceptable in certain circumstances (c) totally unacceptable? Explain your reasons.

2c | Companions

SPEAKING & READING

1 Look at the list of things that some pet owners do with their pets. Work in pairs and discuss the questions.

- celebrating your pet's birthday with a party
- choosing a meal in a restaurant because your pet will enjoy the leftovers
- letting your pet sleep with you in your bed
- taking days off work to stay at home with a sick pet
- talking to your pet on the phone
- watching TV programmes that you think your pet will enjoy

1 Which is the strangest?
2 Would you ever consider doing any of these things?

2 Work in groups of three, A, B and C. Each group read about one pet owner and match the stories 1–3 to the correct picture A–C.

   A: Read about Francis Henry Egerton.
   B: Read about Lionel Walter.
   C: Read about Adolphus Cooke.

3 Tell the other members of your group about your story. How many similarities can you find between the three people?

4 Answer as many of the questions as possible without reading your partners' texts.

1 Who believed he had a talking dog?
2 Who enjoyed strange forms of transport?
3 Whose dogs had personal servants?
4 Who thought he was related to a turkey?
5 Who used to have dinner with his pets?
6 Who kept a large variety of unusual pets?

Now read all three texts to check your answers.

5 Do you think these three pet owners were mad or just eccentric? Which of the three do you think behaved most strangely?

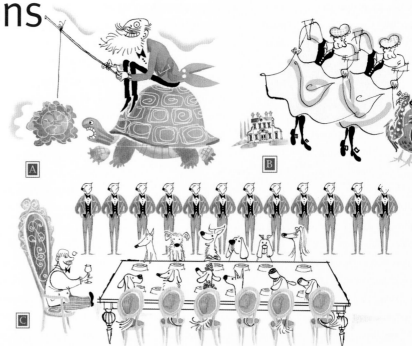

ANIMAL CRACKERS

1

To put it mildly, Francis Henry Egerton (1756–1829), eighth Earl of Bridgewater, liked dogs. At the family home of Ashridge House in Hertfordshire, his twelve dogs would have dinner at the same table as the Earl. Each dog used to have its own personal servant, who would tie a napkin around the animal's neck before serving the meal from silver dishes. However, Egerton did not totally indulge them – any hound whose table manners left something to be desired was immediately banished from the table.

When he was not at home, the Earl spent much of his time in France. He became a familiar sight in Paris, where he would drive in his carriage with half a dozen dogs inside, each sitting on a silk cushion. The dogs also wore handmade leather shoes which were another of Egerton's passions. He used to wear a different pair of shoes for each day of the year and every night they were solemnly placed beside those he had worn the previous day until there were rows and rows of them, all in the correct order.

2

From an early age, Lionel Walter, the second Baron Rothschild (1868–1937), showed an unnatural interest in natural history. On one occasion, as a teenager, he went to the seaside accompanied by his pet opossum and a tame dingo, which he used to take for walks along the seafront. When he began university, he took with him a flock of several dozen kiwis. But as an adult, Lord Rothschild could really indulge his fantasies. He used to like riding on giant tortoises which he persuaded to advance by hanging a lettuce from a stick which he held in front of the tortoises' nose. He also had a carriage which was pulled by three zebras and a pony, and the baron would drive around the country roads near his family home. On a visit to the royal family, Rothschild drove all the way to London in his zebra-drawn carriage, which he parked outside Buckingham Palace, much to the amazement of his royal friends.

3 Irish landowner **Adolphus Cooke** was a firm believer in reincarnation. He was convinced that his late father Robert had returned as a turkey on the family estate at Cookesborough. Following Cooke's strict instructions, his menservants would remove
5 their hats whenever they saw the bird, and his women servants had to curtsey.

Adolphus Cooke owned a large red setter named Gusty who used to run away and mix with common dogs. One day, Cooke decided that enough was enough. He warned the dog of the punishment he
10 had in mind and, to emphasize the point, the dog was shown a rope and a tree. Shortly afterwards, one evening in 1860, Gusty ran away again. Cooke immediately arranged for the dog's trial to take place the following morning. Local workmen were called to give evidence and a special jury found the animal guilty of misbehaviour. Cooke
15 found the dog guilty of ingratitude and sentenced him to death. Just before the sentence was carried out, the executioner claimed that the dog had spoken to him in a foreign tongue. Cooke was convinced that the dog too was a reincarnation and his life was spared.

GRAMMAR: past habits

Use simple past, *used to* + infinitive and *would* + infinitive to talk about past habits.

*The earl **liked** dogs.*
*His dogs **used to have** dinner with him.*
*The servants **would tie** a napkin around their necks.*

Use *used to* to talk about both states and actions. Use *would* to talk about actions only.

*His family **used to have** a house in Hertfordshire.*
Not His family ~~would have~~ a house in Hertfordshire.

> SEE LANGUAGE REFERENCE PAGE 24

1 Read the story below. Look at the verbs in italics and answer these questions.

Which verbs:
a can be replaced by either *used to* + infinitive or *would* + infinitive?
b can only be replaced by *used to* + infinitive?
c cannot be replaced by either *used to* + infinitive or *would* + infinitive?

Every day, I (1) *saw* Ben and his six dogs on the corner of my street. Ben was a busker and he (2) *played* the mouth organ while his dogs (3) *did* all kinds of tricks. He (4) *had* an incredible multicoloured coat that he always (5) *wore*, and the smallest of his dogs, a tiny chihuahua, (6) *slept* in his pocket. I (7) *knew* him quite well because I always (8) *stopped* to talk and I often (9) *gave* him money. Then one day he (10) *disappeared* and so (11) *did* his dogs. I never (12) *found* out what had happened to him or where he'd gone.

2 Find and correct six mistakes in the verbs in the text.

The Lady of the Cross would be a familiar sight on the streets of New Orleans. Every day, she would walk the streets of New Orleans, sometimes crawling on her hands and knees. When she was younger, she also used to carry a large statue of a saint, but she used to give this up when it would become too heavy for her. She lived alone in a large old building which would be a restaurant belonging to her ex-husband. She never used to marry again, but she used to have twelve dogs and three parrots for company. Sadly, only three people used to come to her funeral: her neighbour, a florist from whom she would sometimes buy flowers, and the florist's husband.

3 Work in pairs. Think of seven things that you did as a small child that would seem strange if you did them now. Use the ideas in the box to help you.

clothes   food   games   sleep

I would suck my thumb to go to sleep.

VOCABULARY: strong reactions

1 Look at the dictionary extract on page 147. What does the word *mad* mean in the examples below?

He was really mad when he found out what the dog had done to his garden.
He was completely mad. He was convinced he was a horse and would eat nothing but hay.

2 Decide if the sentences below refer to anger or craziness.

1 She got really worked up.
2 She's round the bend.
3 She needs her head examined.
4 She really blew her top.
5 She was absolutely livid.
6 She's a complete lunatic.
7 She lost her temper.
8 She's totally insane.

3 Work in pairs. Describe someone you know who ...

- does a lot of crazy things.
- often gets angry.

2D | Working animals

LISTENING

1 Work in pairs. Discuss these questions.

- How does the dog help the man in the photo?
- In what other ways do dogs help people?

2 ⊚ **1.14** You are going to hear an interview with a trainer of guide dogs for the blind. Which of the questions below does she answer?

1 How long have you been training guide dogs?
2 How did you first get involved in training guide dogs?
3 What are the most rewarding and the most difficult parts of the job?
4 What advice would you give someone who wants to become a trainer?
5 Do the owners need to have had previous experience of owning a dog?
6 How long does it take for the dogs to get used to their owners and their new homes?
7 What's the hardest thing for a new owner to get used to?
8 What's the hardest thing for the dogs to learn?

3 ⊚ **1.14** Listen again and answer the questions in exercise 2.

4 Would you like to be a guide dog trainer? Why or why not?

GRAMMAR: *be/get used to*

When *used to* is an adjective it is followed by a noun or *-ing* form.
> *It didn't take him long to get **used to his new home**.*
> *I'm **used to getting up** early in the morning.*

Use *be + used to* to talk about situations and actions that are familiar to you.
> *I'm **used to** doing things for myself.*

Use *get + used to* to talk about the process of becoming familiar with a new situation or action.
> *It took us quite a long time to **get used to** each other.*

> ❯ SEE LANGUAGE REFERENCE PAGE 24

1 Read the extracts from the interview. Answer the questions.

1 *I **used to** be a postwoman.*
2 *They're **used to** getting around with a white stick.*
3 *They **get used to** their owners' daily routines.*

Which extract describes:

a a situation that is becoming familiar?
b something that was true in the past?
c a situation that is already familiar?

What part of speech is *used to* in each extract, verb or adjective?

2 Correct the mistakes in the expressions in italics.

I (1) *was used to work* in The Dark Room, a restaurant where people eat in the dark. I wore special night vision glasses and I soon (2) *got used to work* in the dark. But it was more difficult for the customers! They (3) *weren't used to eat* food that they couldn't see and they (4) *used to making* a real mess. They said the strangest thing was not seeing the faces of the other customers. They (5) *were used to judge* people by their appearances, but in the dark they (6) *had to be used to judging* them by their voice and what they said, not what they looked like.

3 Work in pairs. Look at the newspaper headline and answer the questions.

> **Man loses sense of taste**

- How will this change his life?
- What difficulties might it cause?
- What will be the hardest things for him to get used to?

VOCABULARY: collocations with *get*

1 Look at these extracts from the interview and answer the question below.

1 How did you first **get involved** in training guide dogs?
2 He really benefited from **getting** a guide dog.
3 Maybe the dog and the owner just don't **get along**.
4 It's important … that they're used to **getting around** with a white stick.
5 My job's over and the two of them can just **get on with it**.
6 **Get in touch** with the Guide Dogs for the Blind Association on www. guidedogs.org.uk

In which expressions in bold does *get* mean …

a become?
b receive/obtain?
c move/arrive?
d contact?
e do something without assistance?
f have a good relationship?

2 Read the text. Replace the verbs in italics with a different verb or phrase and make any other necessary changes.

Tom (1) *got* Trixie when she was three years old. He (2) *got* interested in the idea of a hearing dog when he (3) *got* a letter from a friend who also had one. Now he doesn't know how he (4) *got* anywhere without her. They (5) *got along* well from the start and Trixie's (6) *getting* particularly good at recognizing people's footsteps. She always knows who's there long before they (7) *get* to the door. She (8) *gets* all kinds of treats and rewards from Tom for all her help. The only danger is that she may (9) *get* fat on all the snacks.

SPEAKING

1 Work in pairs, A and B. Compare and contrast two photos and decide what the link is between the photos.

A: Look at the photo on page 138.
B: Look at the photo on page 140.

> ### Useful language
>
> *My photo shows …*
> *In both photos we can see …*
> *In my photo … , whereas in your photo …*
> *I suppose the link could be …*

2 Work in pairs. How many different ways are animals used by humans? Use the categories in the box to help you think of ideas.

> leisure/entertainment   research
> security   sport   work

3 Compare your ideas in exercise 2 with those of another pair of students. Which of these ways of using animals …

- do you think is the most important for humans?
- do you find unacceptable?

DID YOU KNOW?

1 Work in pairs. Read the information about dogs in Britain and discuss the questions.

The UK has a reputation for being a nation of dog lovers. There are almost five million dogs in the UK and one in four families owns a pet dog. The high point of the year for British dog lovers is Crufts, the world's largest dog show and competition, which attracts more than 21,000 dogs and 120,000 people (and many more who watch on TV).

People in Britain give generously to charities like the Battersea Dogs' Home (which looks after abandoned pets) or the Royal Society for the Prevention of Cruelty to Animals. On average, a dog owner will spend more than £1,750 a year on their pet. In fact, many dog owners claim to get on better with their dog than they do with their partner.

- How many people do you know who own a dog? What kind of dog do they own? What are the most popular breeds? Why?
- Is your country a 'nation of dog lovers'?
- Would you ever give money to a dogs' home?

GRAMMAR

Present habits

We can use a variety of verb forms to talk about present habits (actions that are repeated regularly over a long period of time).

The simple present is the most common form. It is often used with adverbs of frequency (eg *usually, sometimes, once a week*).

> A fox **comes** into our garden **almost every night.**

We use *will/won't* + infinitive to talk about predictable or characteristic behaviour, habits and tendencies.
> A hungry fox **will attack** pet rabbits.

We use *keep* + *verb* + *-ing* to talk about repeated behaviour usually viewed negatively by the speaker.
> If your newspaper **keeps publishing** this type of journalism, you will lose loyal readers.

We use the present continuous + *always/forever/constantly* to talk about annoying habits. We often use this form to exaggerate or complain about behaviour we find annoying.
> The gutter press **is forever filling** its pages with sensationalist stories.

Past habits

We use the past simple, *used to* + infinitive and *would* + infinitive to talk about past habits.

We often use the past simple with adverbs of frequency (eg *every year, normally, on Sundays*).
> **Every night** he and his dogs **sat** down to dinner together.

We can use *used to* + infinitive to talk about both past states and habitual past actions.
> Each dog **used to have** its own personal servant. (state)
> He **used to wear** a different pair of shoes every day. (action)

We can also use *would* + infinitive to talk about habitual past actions.
> He **would drive** in his carriage with half a dozen dogs inside.

We **cannot** use *would* + infinitive to talk about states.
> Adolphus Cooke ~~would be~~ a firm believer in reincarnation.

Be/Get used to

Used to can be a verb (see left) or an adjective. When it is an adjective, it is followed by a noun or a verb + *-ing*.
> When they start their training, the dogs are already **used to busy roads.**
> They get **used to finding** their way through a crowd.

The adjective means *familiar with something because you have often done it before, so it no longer seems difficult or strange*. We use it most commonly with the verbs *be* and *get*.

We use *be* + *used to* to talk about situations or actions that are already familiar. We use *get* + *used to* to talk about the process of becoming familiar with a new situation or action.
> They **are used to** getting around with a white stick.
> (= The action is already familiar to them.)
> They **are getting used** to the white stick.
> (= They are becoming familiar with the new situation.)

FUNCTIONAL LANGUAGE

Expressing opinions

As far as I'm concerned …
Frankly, …
I may be wrong, but …
If you ask me, …
Personally, …
To be perfectly honest, …

We are absolutely convinced (that) …
I don't believe for a minute (that) …
I really don't think (that) …

WORD LIST

Adjectives (character)

aggressive **	/əˈgresɪv/
cold-blooded	/ˌkəʊldˈblʌdɪd/
cuddly	/ˈkʌd(ə)li/
cute	/kjuːt/
docile	/ˈdəʊsaɪl/
ferocious	/fəˈrəʊʃəs/
inquisitive	/ɪnˈkwɪzətɪv/
lovely ***	/ˈlʌvli/
obedient *	/əˈbiːdiənt/
playful	/ˈpleɪf(ə)l/
tame	/teɪm/
vicious *	/ˈvɪʃəs/

Verb idioms

add up	/ˌæd ˈʌp/
butt in	/ˌbʌt ˈɪn/
clear up	/ˌklɪə(r) ˈʌp/
draw the line	/ˌdrɔː ðə ˈlaɪn/
face ***	/feɪs/
miss the point	/ˌmɪs ðə ˈpɔɪnt/

Strong reactions

blow (your) top	/bləʊ ˈtɒp/
insane adj	/ɪnˈseɪn/
livid adj	/ˈlɪvɪd/
lose (your) temper	/luːz ˈtempə(r)/
lunatic n C	/ˈluːnətɪk/
need (your) head examined	/niːd hed ɪgˈzæmɪnd/
round the bend	/raʊnd ðə bend/
worked up	/ˌwɜː(r)kt ˈʌp/

Collocations with *get*

get along	/ˌget əˈlɒŋ/
get around	/ˌget əˈraʊnd/
get in touch with	/ˌget ɪn ˈtʌtʃ ˌwɪð/
get involved	/ˌget ɪnˈvɒlvd/
get on with it	/ˌget ˈɒn wɪð ɪt/

Other words & phrases

abandon v **	/əˈbændən/
absurd adj *	/əbˈsɜː(r)d/
afloat adj	/əˈfləʊt/
anxious adj **	/ˈæŋkʃəs/
assault n C **	/əˈsɔːlt/
autistic adj	/ɔːˈtɪstɪk/
banish v *	/ˈbænɪʃ/
baron n C	/ˈbærən/
bather n C	/ˈbeɪðə(r)/
batter v	/ˈbætə(r)/
bite v **/n C *	/baɪt/
breed v/n C **	/briːd/
break out v	/ˌbreɪkˈaʊt/
bury v **	/ˈberi/
busker n C	/ˈbʌskə(r)/
calf n C *	/kaːf/
carriage n C *	/ˈkærɪdʒ/
clash v **	/klæʃ/
common sense	/ˌkɒmən sens/
convinced adj *	/kənˈvɪnst/
crawl v *	/krɔːl/
cruel adj **	/ˈkruːəl/
cull n C	/kʌl/
curtsey v	/ˈkɜː(r)tsi/
deliberate adj **	/dɪˈlɪb(ə)rət/
dig v **	/dɪg/
dingo n C	/ˈdɪŋgəʊ/
disabled adj **	/dɪsˈeɪb(ə)ld/
disappointedly adv	/dɪsəˈpɔɪntɪdli/
eagle n C *	/ˈiːg(ə)l/
earl n C	/ɜː(r)l/
eccentric adj	/ɪkˈsentrɪk/
estate n C ***	/ɪˈsteɪt/
face facts	/feɪs ˈfækts/
fellow adj **	/ˈfeləʊ/
fence n C **	/fens/
flock of	/ˈflɒk əv/
foreseeable adj	/fɔː(r)ˈsiːəb(ə)l/
fox n C **	/fɒks/
gap n C ***	/gæp/
gel together	/dʒel təˈgeðə(r)/
get rid of	/get ˈrɪd əv/
guinea pig n C	/ˈgɪni ˌpɪg/
habitat n C *	/ˈhæbɪtæt/
hazard n C **	/ˈhæzə(r)d/
hit it off	/ˌhɪt ɪt ˈɒf/
horrific adj	/hɒˈrɪfɪk/
hound n C	/haʊnd/
hutch n C	/hʌtʃ/
inaccurate adj	/ɪnˈækjʊrət/
incident n C ***	/ˈɪnsɪd(ə)nt/
indulge v *	/ɪnˈdʌldʒ/
ironically adv	/aɪˈrɒnɪkli/
irritation n U *	/ɪrɪˈteɪʃ(ə)n/
ivory n U *	/ˈaɪvəri/
kitten n C *	/ˈkɪt(ə)n/
kiwi n C	/ˈkiːwiː/
lead n C ***	/liːd/
leather n C **	/ˈleðə(r)/
local authorities n	/ˌləʊk(ə)l ɔːˈθɒrətɪz/
loyal adj **	/ˈlɔɪəl/
mayor n C **	/meə(r)/
menace v/n C	/ˈmenəs/
messy adj	/ˈmesi/
mildly adv *	/ˈmaɪldli/
misbehaviour n U	/ˌmɪsbɪˈheɪvjə(r)/
napkin n C	/ˈnæpkɪn/
nose butt n C	/ˈnəʊz ˌbʌt/
nuisance n C *	/ˈnjuːs(ə)ns/
obstacle n C **	/ˈɒbstək(ə)l/
opossum n C	/əˈpɒsəm/
ordeal n C *	/ɔː(r)ˈdiːl/
overcome v **	/ˌəʊvə(r)ˈkʌm/
overhanging adj	/ˌəʊvə(r)ˈhæŋɪŋ/
pest n C *	/pest/
petition n C **	/pəˈtɪʃ(ə)n/
plague v	/pleɪg/
pointless adj	/ˈpɔɪntləs/
porpoise n C	/ˈpɔː(r)pəs/
potential adj ***	/pəˈtenʃ(ə)l/
privacy n U *	/ˈprɪvəsi/
punishment n C **	/ˈpʌnɪʃmənt/
pup n C	/pʌp/
puppy n C *	/ˈpʌpi/
red setter n C	/ˌred ˈsetə(r)/
reincarnation n U	/ˌriːɪnkɑː(r)ˈneɪʃ(ə)n/
reputation n C ***	/ˌrepjʊˈteɪʃ(ə)n/
rewarding adj	/rɪˈwɔː(r)dɪŋ/
rip v	/rɪp/
rope n C **	/rəʊp/
row n C	/rəʊ/
scream n C */v **	/skriːm/
shark n C *	/ʃɑː(r)k/
shocked adj *	/ʃɒkt/
shortage n C **	/ˈʃɔː(r)tɪdʒ/
sickened n C	/ˈsɪkənd/
silk n U **	/sɪlk/
slaughter v	/ˈslɔːtə(r)/
smoothly adv	/ˈsmuːðli/
solemnly adv	/ˈsɒləmli/
spare v *	/speə(r)/
spot v **	/spɒt/
stick n C **	/stɪk/
sunbather n C	/ˈsʌnˌbeɪðə(r)/
tackle v **	/ˈtæk(ə)l/
terrifying adj	/ˈterəˌfaɪɪŋ/
the bubble burst	/ðə ˌbʌb(ə)l ˈbɜː(r)st/
tortoise n C	/ˈtɔː(r)təs/
tourist operator n C	/ˈtʊərɪst ˌɒpəreɪtə(r)/
trial n C ***	/ˈtraɪəl/
turkey n C/U *	/ˈtɜː(r)ki/
unhygienic adj	/ˌʌnhaɪˈdʒiːnɪk/
vaccine n C	/ˈvæksiːn/
viciously adj	/ˈvɪʃəsli/
wave n C ***	/weɪv/

3A | Fashion statements

Reading

1 Work in pairs. Look at the people in the photos and discuss the questions.

- What kind of music do they like?
- What other interests do they have?
- Where do they go and what do they do in the evenings and at the weekend?
- What are their homes like?
- Judging from their appearance, what do you think these people believe is important in life?

2 Read the article and explain the title.

3 Match the youth cultures A–D in the text to the words 1–14. Read the article again as quickly as possible to find the answers.

1	beards	8	horror films
2	black	9	leather jackets
3	death	10	make-up
4	drugs	11	racism
5	the East	12	slogans
6	fighting	13	the US
7	hair grease	14	the working class

4 Read the article again and match the highlighted words or phrases to the photos A–G.

5 Work in pairs. Discuss these questions.

- What youth cultures exist in your country?
- How is youth culture different now from ten years ago?

Vocabulary: compound adjectives

1 Complete the beginnings of the compound adjectives 1–7 in column A with an ending a–g in column B.

A		**B**	
1	clean	a	-aged
2	easy	b	-going
3	middle	c	-hand
4	second	d	-lived
5	worn	e	-off
6	well	f	-out
7	short	g	-shaven

2 Match the compound adjectives in exercise 1 to the definitions a–g.

a already used by someone else
b between 40 and 60 years of age
c in poor condition because it's old
d lasting for a short period of time
e relaxed and calm
f rich
g with no beard or moustache

3 Complete the sentences with the compound adjectives from exercise 1.

1 I often buy things in _____ clothes shops.
2 I don't mind wearing clothes that are a bit _____ if I feel comfortable in them.
3 I think that _____ people who wear the latest youth fashions look silly.
4 I hate beards and moustaches: _____ men look much better.
5 Most fashions are so _____ that I can't be bothered to follow them.
6 Clothes don't matter much to me and I'm very _____ about what I wear.
7 I'd love to be _____ so that I could spend what I like on my clothes.

4 Work in pairs. Are the sentences in exercise 3 true for you?

Speaking

1 Work in pairs. Discuss this question.

What should parents do when their teenage children adopt an extreme fashion style?

2 Read the situation and decide what you would say.

Your teenage daughter comes home late one day. She is wearing black lipstick, heavy black make-up, she has a stud in her tongue and she has dyed her hair black and purple. She is wearing a long, ankle-length, ripped black skirt and a tight, black T-shirt with the word 'Lost' in blood-red letters. She says that she wants to go to a Goth festival in the school holidays. You are worried that she is putting her future in danger.

3 Compare your ideas with the rest of the class.

The Lost Tribes of London

These days, there aren't as many punks on the streets of London as there used to be. Despite the postcards in the souvenir shops of extravagantly-hairstyled punks with their studded leather jackets and nose piercings, original punk died as a mass expression of youth culture more than twenty years ago. Punks were just one phase of a series of youth
5 tribes, each distinguished by different clothes, hairstyles and tastes in music. The second half of the twentieth century saw a never-ending stream of fashions, each of which lasted for a few years before becoming terminally old-fashioned. To celebrate the rich heritage of Britain's youth culture, here is our brief guide to some of the most influential tribes of the past fifty years.

A Teds

10 Teddy boys and girls (Teds) began appearing on the streets of Britain in the early 1950s and they were one of the first manifestations of youth culture. They came, on the whole, from working class backgrounds, but spent huge amounts of money on clothes: long, knee-length velvet jackets, straight, flowery
15 waistcoats and wide-collared shirts. The boys wore their hair long and greased back with a prominent quiff at the front and the girls wore American-style ponytails. Teds listened and danced to rock 'n' roll and their appearance scared the British public. In the violent London riots of 1958, Teds took part in the racist attacks on the black population.

B Hippies

20 Disillusioned with corporate America, middle-aged, middle-class values and their country's involvement in the Vietnam War, many young Americans in the late 1960s adopted an alternative lifestyle and came to be known as 'hippies'. They showed their rejection of Western material values by turning to the East. Ethnic, Indian-inspired jewellery and clothes were 'in', with flared
25 denim jeans and loose tops with flowery or psychedelic patterns. Men wore long hair and beards. Some people lived in easy-going communes, others followed Eastern religions and many turned to drugs, which claimed the lives of musical heroes like Jimi Hendrix and Janis Joplin. Young people in Britain soon copied their American counterparts and the hippie slogans of 'Peace and love' and 'No nuclear bombs' became common on this side of the Atlantic.

C Punks

30 Punks made their first appearance in Britain in about 1976. They were anti-fashion, anti-hippie, anti-establishment, anti-everything. To begin with, there was no particular style. Their music was a mixture of rock and reggae among other genres. They wore ripped or scruffy clothes, T-shirts with provocative slogans, and studs or safety pins as jewellery. The most popular band was
35 the Sex Pistols, led by the sneering, cynical Johnny Rotten. Following a TV appearance, when the Sex Pistols shocked the country with their appearance and their swearing, newspapers rushed to report on the new trend. Inspired by the newspaper stories and by the disapproval of their parents, young people across the country adopted the new fashion very quickly. But the creativity and originality of the early punks was soon
40 replaced by unimaginative copying. Studded leather jackets and wild, shocking-pink hairstyles became a uniform and the punks themselves became tourist attractions.

D Goths

Goths first came on the scene in the early 1980s as punk fashions became more and more uniform. Inspired by horror novels and movies, both boys and girls dressed in black nineteenth-century style
45 clothes and wore dark make-up. As a result of their portrayal in the press, it was often thought that Goths worshipped the devil or were obsessed with death, but there was never really any set of beliefs associated with being a Goth. Early Goths listened to The Cure or Siouxsie and the Banshees (originally a punk band), but more recently, they are more likely to be fans
50 of Marilyn Manson.

3B | The right look

SPEAKING

1 Interview other members of your class. Find out how many times in the last three months they have …

- bought new clothes or shoes.
- bought make-up.
- bought perfume or aftershave.
- been to the hairdresser.
- used a sunbed or been sunbathing.
- thought about having cosmetic surgery.

2 Work in pairs. Compare what you have learnt in exercise 1 and report back to the class.

3 Which of these quotations do you agree with most?

You can't judge a book by looking at the cover.
(Blues songwriter, Willie Dixon)

It is only the shallow people who do not judge by appearances.
(19th-century novelist, Oscar Wilde)

LISTENING

1 🌐 **1.15–1.16** Listen to two conversations and complete the summaries.

1 A woman is unhappy about her husband's (1) _____ and she persuades him to (2) _____. However, he insists on wearing (3) _____ that evening.
2 A man suggests to his wife that they (4) _____.
He wants her to buy (5) _____ but she is not interested.
In the end, she decides to (6) _____ with a friend.

2 🌐 **1.15–1.16** Listen again and answer the questions.

Conversation 1

1 Why does the woman want her partner to look smart that evening?
2 How long has the man had his fleece?
3 Which colour does the man not like?

Conversation 2

1 Why is the woman surprised by the man's suggestion?
2 What has the woman seen in the shop window?
3 Why does she not want to buy a skirt?

3 Work in pairs. Discuss these questions.

- Do you know anyone who is not interested in clothes?
- Has anyone ever tried to influence what you wear?
- Do you prefer to go shopping for clothes (a) alone (b) with a friend (c) with your partner?

VOCABULARY: expressions with *look*

1 Look at the underlined words in the conversation extracts. Which sentences are about (a) appearance and which are about (b) eye movement?

1 You could try to <u>look</u> your best for once.
2 I just don't like the <u>looks</u> we get when we're in a posh restaurant.
3 By the <u>look</u> of it, it could have been about ten years ago.
4 It'll only take a minute to <u>look</u> through.
5 I was having a <u>look</u> in the window of Next the other day.
6 You could wear something a bit more feminine-<u>looking</u>, maybe.
7 You want me to go for the *Desperate Housewives* <u>look</u>?

2 Work in pairs. Discuss these questions.

1 When do you look your best?
2 Can you think of a time when you exchanged looks with a friend instead of speaking?
3 Do people ever misjudge you by your look?
4 Do you have a look at the price of clothes before trying them on?
5 Do you ever look through fashion magazines for ideas?
6 Who is the most stylish-looking person you know?
7 What kind of look attracts you in other people?

GRAMMAR: defining & non-defining relative clauses

> **Defining relative clauses**
> Defining relative clauses identify the person or thing that is being talked about.
> - Use the relative pronouns *who* and *that* to refer to people.
>   *You're the only one **who** gets upset about it.*
> - Use *that* or *which* to refer to things.
>   *There's some stuff **that** you'll really like.*
> - Use *that* after superlatives and words like *something, someone, anyone* and *everything*.
>   *There's bound to be **something that** you like.*
> - The relative pronoun can refer to the subject or the object of the relative clause.
>   *A pair of trousers **that** would go well with my white jacket.* (subject)
>   *The one **which** you gave me on my birthday.* (object)
> - You can omit the pronoun if it refers to the object.
>   *The one ~~which~~ you gave me on my birthday.*
>
> **Non-defining relative clauses**
> Non-defining relative clauses give additional information about the person or thing that is being talked about. This information is not central to the main meaning of the sentence.
>   *That one's brown, **which is probably my least favourite colour.***
> - Never omit the pronoun.
> - Use a comma before the relative pronoun.
> - Use *which* (not *that*) to refer to things.

> ❯ SEE LANGUAGE REFERENCE PAGE 34

1 Complete the sentences with a relative pronoun. Use the information above to help you.

1 Can't you wear something _____ is a bit smarter?
2 You're the only person _____ I know with only one pair of trainers.
3 She offered to buy him the black jacket, _____ only costs £70.
4 That colour only looks good on people _____ have got brown hair.
5 That's the sixth time _____ you've worn that fleece this week.
6 He's having a meal with his parents-in-law, _____ attach a lot of importance to looks.

2 Which sentences in exercise 1 contain defining relative clauses? In which sentences can you omit the relative pronoun?

3 Use your own ideas to complete the sentences with a defining or non-defining relative clause.

1 The best clothes shops are in the town centre, which _____.
2 I usually look best in clothes that _____.
3 I'd never wear anything which _____.
4 My parents used to buy me clothes that _____.
5 I'd never go out with someone who _____.
6 I have lots of shoes in the back of my wardrobe that _____.
7 I love expensive designer clothes, which _____.
8 I got a yellow scarf for my birthday, which _____.

4 Work in pairs. Read aloud, in a different order, the relative clauses that you wrote for exercise 3. Your partner must guess which sentence they belong to.

DID YOU KNOW?

1 Work in pairs. Read the information and discuss the questions.

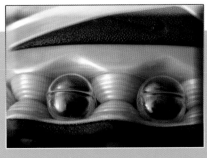

Nike, the world's most famous brand of trainers, is an American company that is named after the Greek goddess of victory. Nike succeeded in transforming the sports shoe into an essential fashion accessory. Now a global business with sales of over $13 billion, its first store opened in California in 1966. Over its history, Nike has signed contracts with many of the world's top stars – ranging from golf legend, Tiger Woods, to the Brazilian national football team. Its advertisements, with their slogan 'Just do it', have become almost as famous as the shoes they sell.

- What trainers do you own? Which do you prefer and why?
- When is it not appropriate to wear trainers?
- What are the most and the least fashionable trainers at the moment?
- What do you think of people who spend over $500 on a pair of trainers?

3c | Mirror images

READING

1 Work in pairs. Look at the photos and discuss this question.

Why do people think the women in the photos are so attractive?

2 Read the article and answer the questions.

1 What is Imagined Ugly Syndrome?
2 Who suffers from it?
3 Why do they suffer from it?

3 Read the article again and complete the sentences below with the appropriate name, Gerri (G), Glenn (Gl), Liz (L), Uma (U) or Winona (W).

1 _____ has recently had a baby.
2 _____ says that being beautiful and famous can be stressful.
3 _____ says that famous people often feel they've got something to prove.
4 _____ has worked with a lot of celebrities.
5 _____ felt she looked different to the other kids at school.
6 _____ thinks that teenage stars are particularly at risk.
7 _____ says that normal people don't really understand the problem.
8 _____ thought that losing weight and keeping fit are the answer to the problem.

4 Match the words and phrases highlighted in the text to the definitions 1–8.

1 being filmed
2 clothes
3 an imperfection
4 likely to suffer from
5 make them want to become famous
6 making it difficult for them to think clearly
7 medical conditions such as anorexia
8 have secret reasons

5 Work in pairs. Discuss this question.

Do you think this is a serious medical problem and that governments should pay for research into it?

Imagined Ugly Syndrome

These women think they're ugly

Why do some of the world's most beautiful women think they're unattractive? *Heat* **looks at the syndrome clouding their judgement.**

Last month, stunning actress Uma Thurman surprised her fans when she confessed that she thinks she's fat and ugly. 'Ever since I had my baby I've had that Body Dysmorphic Disorder,' she told an interviewer. 'I see myself as fat.' She has felt insecure about her looks since her school
5 days. 'I didn't fit in,' she said. 'Nor would you if you were about a foot too tall and you had one eye on each side of your head, an extremely large nose and big thick lips in the middle.'

The Body Dysmorphic Disorder (BDD) Uma refers to is the medical term for Imagined Ugly Syndrome. This syndrome causes
10 people normally thought of as being extremely attractive to look in the mirror and see faults in their faces and figures that no one else can see. People suffering from the syndrome become obsessed with these imaginary physical
15 defects and will do anything to hide them or compensate for them.

Geri Halliwell, formerly known as Ginger Spice, has spoken at length about the eating disorders and deep-rooted
20 insecurities suffered by victims of BDD. 'I have never liked myself and I have always had self-doubt so I thought that if I am as fit as I can be – and thin – then maybe I'll be good enough.'

25 And being beautiful is no defence against Imagined Ugly Syndrome, quite the opposite. 'Think about it,' says celebrity psychologist Glenn Wilson. 'A minor imperfection stands
30 out more on a beautiful person. You're more likely to notice a blemish on perfect skin and when you're in the public eye, everyone from tabloid journalists to make-up artists inspects
35 and comments on every aspect of your face and body.'

Living

Winona Ryder, another celebrity sufferer, blames her dysmorphia on the abnormal pressures of life she had to suffer as a teenage movie star. 'I basically went through puberty on-screen. It's a situation
40 where if you're on a set and you have a pimple, they have to switch the lighting. You shouldn't have to deal with that kind of pressure at that age.'

And apparently it's a pressure that's incomprehensible to ordinary people living their normal lives. As Elizabeth Hurley, paid three
45 million pounds a year to be the face of beauty label Estée Lauder, told a friend, 'You wouldn't understand. You're a civilian.' Liz admits that she has fought a constant battle with her appearance since she became famous. 'I threw away two-thirds of my wardrobe and lost fifteen pounds after I first saw paparazzi pictures of myself.'

50 But if these women really believe they are so ugly, why do they put themselves through the constant stress and pressure of appearing on screen and in magazines?

'Often the insecurities that leave celebrities susceptible to Imagined Ugly Syndrome
55 are the same ones that drive them into the spotlight,' explains Glenn Wilson. 'People who crave attention, fame and success often have hidden agendas, they want to show the school bully how far they've
60 come, they want to make their estranged father proud of them, they want to show the world they've conquered the eating disorder.'

GRAMMAR: participle clauses

We can make participle clauses with *-ing* participles and *-ed* participles.

- Use *-ing* participle clauses to replace relative clauses with active verbs.
  *People **suffering from the syndrome** (= who are suffering from the syndrome) become obsessed.*
  *It's incomprehensible to ordinary people **living their normal lives** (= who live normal lives).*
- Use *-ed* participle clauses to replace relative clauses with passive verbs.
  *She has spoken about the deep-rooted insecurities **suffered by** (= which are suffered by) **victims of BDD**.*
  *Elizabeth Hurley, **paid 3 million pounds a year to be the face of beauty label Estée Lauder**, told a friend …*
- You can add adverbs at the beginning of the clause.
  *Geri Halliwell, **formerly** known as Ginger Spice, has spoken …*
  *It causes people **normally** thought of as being extremely attractive to look in the mirror.*

> SEE LANGUAGE REFERENCE PAGE 34

---

1 Choose the correct participles to complete the text.

Body Dysmorphic Disorder, most commonly (1) *associated / associating* with famous actresses, also affects men. In men, it can take the special form of muscle dysmorphia, a syndrome (2) *driven / driving* more and more men to compulsive exercising. Men (3) *suffered / suffering* from muscle dysmorphia think they are weak and thin even when everyone else thinks they look fit and muscular.

For both men and women, BDD can lead to an addiction to cosmetic surgery, (4) *seen / seeing* as the easy solution to all their problems. Often the operation just makes things worse and the patients, now (5) *thought / thinking* they're even uglier, go back for more. Some cosmetic surgeons advise clients (6) *asked / asking* for repeat cosmetic surgery to seek psychiatric help instead.

2 Rewrite the phrases in italics using participle clauses.

1 Magazines *which feature top models on their cover pages* sell millions of copies.
2 Celebrities *who are always dressed in designer clothes* must spend a fortune every month.
3 Movies *which star skinny, young blondes* give the wrong message to young people.
4 TV stars *who are dropped for putting on weight* often suffer greatly.
5 Pop idols *who are chosen for their looks and not their talent* often don't last long.
6 Adverts *which sell images of youth and happiness* are very common on TV.

3 Look at the list in exercise 2 again.

Which magazines/celebrities/TV stars/pop idols have the most powerful influence on our lives and ideas of beauty these days?

SPEAKING

1 Work in pairs. Turn to page 145. Look at a photo of a man who is thinking of having a complete makeover. What do you think he will want to change?

2 Turn to page 147. Look at another photo of the same man. Discuss the changes he has made. Are they an improvement? Why or why not?

3D | Model behaviour

LISTENING

1 Work in pairs. Discuss these topics.

- ☐ The different kinds of work that a model can do
- ☐ The best things about being a model
- ☐ The worst things about being a model
- ☐ Becoming a model
- ☐ The impressions that models have of themselves
- ☐ The attitudes of other people towards models

2 🔘 **1.17** Listen to an interview with a model. Put the six topics in exercise 1 in the order in which she discusses them.

3 🔘 **1.17** Listen to the interview again. Write down the most important words (four maximum) in the model's answer to each question.

4 Work in pairs. Compare your notes from exercise 3 and use them to answer the questions in exercise 1.

5 Do you think that supermodels deserve the high salaries they receive?

VOCABULARY: slang

1 Replace the words in italics in sentences 1–8 with a slang expression from the box.

airhead	beat	blow	a drag
dumb	grand	nuts	psyched up

1 You have to be *mentally prepared* to do catwalk work.
2 Sometimes, she could make two or three *thousand dollars* in one week.
3 She used to *spend* all the money.
4 She thought the photographer's idea was *stupid*.
5 The photographer went *crazy* when she disagreed with him.
6 Some of the photographers can be *boring or annoying*.
7 Some people treated her like an *idiot*.
8 She was feeling *very tired* because she'd been working non-stop.

Check your answers in tapescript 1.17 on page 152.

2 What other English slang words or expressions do you know?

FUNCTIONAL LANGUAGE: addition

- Use the following expressions at the beginning of a clause or sentence to show that you are going to add extra information:
  Besides, ...
  What's more, ...
  On top of that, ...
  In addition, ...

- Use the following expressions to join two or more pieces of information in one sentence:
  besides + noun/gerund
  in addition to + noun/gerund
  as well as + noun/gerund

❯ SEE LANGUAGE REFERENCE PAGE 34

1 Choose the correct linker to complete the sentences.

1 She was very shy and, *in addition / in addition to*, she was too short for the catwalk.
2 *Besides / What's more* her work in New York, she travelled to Greece and Italy.
3 *Besides / In addition* her own apartment, she also had a lot of independence.
4 Some photographers were very demanding. *As well as / What's more*, some of their ideas were stupid.
5 *As well as / On top of that* being very curious, some people thought she was very strange.
6 Her hair was dirty. *In addition to / On top of that*, she had a spot on her chin.

2 Use linkers and the information below to write a short paragraph.

Becoming a model
- The first requirement, of course, is to have a beautiful or interesting face.
- You must be able to change your facial expression very quickly.
- You need to be extremely slim.
- You need to be quite tall.
- You should be under 30, or at least look as if you are.
- You are never allowed to have spots or look tired. You must do exactly as you are told.
- You must be very tolerant of the people around you.

3 Choose one of the topics below. You are going to talk about it for one minute. First, spend a few minutes planning what you want to say. Think of at least five things to say.

- Your favourite clothes shop
- How you decide what to wear in the morning
- The clothes that you take with you on holiday
- Should we judge people by their appearance?

Work in groups and take it in turns to talk for one minute.

Useful language

Oh, I nearly forgot, …
What else?
Oh, and another thing, …
Now I come to think of it, …

PRONUNCIATION: consonant clusters

1 Complete the words with the missing letters c, k, p, r, h, l or t.

1 s ____ ar
2 s ____ ____ ess
3 s ____ hool
4 s ____ in
5 s ____ ____ een
6 s ____ oken
7 s ____ ot
8 s ____ ____ ay

2 🌐 **1.18** Listen to the recording to check your answers. Did you have the same words as those on the recording, or different ones?

3 How many other English words can you think of which begin with the same combination of consonants?

4 Work in pairs. You are going to play a game. Turn to page 149 for the instructions.

SPEAKING

1 Work in pairs. Put the following characteristics in order of importance in determining how good-looking a man is.

☐ above-average height
☐ attractive hair
☐ fashionable clothes
☐ interesting facial structure
☐ kind or intelligent eyes
☐ muscular physique
☐ tanned, healthy complexion
☐ warm smile

2 🌐 **1.19** Listen to the recording then work in pairs.

- What can you remember about the topics in exercise 1?
- Is it more important for a man or for a woman to be good-looking?

3 | Language reference

GRAMMAR

Defining & non-defining relative clauses

We use relative clauses to give information about a noun (a person or thing). We put the relative clause immediately after the noun. Relative clauses often begin with a relative pronoun:

that, who, which	used to refer to people and things (see notes below)
whose	possessive pronoun (used to replace *her, his, their*, etc)
when, where	used to refer to times and places

Defining relative clauses

Defining relative clauses identify the person or thing that is being talked about.

We use the relative pronouns *who* and *that* to refer to people.
> She has a boyfriend **who** plays in a band.

We use *that* or *which* to refer to things.
> It's a photo **that** was taken in the 1980s.

We use *that* after superlatives and words like *something, someone, anyone, everything*.
> We invited everyone **that** we knew.

We do not use a comma between the noun and the relative clause.

Omitting the relative pronoun

The relative pronoun can refer to the subject or the object of the relative clause
> I bought some trainers **that** were very expensive. (*that* is the subject of *were*)
> I lost the trainers **that** I bought last week. (*that* refers to the object of *bought* – the subject is *I*)

We can omit the pronoun if it refers to the object.
> I lost the trainers (**that**) I bought last week.

Non-defining relative clauses

Non-defining relative clauses give additional information about the person or thing that is being talked about. This information is not central to the main meaning of the sentence.

> The jacket, **which he has had for years,** is covered in studs.
> His wife, **who rides a Harley Davidson**, also wears leather.

We never omit the pronoun in non-defining clauses. We use a comma before the relative pronoun. We usually use *which* (not *that*) to refer to things.

We can also use *which* to refer to an entire clause. We often use this structure to make a comment.
> They were very well-off, **which we found very surprising**.
> She kept her cool, **which is more than I can say for myself.**

Participle clauses

We can use participle clauses in place of some relative clauses. We make participle clauses with present participles (-*ing*) and past participles (-*ed*).

We use -*ing* participle clauses to replace relative clauses that contain active verbs.
> No entry to people **wearing** (= who are wearing jeans) *jeans*.
> She wants to be a top model **earning** (= who earns/is earning) *millions of dollars*.

We use -*ed* participle clauses to replace relative clauses that contain passive verbs.
> I don't want anything **made** (= that has been/is made of) *of artificial fibres*.
> His first song, **called** (= which was called) *'No Future', became an instant hit.*

FUNCTIONAL LANGUAGE

Addition

We use the following expressions at the beginning of a clause or sentence to show that we are going to add extra information: *besides, what's more, on top of that, in addition.*

> He's a punk. **On top of that**, he's got a criminal record.

What's more is used in spoken language and is the most informal of these expressions.

We use the following expressions to join two or more pieces of information in one sentence:

besides + noun/gerund
in addition to + noun/gerund
as well as + noun/gerund

> **Besides being** a punk, he's got a criminal record.
> **In addition to his appearance**, he's got a criminal record.

WORD LIST

Compound adjectives

clean-shaven	/ˌkliːnˈʃeɪv(ə)n/
easy-going	/ˌiːziˈɡəʊɪŋ/
middle-aged *	/ˌmɪd(ə)lˈeɪdʒd/
second-hand **	/ˌsekəndˈhænd/
short-lived	/ˌʃɔː(r)tˈlɪvd/
well-off	/ˌwelˈɒf/
worn-out	/ˌwɔː(r)nˈaʊt/

Expressions with *look*

by the look of it	/baɪ ðə ˈlʊk əv ɪt/
feminine-looking	/ˈfemənɪnˌlʊkɪŋ/
have a look	/ˌhæv ə ˈlʊk/
look your best	/ˌlʊk jə(r) ˈbest/
look through	/ˌlʊk ˈθruː/
looks *n pl*	/lʊks/
the (sth) look	/ðə ˈlʊk/

Slang

airhead *n C*	/ˈeə(r)ˌhed/
beat *adj*	/biːt/
blow *n C*	/bləʊ/
a drag *n s*	/ə ˈdræɡ/
dumb *adj*	/dʌm/
grand *n C*	/ɡrænd/
nuts *adj*	/nʌts/
psyched up *adj*	/ˌsaɪkt ˈʌp/

Other words & phrases

abnormal *adj* *	/æbˈnɔː(r)m(ə)l/
accessory *n C* **	/əkˈsesəri/
aftershave *n C/U*	/ˈɑːftə(r)ˌʃeɪv/
anorexia *n U*	/ˌænəˈreksiə/
beard *n C* *	/bɪə(r)d/
big mouth *n C*	/ˌbɪɡ ˈmaʊθ/
blame *v* ***	/bleɪm/
blemish *n C*	/ˈblemɪʃ/
bothered *adj*	/ˈbɒðə(r)d/
bound to	/ˈbaʊnd tə/
brand *n C* **	/brænd/
brandy *n C* *	/ˈbrændi/
bully *n C* *	/ˈbʊli/
catwalk *n C*	/ˈkætˌwɔːk/
chuck *v*	/tʃʌk/
commune *n C*	/ˈkɒmjuːn/
compensate *v* *	/ˈkɒmpənseɪt/
complexion *n C* *	/kəmˈplekʃ(ə)n/
compulsive *adj*	/kəmˈpʌlsɪv/
conquer *v* *	/ˈkɒŋkə(r)/
corporate *adj* ***	/ˈkɔː(r)p(ə)rət/
counterpart *n C* **	/ˈkaʊntə(r)ˌpɑː(r)t/
crave *v*	/kreɪv/
cynical *adj* *	/ˈsɪnɪk(ə)l/
dare *v* **	/deə(r)/
deep-rooted *adj*	/ˌdiːpˈruːtɪd/
defect *n C* **	/ˈdiːfekt/
denim *n U*	/ˈdenɪm/
disapproval *n U*	/ˌdɪsəˈpruːv(ə)l/
disillusioned *adj*	/ˌdɪsɪˈluːʒ(ə)nd/
dye *v*	/daɪ/
dysmorphia *n U*	/dɪsˈmɔːfɪə/
estranged *adj*	/ɪˈstreɪndʒd/
ethnic *adj* **	/ˈeθnɪk/
fit in *v*	/ˌfɪt ˈɪn/
flared *adj*	/fleə(r)d/
fleece *n C*	/fliːs/
formerly *adv* **	/ˈfɔː(r)mə(r)li/
frustrated *adj* *	/frʌˈstreɪtɪd/
Goth *n C*	/ɡɒθ/
grease *n U*	/ɡriːs/
heritage *n U* **	/ˈherɪtɪdʒ/
incomprehensible *adj*	/ɪnˌkɒmprɪ-ˈhensəb(ə)l/
insecure *adj*	/ˌɪnsɪˈkjʊə(r)/
inspire *v* **	/ɪnˈspaɪə(r)/
involvement *n U* ***	/ɪnˈvɒlvmənt/
keep your cool	/ˌkiːp jə(r) ˈkuːl/
linen *n U* *	/ˈlɪnɪn/
lipstick *n C*	/ˈlɪpˌstɪk/
loose *adj* **	/luːs/
manifestation *n C* *	/ˌmænɪfeˈsteɪʃ(ə)n/
never-ending *adv*	/ˌnevə(r)ˈendɪŋ/
pearl *n C/U* *	/pɜː(r)l/
phase *n C* ***	/feɪz/
photo shoot *n C*	/ˈfəʊtəʊ ˌʃuːt/
photogenic *adj*	/ˌfəʊtəʊˈdʒenɪk/
piercing *n C*	/ˈpɪəsɪŋ/
pimple *n C*	/ˈpɪmp(ə)l/
ponytail *n C*	/ˈpəʊniˌteɪl/
portrayal *n C*	/pɔː(r)ˈtreɪəl/
posh *adj*	/pɒʃ/
provocative *adj*	/prəˈvɒkətɪv/

psychedelic *adj*	/ˌsaɪkəˈdelɪk/
puberty *n U*	/ˈpjuːbə(r)ti/
punk *n C* *	/pʌŋk/
quiff *n C*	/kwɪf/
range *v* **	/reɪndʒ/
rejection *n C/U* **	/rɪˈdʒekʃ(ə)n/
requirement *n C* ***	/rɪˈkwaɪə(r)mənt/
riot *n C* **	/ˈraɪət/
rough *adj* ***	/rʌf/
safety pin *n C*	/ˈseɪfti ˌpɪn/
scruffy *adj*	/ˈskrʌfi/
skinny *adj*	/ˈskɪni/
slogan *n C* *	/ˈsləʊɡən/
sneer *v*	/snɪə(r)/
spot *n C* ***	/spɒt/
spotlight *n*	/ˈspɒtˌlaɪt/
stream *n C* **	/striːm/
stud *n C* *	/stʌd/
studded *adj*	/ˈstʌdɪd/
stunning *adj*	/ˈstʌnɪŋ/
susceptible to *adj*	/səˈseptəb(ə)l tuː/
swear *v* **	/sweə(r)/
syndrome *n C* *	/ˈsɪnˌdrəʊm/
tabloid *n C*	/ˈtæblɔɪd/
tanned *adj*	/tænd/
tight *adj* **	/taɪt/
treat *v* **	/triːt/
tribe *n C* **	/traɪb/
velvet *n U*	/ˈvelvɪt/
waistcoat *n C*	/ˈweɪs(t)ˌkəʊt/
wide-collared *adj*	/ˌwaɪdˈkɒlə(r)d/
worship *v*	/ˈwɜː(r)ʃɪp/
worship *n U* *	/ˈwɜː(r)ʃɪp/

4A | Living in fear

SPEAKING

1 Work in pairs. Look at the list of phobias in the box. Which one would be the most difficult to live with? Why?

fear of dentists	fear of spiders
fear of the dark	fear of water
fear of needles	fear of heights

2 🔊 **1.20–1.25** Listen to six people answering one of the questions. Which question are they each answering, 1 or 2?

1 What are you afraid of?
2 What were you afraid of as a child?

3 Work in pairs. Discuss the questions in exercise 2.

4 Do you know of anyone who suffers from an extreme or an unusual fear?

READING

1 Work in pairs. Look at the questions 1–5. Which can you answer?

1 What is the difference between a fear and a phobia?
2 Are phobias hereditary?
3 Can phobias be treated successfully?
4 Which is the most common phobia?
5 What is the weirdest phobia?

2 Read the text and match the questions 1–5 in exercise 1 to the answers A–E in the text.

3 Complete the text with the phrases a–g in the gaps 1–7.

a getting into a car is no better
b and cause so much distress
c that is far out of proportion to the actual risk that it involves
d and they never do crosswords
e but it is also true that anxious behaviour is learnt
f no matter how many floors they have to climb
g with the object that triggers their fears

4 What information would you expect to find on the other pages of a section of a health magazine about fears and phobias?

FEARS & PHOBIAS FAQS

A It is certainly true that the children of phobics are more likely to be fearful and anxious, but it's difficult to say whether this is genetic or learnt. As the capacity to be anxious or fearful depends on a chemical balance in
5   the brain, it is possible that this chemical imbalance is passed down from parent to child, (1) _____. Children learn by watching how their parents, and other adults, react to the world around them. Parents need to be careful not to be too cautious or overemphasize danger,
10 otherwise their children may be prone to developing phobias as they grow older.

B Claustrophobia – the fear of enclosed spaces. Sufferers' basic fear is not of the enclosed space itself, but that they are not going to be able to escape from
15 it. Even at home they often need to sit next to an open door so that they know that they'll be able to get out if they need to. Travelling on public transport is impossible – (2) _____. Claustrophobics need to feel that they can get out of the car at a moment's notice, otherwise they
20 suffer severe panic attacks. This can be very difficult on a motorway! And of course, they never take a lift, (3) _____, just in case it breaks down.

C Yes, of course they can. A phobia is a conditioned reflex, so the best treatment is to reverse the
25 conditioning. In order to do so, sufferers of this phobia must try to establish positive associations (4) _____. This can be a very long and painful process and is based on gradual exposure to the object, linked to the practice of a range of relaxation techniques. Many sufferers have
30 turned to hypnotism or acupuncture in order to help them.

D It's a question of degree. Fear is a normal human reaction to danger. A phobia is an intense, unreasonable fear of a thing or a situation (5) _____. The object of the
35 phobia may even be totally harmless, everyday objects like a tap or a light bulb. For a fear to be considered a phobia, it has to be so extreme (6) _____ that it seriously limits a person's normal life.

E One of the weirdest is hippopotomonstros
40 esquippedaliophobia: the fear of long words. You can't help thinking that the name was chosen so that sufferers couldn't talk about their problem! People who suffer from this phobia often use abbreviations and acronyms – (7) _____! They ask friends to check their
45 letters, postcards or emails in case they contain long words. And then they ask them to delete or cross them out, otherwise they won't be able to read their mail!

VOCABULARY: word building

1 Complete the table with words from the text.

noun	adjective	negative adjective
(1) _____	(2) _____	fearless
anxiety	(3) _____	
(4) _____	risky	
reason	(5) _____	(6) _____
caution	(7) _____	
harm	harmful	(8) _____

2 Complete the sentences with a word from the table.

1 The last time I felt really _____ about an exam was *when I took my driving test.*
2 I know that *frogs are basically* _____, but I don't like touching them.
3 I would never take a _____ with *money.*
4 I'd really like to overcome my _____ of *heights.*
5 The only thing I do that is _____ to my health is *smoke.*
6 I'm quite _____ about spending money when *I'm on holiday.*
7 There is no _____ why I would ever *leave my job.*

3 Replace the phrases in italics in exercise 2 so that they are true for you. Then compare your sentences in pairs.

FUNCTIONAL LANGUAGE: explaining reasons (*so that, in order to, in case, otherwise*)

1 Work in pairs. Look at the examples of *so that, in order to, in case* and *otherwise* in the text. Then complete the grammar box with the appropriate linkers.

Use *so that, in order to, in case* and *otherwise* to explain the reasons for your actions.

- Use (1) _____ to talk about what will happen if you don't do something.
- Use (2) _____ to talk about a situation you want to be prepared for.
- Use (3) _____ and (4) _____ to talk about why you do something.
- Use (5) _____, (6) _____ and (7) _____ + clause.
- Use (8) _____ + infinitive.

❯ SEE LANGUAGE REFERENCE PAGE 44

2 Complete the text with the correct linkers *so that, in order to, in case* or *otherwise.*

Jenny gets up every two hours during the night (1) _____ check that all the windows and doors are locked. She sets an alarm clock (2) _____ she forgets and oversleeps. She has to ask her sister to come and house-sit for her, (3) _____ she can't go out to do the shopping. She has had closed circuit TV installed in all the rooms (4) _____ she can keep an eye on what's happening in the house at all times. She's got three back-up alarm systems installed (5) _____ the main system fails. It takes her almost an hour to set the alarms before she goes to bed.

What is Jenny afraid of?

3 Work in two groups, A and B. You will be discussing phobias.

Group A: Turn to page 139.
Group B: Turn to page 146.

Roleplay

1 Work in pairs (one student from Group A and one student from Group B). Use the questions below to interview your partner about their phobia.

- What phobia do you suffer from?
- How long have you suffered from it?
- How did it start?
- How does it affect your day-to-day life?

Useful language

You poor thing!
That must be really difficult for you.
That can't be easy.
How do you manage that?
What a pain!

4B | Gladiators

SPEAKING

1 Work in pairs. Divide the adjectives into three categories. Use a dictionary to help you.

> assertive   reserved   confident
> domineering   self-assured   shy
> bossy   aggressive   timid

2 Think of a person you know who fits each category in exercise 1. Tell your partner about them. How would each person react in the situations below?

1 They are in a restaurant and order a steak medium-rare but it is served to them well-done.
2 They are a customer waiting in a queue in their busy lunch hour. A frail old lady steps in line ahead of them and claims that she is in a hurry.
3 After walking out of a store, they discover they were short-changed by £3.
4 They are in the middle of watching a very interesting television programme when their partner asks them for a favour which means missing the rest of the programme.
5 A friend drops in to say *hello*, but is staying too long, preventing them from finishing an important work project.

3 How would you react? Which situation would you find most difficult to deal with? Why?

4 Work in groups. Discuss these questions with the other members of your group.

- Can you think of a situation you have been in recently where you had to assert yourself?
- Who is the most assertive person that you know?

LISTENING

1 🔘 **1.26** Listen to a conversation between two friends. What is the link between their conversation and the photo below?

2 🔘 **1.26** Listen again and complete the sentences with the correct name, Kay (K), Jan (J) or Suzi (S).

1 _____ is going to do a gladiator course.
2 _____ is doing a gladiator course.
3 _____ would never consider doing a gladiator course.
4 _____ is working in Rome.
5 _____ has never been to Rome.
6 _____ has been to Rome a couple of times.
7 _____ needs to learn to be more confident.
8 _____ thinks she doesn't need to do an assertiveness course.

3 Look at these expressions in tapescript 1.26 on page 153 and explain what they mean in your own words.

1 That's so Suzi.
2 It's supposed to be the latest thing.
3 You can say that again.
4 Suzi's really into it.
5 This woman walked all over her.
6 No way!

4 Work in pairs. Discuss these questions.

- Do you know anyone who would enjoy a gladiator course?
- What other ways can you think of to increase your self-confidence?

GRAMMAR: present perfect & past simple

1 Choose the correct form of the verb to complete the sentences.

1 How's Suzi getting on? *Have you heard / Did you hear* from her recently?
2 She*'s phoned / phoned* last night and *said / 's said* she's really enjoying it.
3 How long *has she been / was she* out there?
4 *Have you been / Did you go* out to see her yet?
5 The first time she actually *has fought / fought* in front of an audience *has been / was* fantastic.
6 She *has signed / signed* up two months ago, and she*'s been / was* really happy with it from the word 'go'.
7 She *already fought / 's already fought* her a couple of times and she *has lost / lost* on both occasions.
8 I *just heard / 've just heard* that I've got to give a presentation at work.
9 I *never did / 've never done* anything like that before and the thought absolutely terrifies me!

Check your answers in tapescript 1.26 on page 153.

2 Complete the text with the verbs in the correct form, present perfect or past simple.

So, here I am – at gladiator camp! We (1) _____ (*meet*) the other participants – all men! And we (2) _____ (*pick up*) our tunics and swords. They are heavy! When I first (3) _____ (*try*) to pick them up, I literally (4) _____ (*fall*) over under their weight! They (5) _____ (*put*) me in the beginners group yesterday – obviously – and Suzi's in the advanced group. She (6) _____ (*fight*) against one of the men last night in a kind of welcome party. She (7) _____ (*be*) very, very impressive. We (8) _____ (*only / be*) here 12 hours, but we (9) _____ (*try*) out all the weapons. We (10) _____ (*do*) two hours of sword training earlier this morning and my shoulders are in agony! We've got our first fights this afternoon. I'll let you know how I get on. Wish me luck! Jan.

3 Look at the time expressions in the box. Which are usually used with the present perfect and which are used with the past simple?

yet   already   over the last three weeks   just
never   yesterday morning   earlier this evening
this week   so far   last night   for three years

4 Look at the actions in the box. Choose five and write sentences about them using some of the time expressions in exercise 3.

I've never spoken in public.

speak in public   go to the gym   have lunch
send a text message   have an argument
take an exam   get angry   really enjoy yourself

Use the present perfect

* to talk about actions and states that started in the past and continue in the present.
  I've worked here for over three years now.
  She's been really stressed since she started her new job.
* to talk about actions that happened during a period of time which is unfinished.
  I've seen him at least three times this week.
* to talk about past actions when the time is not stated.
  I've been to Rome twice before.

Use the past simple

* to talk about a finished action in the past.
  I worked there for over three years. (= I don't work there now.)
* to talk about past actions when the time is stated.
  I saw him last night.

> SEE LANGUAGE REFERENCE PAGE 44

DID YOU KNOW?

1 Work in pairs. Read the text and discuss these questions.

It is often said that the British have a 'stiff upper lip'. They are said to hide their emotions, especially in difficult or unpleasant situations; they remain calm and do not like to complain. Many British people are proud of this characteristic even though they make jokes about it. However, it has been suggested that it is less true of the British now than it was in the past. When Princess Diana died in 1997, hundreds of thousands of British people cried openly in the streets, and emotional openness is increasingly seen as natural and healthy.

* Do you know anyone who has a stiff upper lip?
* How do people in your country see the British?
* Are people in your country emotionally reserved or the opposite?

4c | The land of the brave

SPEAKING & VOCABULARY: word class

1 Work in pairs. Which of the following freedoms is most important to you? Why?

> financial freedom   freedom of movement
> freedom of speech   political freedom
> religious freedom

2 Choose the correct word to complete the sentences.

1 Sometimes even to live is an act of *courage / courageous*. (Seneca)
2 Better to starve free than be a fat *slave / slavery*. (Aesop)
3 It is easy to be *brave / bravery* from a safe distance. (Aesop)
4 You can't separate peace from *free / freedom* because no one can be at peace unless he has *free / freedom*. (Malcolm X)
5 It is through *disobedience / disobey* that progress has been made, through *disobedience / disobey* and through rebellion. (Oscar Wilde)
6 The time has come for us to civilize ourselves by the total, direct and immediate *abolish / abolition* of poverty. (Martin Luther King, Jr)
7 I prefer *liberate / liberty* with danger than peace with slavery. (Jean-Jacques Rousseau)
8 *Equal / Equality* rights for all, special privileges for none. (Thomas Jefferson)

3 Work in pairs. How strongly do you agree or disagree with the statements in exercise 2?

4 Do you think that the United States gives a good example of equality to the world? Why or why not?

READING

1 Read the magazine page and answer these questions.

1 What exactly did Rosa Parks do?
2 Why was her action considered brave?
3 How did the black community react?
4 What effect did this have on American laws?

2 Read the page again and say if the sentences are true or false.

1 Rosa Parks was the first person to defy the segregation laws on the buses.
2 Segregation laws continued after the abolition of slavery.
3 Many blacks refused to give up their seats on the buses after Rosa's arrest.
4 Segregation laws governing buses travelling between states were made illegal in 1952.
5 According to the segregation laws, blacks could only sit in the back four rows of seats.
6 Martin Luther King was a key figure in the Montgomery bus boycott.
7 King was awarded the Nobel Peace Prize the year after the Civil Rights Bill was signed.
8 The Civil Rights Bill was passed more than 100 years after the abolition of slavery in the US.

3 Complete the sentences with the highlighted words or phrases in the magazine page.

1 A huge number of people decided to _____ the bus boycott.
2 It took a great deal of courage for black citizens to _____ for what they believed in and fight for their rights.
3 Segregation laws governing interstate train services were _____ in 1952.
4 Ten years of civil rights protests _____ in the signing of the Civil Rights Bill in 1964.
5 The Montgomery bus boycott _____ a significant change in the black community's attitude to segregation.
6 The Supreme Court ruling in 1956 _____ all passengers the same status.

4 Think of a courageous person in the history of your country. Talk to your partner about what this person did.

It happened on ...
December 1

1955: Rosa Parks, mother of the American Civil Rights Movement, arrested for challenging race laws on a bus in Alabama

On Thursday, December 1, 1955, Rosa Parks got on a city bus in Montgomery, Alabama, and sat with three other blacks in the fifth row – the first row that blacks were allowed to occupy according to the transport segregation laws in Montgomery. The front rows filled up with whites and a few stops later, a white man got on and was left standing. The law stated that blacks and whites could not sit in the same row, so the driver asked the four black passengers seated in the fifth row to move and make way for the one white passenger. Three of the passengers stood up, but Rosa Parks refused to give up her seat.

The police arrived and Rosa was arrested. She was not the first black passenger to disobey a bus driver. Blacks had been arrested and even killed for disobeying drivers in the past, but Rosa was a well-known and respected figure in the black community and her arrest sparked a mass boycott on the city buses that lasted over a year and culminated in a Supreme Court ruling which abolished segregation on public transport throughout the United States.

Rosa Parks's brave decision marked the beginning of the American Civil Rights Movement. On the evening before she was due in court, a young reverend, Martin Luther King, stood up in a meeting in Montgomery and called for the black community to back Rosa Parks and fight for equal rights on the buses. Almost ten years later, in 1964, President Johnson signed the Civil Rights Bill which granted equal rights to all American citizens regardless of the colour of their skin. In the same year, Martin Luther King was awarded the Nobel Peace Prize for his role in the Civil Rights Movement.

'When he saw me still sitting, he asked if I was going to stand up and I said, "No, I'm not." And he said, "Well, if you don't stand up, I'm going to have to call the police and have you arrested." I said, "You may do that."'

The Civil Rights Movement
Slavery was officially abolished in the USA in 1865. But black Americans, although no longer slaves, continued to be treated as second-class citizens for almost 100 years. Segregation laws in the southern states allowed for racial separation in schools, parks, playgrounds, restaurants, hotels, theatres, public transport and so on. This situation continued until the 1950s and the birth of the Civil Rights Movement, headed by Martin Luther King. The movement would fight for liberty and equality for the next ten years until these laws were finally overturned in 1964.

Other events

1640: Portugal regains independence

1835: Hans Christian Anderson publishes first book of fairy tales

1919: Lady Astor becomes Britain's first female MP

1973: Israel's founding father, David Ben-Gurion, dies

1990: Channel Tunnel links France & UK

2005: marriage equality for same sex couples in South Africa

Segregation on public transport
In 1952, segregation on interstate railways was abolished by the US Supreme Court. In 1954, a similar judgment was passed concerning interstate buses. However, states in the Deep South continued their policy of transport segregation. This usually involved whites sitting in the front and blacks in the back. Blacks sitting nearest the front had to give up their seats to whites that were standing. Anyone breaking the law could be arrested and fined.

'Right here in Montgomery when the history books are written in the future, somebody will have to say "There lived a race of people ... who had the moral courage to stand up for their rights."'

(Martin Luther King addressing a meeting in Montgomery on December 5th, 1955)

LISTENING

1 Work in pairs. Put the actions in order from 1 (the action which requires the most courage) → 4 (the action which requires the least courage).

☐ holding a rattlesnake in your hands
☐ eating a dish of fried rattlesnake
☐ going for a walk in an area where there are known to be rattlesnakes
☐ sitting in a bath with dozens of rattlesnakes

Which of these things would you be willing to do? Under what circumstances?

2 Look at the photos and say what you think is happening.

3 🔊 **1.27** Listen to the recording to check your answers.

4 🔊 **1.27** Listen to the recording again and make notes about the following:

1 Sweetwater, Texas
2 Crotelus Atrox
3 Nolan County Coliseum
4 Jaycees (Junior Chamber of Commerce)
5 Jackie Bibby

Work in pairs and compare the information in your notes.

5 Work in pairs. Discuss the questions.

● Which adjective in the box best describes the people who participate in the Rattlesnake Sacking Championships?

brave	cruel	foolish	mad

● Have you ever seen a TV show where people try to get into the *Guinness Book of World Records*? What records were they trying to break?

GRAMMAR: present perfect simple & continuous

The present perfect continuous is used in very similar ways to the present perfect simple (see page 44), but there is a difference in emphasis.

● Use the continuous form to emphasize the action, or the duration of the action.
● Use the simple form (a) to emphasize the result of the action; (b) to talk about single completed actions; (c) with stative verbs.

In recent weeks we've been exploring America's Deep South, ... and our journey has taken us through Florida, Georgia and Alabama.
Hunters have been bringing in snakes since the show opened ...
... they have already weighed over 700 kilos.
We've been driving around Texas for over a month
... we've done hundreds and hundreds of miles.

❯ SEE LANGUAGE REFERENCE PAGE 44

1 In the text below, change four of the verbs in bold which should be in the present perfect simple.

For many years, campaigners in America **have been trying** to get rattlesnake round ups banned. They say that round ups **have been becoming** commercial events that promote cruelty to animals. A number of pressure groups **have been working** together to organize demonstrations. They **have** also **been speaking** to local politicians and companies that sponsor the shows. They **have been scoring** an important victory in Pennsylvania where the state **has been banning** the killing of snakes during competitions. Campaigners say that this proves that they **have been getting** their message across, but people in Texas **have been being** less responsive.

2 Work in pairs. Think of two possible responses (one with present perfect continuous and one with the present perfect simple) to the comments below.

1 A: You look exhausted!
B: I've been working really hard. I haven't slept for two days.

1 You look exhausted!
2 Why are your eyes so red?
3 Your shoes are really dirty!
4 How come you're so wet?
5 You've got tomato sauce on your T-shirt!
6 You look really worried!
7 You're hot! Are you OK?

3 Write six sentences about yourself (four true and two false) using the present perfect continuous. If necessary, use the verbs in the box to help you.

hope	feel	live	look for	plan
study	try	wear	work	

Read your sentences to a partner. Your partner must guess which of your sentences are false.

VOCABULARY: homophones

1 Choose the correct word to complete the sentences.

1 The rattle on the end of the *tail / tale* is a warning signal.
2 Don't move and he'll stay still, too. In *principal / principle* anyway!
3 They generally swallow their *pray / prey* whole.
4 We need to *ensure / insure* that we give people the right antidote.
5 Fried rattlesnake, rattlesnake kebabs, barbecued rattler, or just *plain / plane* baked rattlesnake.
6 You could have a three-*coarse / course* meal and eat nothing but snake.
7 The idea is to pick it up with your *bare / bear* hands and throw it in the sack.
8 I'm getting tired of the *hole / whole* thing.

Check your answers in tapescript 1.27 on page 153.

2 Complete the sentences with a word that you did not use in exercise 1.

1 Some passengers began to ____ as the ____ took off.
2 The film's use of ____ language was my ____ reason for not liking it.
3 The rain came through a ____ in the roof and we had forgotten to ____ against water damage.
4 Goldilocks is a children's ____ about a little girl who goes into a house belonging to a ____ family.

3 Do you know any other English words that have the same pronunciation but a different spelling?

PRONUNCIATION: word stress

1 Find eighteen words in the wordsnake and put them in the correct column below according to their stress pattern.

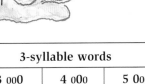

2-syllable words		3-syllable words		
1 oO	**2** Oo	**3** oOo	**4** Ooo	**5** Ooo
____	____	____	____	____
____	____	____	____	____
____	____	____	____	____
____	____	____	____	____

🔊 **1.28** Listen to the recording to check your answers.

2 Can you add two more words to each of the columns?

3 Look at tapescript 1.27 on page 153. Find five words with more than three syllables. What are their stress patterns?

SPEAKING

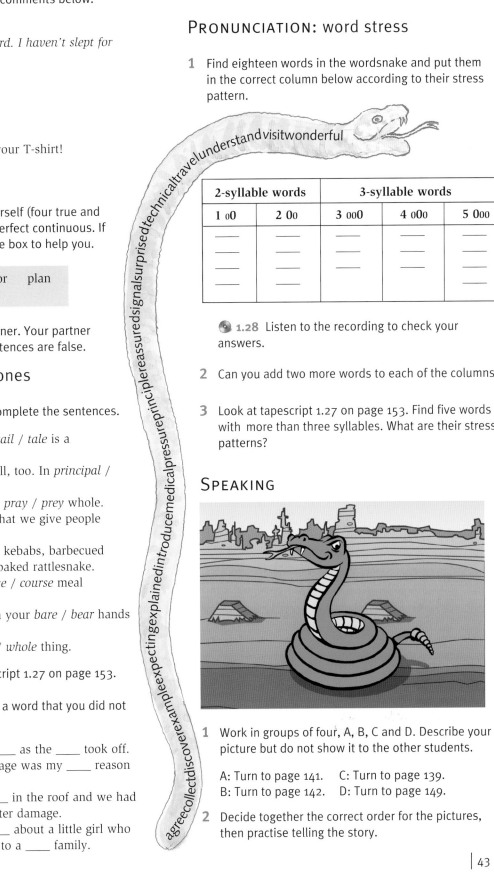

1 Work in groups of four, A, B, C and D. Describe your picture but do not show it to the other students.

A: Turn to page 141.   C: Turn to page 139.
B: Turn to page 142.   D: Turn to page 149.

2 Decide together the correct order for the pictures, then practise telling the story.

Grammar

Present perfect & past simple

Present perfect

We use the present perfect to talk about
- actions or states that started in the past and continue in the present.
  I've lived here all my life (= and I continue to live here now).
- actions that happened during a period of time which is unfinished.
  She's already fought her a couple of times this week.
  (= This week has not yet finished.)
- actions that happened in the past but the time when they happened is not stated and is not considered important.
  I've been to Rome. (= We don't know when.)
If the time is stated the verb form changes to the past simple.
  I went to Rome last year.
Time expressions which are often used with the present perfect include *already, just, ever, never, yet, since, for, recently.*

Past simple

We use the past simple to talk about states and actions in the past. The use of the past simple shows that the state or action is finished or complete, and that it took place in a finished period of time.
  I worked there for three years. (= I don't work there now.)
  I was a real fan when I was younger. (= I'm not anymore.)
We often use the past simple
- to describe the main events in a story.
- to talk about past habits.
- with past time expressions (eg *yesterday, two years ago, when he was a child*).

Present perfect simple & continuous

Similarities

The present perfect continuous is used in very similar ways to the present perfect simple (see above). We use both forms to talk about
- actions that started in the past and continue into the present.
  We've been living here for almost six years now.
  We've worked together for ages.
- actions that were in progress, or repeated actions, in a period of time which is unfinished.
  We've been working together a lot this week.
Questions often begin with *how long* ...
  How long have you been working here?
We can use *for* (+ a period of time) and *since* (+ the point in time when the action started) in the answers.
  For the last ten years.
  Since I finished college.

Differences

There is a difference in emphasis and meaning between the present perfect continuous and the present perfect simple.

We use the present perfect continuous (and not the present perfect simple)
- to emphasize the action, or the duration of the action.
  We've been travelling for six months.
  (= The emphasis is on the length of the trip and the action of travelling.)
  So far we've visited eight countries.
  (= The emphasis is on what they've achieved, ie the number of countries they've visited.)
  Not *So far we've been visiting eight countries.*
- to talk about actions that have been in progress recently.
  We've recently been working on a new project.
We use the present perfect simple (and not the present perfect continuous)
- to emphasize the result of an action (eg with a definite number or quantity).
  I've sent him three emails but I haven't had a reply. (= The emphasis is on the number of emails.)
  I've been trying to get in touch all morning. (= The emphasis is on the action, ie getting in touch.)
- to talk about single completed actions.
  I've finished the report.
- with stative verbs.
  I've known him since we were at school.
- with superlatives.
  It's the funniest thing I've ever seen.

FUNCTIONAL LANGUAGE

Explaining reasons

So that, in order to, in case, otherwise

We use *so that* and *in order to* to talk about why we do something.

> They sit near an open door **so that** they can get out quickly.
> **In order to** overcome their phobia they have to confront the object of their fears.

We use *in case* to indicate a situation we want to be prepared for or avoid.

> They never take a lift **in case** it breaks down.

We use *otherwise* to talk about what will happen if we don't do something.

> Parents need to be careful, **otherwise** their children could develop phobias.

We use *in case*, *otherwise* and *so that* with a clause.

We use *in order (not) to* + infinitive.

WORD LIST

Word building

anxiety *n U* **	/æŋ'zaɪəti/
anxious *adj* **	/'æŋkʃəs/
caution *n U* **	/'kɔːʃ(ə)n/
cautious *adj* *	/'kɔːʃəs/
fear *n U* ***	/fɪə(r)/
fearful *adj*	/'fɪə(r)f(ə)l/
fearless *adj*	/'fɪə(r)ləs/
harm *n* **	/hɑː(r)m/
harmful *adj* *	/'hɑː(r)mf(ə)l/
harmless *adj* *	/'hɑː(r)mləs/
reason *n C* ***	/'riːz(ə)n/
reasonable *adj* ***	/'riːz(ə)nəb(ə)l/
risk *n C* ***	/rɪsk/
risky *adj* *	/'rɪski/
unreasonable *adj* *	/ʌn'riːz(ə)nəb(ə)l/

Word class

abolish *v* **	/ə'bɒlɪʃ/
abolition *n U*	/æbə'lɪʃ(ə)n/
brave *adj*	/breɪv/
bravery *n U*	/'breɪvəri/
courage *n U* **	/'kʌrɪdʒ/
courageous *adj*	/kə'reɪdʒəs/

disobedience *n U*	/dɪsə'biːdiəns/
disobey *v*	/dɪsə'beɪ/
equal *adj* ***	/'iːkwəl/
equality *n U* **	/ɪ'kwɒləti/
free *adj* ***	/friː/
freedom *n C* ***	/'friːdəm/
liberate *v*	/'lɪbəreɪt/
liberty *n C* **	/'lɪbə(r)ti/
slave *n C* **	/sleɪv/
slavery *n U*	/'sleɪvəri/

Homophones

bare *adj* **	/beə(r)/
bear *n C* **	/beə(r)/
coarse *adj* *	/kɔː(r)s/
course *n C* ***	/kɔː(r)s/
ensure *v* ***	/ɪn'ʃɔː(r)/
hole *n C* ***	/həʊl/
insure *v* *	/ɪn'ʃʊə(r)/
plain *adj* **	/pleɪn/
plane *n C* ***	/pleɪn/
pray *v* **	/preɪ/
prey *n C* **	/preɪ/
principal *adj* ***	/'prɪnsəp(ə)l/
principle *n C* ***	/'prɪnsəp(ə)l/
tail *n C* ***	/teɪl/
tale *n C* **	/teɪl/
whole *adj* ***	/həʊl/

Other words & phrases

acronym *n C*	/'ækrənɪm/
acupuncture *n U*	/'ækjʊˌpʌŋktʃə(r)/
AGM *n C*	/ˌeɪ dʒiː 'em/
agony *n U*	/'ægəni/
antidote *n C*	/'æntɪˌdəʊt/
antivenin *n U*	/ˌænti'venɪn/
arena *n C*	/ə'riːnə/
assertive *adj*	/ə'sɜː(r)tɪv/
award *v* ***	/ə'wɔː(r)d/
back *v* ***	/bæk/
bake *v*	/beɪk/
balance *n C* ***	/'bæləns/
boost *v* **	/buːst/
bossy *adj*	/'bɒsi/
boycott *n C*	/'bɔɪˌkɒt/
break down *v*	/ˌbreɪk 'daʊn/
bust *v*	/bʌst/
buzz *n s*	/bʌz/
conditioned *adj*	/kən'dɪʃ(ə)nd/
confront *v*	/kən'frʌnt/
cookout *n C*	/'kʊkˌaʊt/
culminate *v*	/'kʌlmɪneɪt/
daunting *adj*	/'dɔːntɪŋ/
deep-fried *adj*	/ˌdiːp 'fraɪd/
defy *v*	/dɪ'faɪ/
distress *n U*	/dɪ'stres/
domineering *adj*	/ˌdɒmɪ'nɪərɪŋ/
drop in *v*	/ˌdrɒp 'ɪn/
enclosed *adj*	/ɪn'kləʊzd/
establish *v* ***	/ɪ'stæblɪʃ/

fairy tale *n C* *	/'feəri ˌteɪl/
fang *n C*	/fæŋ/
fine *v* *	/faɪn/
folks *n pl* **	/fəʊks/
frail *adj* *	/freɪl/
genetic *adj* **	/dʒə'netɪk/
gladiator *n C*	/'glædiˌeɪtə(r)/
gradual *adj* *	/'grædʒuəl/
grant *v* ***	/grɑːnt/
herpetologist *n C*	/ˌhɜː(r)pə'tɒlədʒɪst/
homeless *adj* *	/'həʊmləs/
hypnosis *n U*	/hɪp'nəʊsɪs/
in a hurry	/ˌɪn ə 'hʌri/
interstate *adj*	/ˌɪntə(r)'steɪt/
medium-rare *adj*	/ˌmiːdiəm'reə(r)/
needle *n C* *	/'niːd(ə)l/
openness *n U* *	/'əʊpənnəs/
overemphasize *v*	/ˌəʊvər'emfəˌsaɪz/
oversleep *v*	/ˌəʊvə(r)'sliːp/
overturn *v*	/ˌəʊvə(r)'tɜː(r)n/
pass down *v*	/ˌpɑːs 'daʊn/
phobia *n C*	/'fəʊbiə/
privilege *n C*	/'prɪvəlɪdʒ/
proceeds *n pl* *	/'prəʊsiːdz/
prone to *adj* *	/'prəʊn ˌtuː/
rancher *n C*	/'rɑːntʃə(r)/
rattle *n C*	/'ræt(ə)l/
rattler *n C*	/'ræt(ə)lə(r)/
rattlesnake *n C*	/'ræt(ə)lˌsneɪk/
rave about (sth) *v*	/'reɪv əˌbaʊt/
reflex *n C*	/'riːfleks/
regain *v*	/rɪ'geɪn/
regardless *adv*	/rɪ'gɑː(r)dləs/
reserved *adj*	/rɪ'zɜː(r)vd/
reverend *n C*	/'rev(ə)rənd/
reverse *v* **	/rɪ'vɜː(r)s/
rodeo *n C*	/'rəʊdiəʊ/
rope (sb)	/ˌrəʊp 'ɪntə/
into sth	
roundup *n C*	/'raʊndʌp/
rule *v* ***	/ruːl/
sacking *n C*	/'sækɪŋ/
scout *n C* *	/skaʊt/
segregation *n U*	/ˌsegrɪ'geɪʃ(ə)n/
self-assured *adj*	/ˌselfə'ʃɔː(r)d/
short-changed *adj*	/ˌʃɔː(r)t'tʃeɪndʒd/
spark *v* *	/spɑː(r)k/
stand up for *v*	/ˌstænd 'ʌp fɔː(r)/
starve *v*	/stɑː(r)v/
stiff *adj* **	/stɪf/
strike (sb) as *v*	/'straɪk ˌəz/
sword *n C* **	/sɔː(r)d/
toga *n C*	/'təʊgə/
treat (sb) *v* ***	/triːt/
trigger *n C*	/'trɪgə(r)/
tunic *n C*	/'tjuːnɪk/
venom *n U*	/'venəm/
venue *n C* **	/'venjuː/
weigh-in *n C*	/'weɪˌɪn/
well-done *adj*	/ˌwel'dʌn/

5A | Performance art

VOCABULARY: art

1 Complete the questions with a word from the box.

> abstract   collection   dealers   exhibition
> landscapes   patrons   sculptures

1   Which gallery or museum in your country has the largest _____ of fine art?
2   Are there any large _____ or murals in the streets and squares of your town? What do they look like?
3   Who is the most famous painter in your country? Was he/she a figurative or an _____ artist?
4   Who are the most famous _____ of the arts in your country?
5   In which part of your town can you find private galleries and art _____?
6   What was the last art _____ that you went to? Did you like it?
7   In general, do you prefer _____, still lifes or portraits? Or something else?

2 Work in pairs. Ask and answer the questions in exercise 1.

READING

1 Look at the photo and decide if you think the sentences are true or false.

1   She is a well-known artist.
2   Her paintings are very expensive.
3   Her work is famous because it is shocking.
4   There is a serious message in her work.

Read the article to find out if you were correct.

2 Read the article. Put the events in the order in which they happened.

☐ She became internationally famous.
☐ Orlan's performance at an art fair in Paris caused a scandal.
☐ She began changing her appearance.
☐ Her work was taken to an arts centre in an ambulance.
☐ She needed emergency surgery.
☐ She began teaching at a college in Dijon.
☐ She was fired.

3 Work in pairs. Discuss these questions.

• Would you like to see one of Orlan's videos?
• Would you be happy if your government sponsored her work?

Orlan

A worldwide satellite audience watched the live broadcast in fascination and horror. A woman was lying on a surgical table in an operating theatre and was reading texts from French philosophers. As the doctors, who were wearing costumes
5 that had been designed by Paco Rabanne, prepared their tools, an African man danced around the table.

Orlan, the star of the video, is probably the world's most well-known performance artist. She has had dozens of exhibitions around the world, she appears in fashion
10 magazines and TV talk shows and collectors pay high prices for her pictures. She is a professor of fine arts at a prestigious college in Dijon and her work is supported by the French Ministry of Culture.

She was born in central France in 1947 and did her first
15 performances at the age of eighteen. She later became a teacher but lost her job in 1977, as a result of a work that she had performed at an art fair in Paris. In the work, 'The kiss of the artist', she had sat behind a life-size photograph of her body and sold kisses to the audience. At the end of each kiss,
20 an electronic siren deafened the gallery. The work succeeded in shocking the public but Orlan was out of a job.

Orlan was getting more and more attention, but art lovers were unprepared for what came next. Her next major work – a video – was shown at the Lyons Centre of Contemporary Art.
25 An ambulance had rushed the video to the Centre from the hospital where Orlan had just had an emergency operation. She had installed a video camera in the operating theatre, and the film became the first of her surgical performances.

By the mid-1980s, her fame had led to work for the Ministry
30 of Culture and a teaching position at Dijon, but international stardom came later, in the 1990s, after changing her appearance. Returning to the operating theatre, she began a series of plastic surgery operations that continued for the next ten years. In each operation, a part of Orlan's body was
35 changed, so that it looked like a beautiful bit of her favourite paintings – the forehead of Leonardo's *Mona Lisa* or the chin of Botticelli's *Venus*, for example.

Galleries around the world showed films of the operations and Orlan's fame grew. Her self-portraits are her most
40 recognizable paintings, but her work is conceptual, rather than figurative. She describes herself as a feminist and says that her intention is to challenge traditional ideas of beauty. In the tradition of Marcel Duchamp, her work is designed to shock and provoke, not simply to be admired.

GRAMMAR: narrative tenses

1 Read the article and choose the best headline.

Artist turns off the tap

Water protest to end

Artist Mark McGowan (1) *said / had said* that he
(2) *was expecting / had expected* his exhibition,
'The Running Tap' at the House Gallery in
south-east London, to close in the next few days.
The exhibition (3) *started / was starting* one month
ago when Mark (4) *opened / was opening* a tap in
the kitchen area of the gallery and (5) *left / had left*
it running. McGowan (6) *intended / had intended*
to leave the tap running for a year, but after
receiving a letter from the Thames Water Authority,
the gallery owners (7) *were thinking / had thought*
about shutting the exhibition down. The exhibition
(8) *was wasting / had wasted* over 700 litres of
water every hour, and over half a million litres
(9) *were already / had already been* used.
McGowan (10) *was designing / had designed* his
artwork to draw attention to the way that people
waste water.

2 Now choose the best verb forms to complete the text in exercise 1.

3 Put the verbs in brackets into the past simple, past continuous or past perfect. Sometimes more than one tense is possible.

I (1) ____ (*walk*) home yesterday when I (2) ___ (*see*)
a group of people in front of the church. They
(3) ____ (*laugh*) and one man with a video camera
(4) ____ (*film*) something, so I (5) ____ (*go*) to have
a closer look. Three people (6) ____ (*hold*) long sticks
and they seemed to be attacking a traffic warden!
The man with the video camera (7) ____ (*notice*) the
look of horror on my face. He (8) ____ (*come*) over
to me and (9) _____ (*explain*) that it was a piece of
performance art. The traffic warden was really an
artist called Mark McGowan, who (10) ____ (*dress*) up
in a warden's uniform. He (11) ____ (*advertise*) the
event on a website, inviting people to come along and
hit him with wooden sticks.

- Use the past simple to talk about the main events in a story.
  *The doctors **prepared** their tools. An African man **danced** around the table.*
- Use the past continuous to describe 'background' events and actions that were in progress at the time of the main events.
  *She **was lying** on a surgical table.*
  *The doctors **were wearing** costumes.*
- Use the past perfect to show that a past action took place before another past action.
  *She lost her job as a result of a work she **had performed** in Paris.*

❯ SEE LANGUAGE REFERENCE PAGE 54

SPEAKING

1 Work in two groups. Put the events in any order to create an interesting life story for the woman in the photo.

Group A: Turn to page 139. Group B: Turn to page 141.

2 Work with a partner from another group. Compare your stories. Then, combine them to make one story.

3 🔘 **1.29** Listen to a short biography of the woman in the photo. How similar was your version to the real story?

4 Work in pairs. How much of the real story can you remember?

5B | Priceless!

Listening

1 Work in pairs. Discuss these questions.

- What pictures or photos do you have on the walls of your home?
- Which picture has the greatest personal value?
- Which do you like most and least? Why?

2 🔘 **1.30** Listen to an interview with an art consultant and curator. Answer the questions.

1 Why has the woman been invited to take part in the interview?
2 What does she do in her job?
3 What does she think about public art projects?

3 Complete the sentences.

1 The hospital has appointed an arts curator with a salary of _____ a year.
2 The hospital recently unveiled a _____ _____ outside the entrance.
3 Lucy does not think that £70,000 is _____ _____ for the piece of art.
4 The money for the art curator's salary comes from _____ _____.
5 Some countries, like _____, already have many public art projects.
6 These projects encourage people to _____ _____ _____.
7 Lucy is very critical of a project in a _____ _____.

🔘 **1.30** Listen again and check your answers.

4 Work in pairs. Discuss these questions.

- Do you think it is a good idea to spend money on public art projects?
- Do you think your work place (or place of study) would benefit from an art project? If yes, what kind of art? If no, why not?

Vocabulary: -*ever* words

- Use the words *whoever, whatever, whenever, wherever* and *however* to say 'it doesn't matter who/it doesn't matter what, etc'.
  *They can think **whatever** they like.*
  ***Whatever** you think of it, I don't think that anybody would say it's a masterpiece.*
  ***Wherever** you go, you see large public arts projects.*
  ***Whenever** we unveil a work of art, people always get together and talk about it.*

> **See Language Reference page 54**

1 Match the responses a–f to the questions 1–6 to make a conversation.

1 When do you want to go for dinner?
2 What time suits you?
3 Yes, good idea. Who shall we invite with us?
4 Yes, OK. Where shall we go?
5 Fine, let's say the Criterion. How shall we get there? Taxi?
6 What shall we eat?

a However you suggest. Taxi's fine by me.
b A little later, perhaps? Whenever you feel like it.
c Wherever you choose. You know better than me.
d Whoever you like. You're paying.
e Oh, I don't know. Whatever they recommend.
f Whatever time suits you. Nine o'clock, say?

2 🔘 **1.31** Listen to the recording to check your answers.

3 Complete the quotations with -*ever* words.

1 Some people cause happiness _____ they go, others _____ they go. (Oscar Wilde)
2 Sir, I will go _____ I am needed _____ you give the order. (Colonel A Burke)
3 _____ said money can't buy you happiness simply didn't know where to go shopping. (attributed to Bo Derek)
4 _____ your car, _____ you are, get instant online quotes and cover at Quantum Quotes. (Anon)
5 _____ you say, say it with conviction. (Mark Twain)
6 The future is something which everyone reaches at the rate of 60 minutes an hour, _____ he does, _____ he is. (CS Lewis)

FUNCTIONAL LANGUAGE: evaluating

1 Put the phrases 1–8 into two groups: one positive (P), one negative (N).

1 It has no redeeming features.
2 It's a load of rubbish.
3 It's a masterpiece.
4 It's absolutely worthless.
5 It's extremely valuable.
6 It's not worth anything at all.
7 It's priceless.
8 It's worth a fortune.

2 Work in groups. The following items are going to be auctioned online. Use the expressions in exercise 1 to say how much you think they are worth.

1 'Hanging Spirit' by Stephen Knapp (see photo)
2 'Horse' by Diocletus the Etruscan (see photo)
3 'Symmetry #17' by Charles Andrews (see photo)
4 a self-portrait of Vincent Van Gogh
5 an autographed photo of Elton John
6 an original recording of 'Can't buy me love' by The Beatles
7 Luke Skywalker's original light sabre from *Star Wars*

SPEAKING

Roleplay

1 Work in groups of three, students A–C. Decide which two works you like best.

'Symmetry #17' by Charles Andrews

'Hanging Spirit'
by Stephen Knapp

'Horse' by Diocletus the Etruscan

2 You work for a large company which has decided to spend $25,000 on a work of art to decorate the reception area. An art dealer has offered you three works, with an estimated value of $25,000 each.

A: Turn to page 139 and answer the questions.
B: Turn to page 141 and answer the questions.
C: Turn to page 144 and answer the questions.

3 Discuss the possibilities with the other members of your group and decide together which work of art you will buy.

Take it in turns to …
• introduce yourself and describe your position in the company.
• say which work of art you think the company should buy.

> ### Useful language
>
> *I'm the … in the company, and I think …*
> *I've been told that …*
> *A lot of people have told me that …*
> *I think you ought to know that …*
> *What I really like about X is …*
> *X would be the best choice because …*
> *I'm sorry, but I really don't agree with you there.*

4 🔘 1.32 Listen to find out which work of art is worth the most.

5c | A good read

SPEAKING & READING

1 Work in pairs. Look at the painting and discuss these questions.

- What does it show?
- How would you describe the personality of the girl?
- Would you hang it in your home? If yes, where?
- If it were in a calendar, which month would it represent?

2 The painting has inspired a novel of the same name, *Girl with a Pearl Earring*. Here are some key events from the story. Put them in the correct order.

☐ a Things had been going well and it seemed that the painting was almost ready. But Vermeer was not totally happy. Something was missing.

☐ b Griet had been working as a maid at Vermeer's house for a little over a year. She was serving drinks at a party when the artist's patron singled her out for special attention.

☐ c He had been searching for the answer for some time when he finally realized what was missing – a pearl earring. A small detail, but one that would cost Griet dearly.

☐ d Vermeer had not been planning to paint Griet, but he complied with his patron's request and set about preparing a portrait of his maid.

3 Match the extracts 1–4 to the events a–d in exercise 2.

1 He was looking at a book and did not notice as I slipped into my chair. I arranged myself as I had been sitting before. As I turned my head to look over my left shoulder, he glanced up. At the same time the end of the yellow cloth came loose and fell over my shoulder.
'Oh' I breathed, afraid that the cloth would fall from my head and reveal all my hair. But it held – only the end of the yellow cloth dangled free. My hair remained hidden.
'Yes,' he said then. 'That is it, Griet. Yes.'

2 Late in the evening, Van Ruijven managed to corner me in the hallway as I was passing along it with a lighted candle and a wine jug. 'Ah, the wide-eyed maid,' he cried, leaning into me. 'Hello, my girl.' He grabbed my chin in his hand, his other hand pulling the candle up to light my face. I did not like the way he looked at me.
'You should paint her,' he said over his shoulder.

3 'You must wear the other one as well,' he declared, picking up the second earring and holding it out to me.
For a moment I could not speak. I wanted him to think of me, not the painting.
'Why?' I finally answered. 'It can't be seen in the painting.'
'You must wear both,' he insisted. 'It is a farce to wear only one.'
'But – my other ear is not pierced,' I faltered.
'Then you must tend to it.' He continued to hold it out.
I reached over and took it. I did it for him. I got out a needle and clove oil and pierced my other ear. I did not cry, or faint, or make a sound. Then I sat all morning and he painted the earring he could see, and I felt, stinging like fire in my other ear, the pearl he could not see.

4 He had been working on the painting for almost two months, and though I had not seen it, I thought it must be close to done. He was no longer having me mix quantities of colour for it, but used tiny amounts and made few movements with his brushes. As I sat, I thought I had understood how he wanted me to be, but now I was not so sure. Sometimes he simply sat and looked at me as if he were waiting for me to do something. Then he was not like a painter, but like a man, and it was hard to look at him.
One day he announced suddenly, as I was sitting in my chair, 'This will satisfy van Ruijven, but not me.'

4 Work in pairs. Decide whether the statements below are true. Underline the passages that justify your answers.

1 The portrait did not take long to paint.
2 The artist was a perfectionist.
3 The girl didn't want to show her hair.
4 The earrings belonged to the girl.
5 The girl enjoyed wearing the pearl earrings.

5 Work in pairs. Discuss these questions.

- Which extract do you think would be the most difficult to transfer to film? Why?
- Have you seen the film of the novel? If yes, what did you think of it? If not, would you be interested in seeing it?

GRAMMAR: past perfect continuous

- Use *had* + *been* + verb + *-ing* to form the past perfect continuous.
  *She **had been washing** the steps.*
- Use the past perfect continuous to talk about actions that were in progress before or up to a certain point in the past.
  *She **had been cleaning** his studio when Tanneke called her down to the kitchen.*
- Use the past perfect simple and not the continuous to talk about a completed action.
  *He **had decided** to paint her and no one could change his mind.*

⟩ SEE LANGUAGE REFERENCE PAGE 54

1 Find six examples of the past perfect continuous in the extracts from the novel and in Reading exercise 2.

2 Change five of the verbs in italics to the past perfect continuous.

In the Vermeer household, one of Griet's regular tasks (1) *had been* to go to the market to buy fish and meat. There she (2) *had met* Pieter, the butcher's son. He (3) *had noticed* her some time before and (4) *had waited* for a chance to speak to her.
Pieter (5) *had gone* to her parents' church for a few months when Griet's mother invited him to eat with them one Sunday. He (6) *had accepted* immediately, but Griet was not so happy about the invitation. Her family were poor and her mother (7) *had saved* for weeks to buy a little fish for their Sunday dinner.
The dinner (8) *had been* a success and Griet and Pieter started seeing each other regularly. On Griet's 18th birthday, Pieter decided that he (9) *had waited* long enough and he asked her father for her hand in marriage. When Griet got into trouble at the Vermeers she finally made the decision she (10) *had avoided* for so long.

3 Work in pairs. Think of three photos of yourself. Describe ...

- what was happening in each photo.
- what you had been doing before each photo was taken.
- what you did after each photo was taken.

Which of these photos do you prefer? Why?

PRONUNCIATION: long vowels

1 Work in pairs. Underline the word that does not go with the groups 1–5.

1 /ɜ:/ girl   blue   pearl   serving
2 /ɔ:/ hallway   almost   artist   thought
3 /ɑ:/ answered   market   hard   portrait
4 /i:/ needle   seen   working   speak
5 /u:/ loose   two   used   seemed

Which groups 1–5 should the odd word for each group be in?

2 🔊 1.33 Find at least one example of each of the five sounds in the movie trailer. Then listen and check.

Drawn into the intimate world of her master's art, Griet falls madly in love. What can she do but comply with her master's every desire? She will only be set free when the painting is finished. But what will become of her then?

3 Practise reading the trailer aloud with your partner.

5D | Bookworm

SPEAKING

1 Work in pairs. Look at the photos of the reading material and discuss these questions.

1 Which do you read for pleasure?
2 Which do you read for work?
3 What else do you read?

2 Use the questions to interview your classmates on their reading habits. Find the person in the class whose reading habits are most similar to yours.

1 How many books do you read a year?
2 Do you enjoy reading? Or do you just read for work or study?
3 Where or when do you usually do your reading?
4 Do you usually take a book with you on holiday? Why or why not?
5 If you do, what kind of book do you usually take?
6 What are you reading at the moment? Would you recommend it? Why or why not?

LISTENING

1 🔘 **1.34** Listen to a radio programme about the talk show host, Oprah Winfrey, and answer these questions.

1 Why is Oprah Winfrey an important figure in American society?
2 What sort of childhood did she have?
3 What does she like reading?

2 🔘 **1.34** Listen again and put the events in the correct order.

☐ Oprah was the victim of abuse.
☐ Hundreds of thousands of people followed Oprah's example.
☐ She read a book every week and wrote a report on it.
☐ She recommended Tolstoy's *Anna Karenina*.
☐ Her TV show won its first award.
☐ She began the Oprah Winfrey Book Club.
☐ She changed the kind of books that she put forward.
☐ She worked as a TV reporter and newsreader.

3 Would you follow the advice of a talk show host? Would you consider joining a book club? Why or why not?

VOCABULARY: phrasal verbs 1

1 Rearrange the words to make sentences.

1 a her life no one out success such thought turn would.
2 her immediately public the to took.
3 a book club came idea of Oprah the up with.
4 contemporary enough expectations her lived not novels to up.
5 book's off 837 pages put shouldn't the them.
6 have of own people reading groups set their thousands up.
7 chance down novelist one the turned.

Check your answers in the tapescript 1.34 on page 155.

2 Replace the words in italics with a phrasal verb from the box in the correct tense.

> come up with   live up to   put me off
> set up   take to   turn me down   turn out

1 I was so disappointed when they decided to *refuse me*.
2 I thought I'd never find the answer, but I *found* the solution in the end.
3 I *begin to like* some people very quickly, but sometimes it takes longer.
4 I never thought my life would *develop* as it has.
5 I'm sorry, but it's beginning to *stop me enjoying* my food.
6 It's extremely hard to *be as good as* their expectations.
7 I'd like to *establish* my own business in a few years.

3 Work in pairs. Have you ever said or thought any of the sentences in exercise 2?

SPEAKING

1 Work in pairs. You are going to present something you have read to the class. Follow the instructions below.

Choose something you have both read or would like to read (it doesn't have to be a novel – it could be a comic, a magazine, a film script etc) that you think your classmates will find interesting.

Make notes on anything you know about ...

- the contents.
- why you think it's interesting.
- why you think your classmates would enjoy reading it.

Prepare to present your choice to the class.

Useful language

We've chosen ... because we think ...
We think you'll find it ...
First of all it's really ...
But above all it's ...
So, to sum up ...

2 Present your choice to the class. The class will vote on which they're most interested in reading.

DID YOU KNOW?

1 Work in pairs. Read the text and discuss these questions.

The Man Booker Prize for Fiction is one of the world's most important literary prizes. It is awarded each year for the best original full-length novel written by a citizen of the Commonwealth or the Republic of Ireland in the English language. A panel of judges choose a short list of six novels from over 200 entrants. The short list is announced in September, and then a month later the prize is awarded in a special, televised ceremony. The winner of the Man Booker Prize receives £50,000. In addition, both the winner and the short-listed authors are guaranteed a worldwide readership and a dramatic increase in book sales.

- What literary prizes are awarded to writers in your language?
- Who are the best known writers a) of the moment b) of all time? Have you read any of their books? What did you think of them?
- Which is the most widely translated work of literature in your language? Would you recommend it? Why or why not?

Grammar

Narrative tenses

When we are telling a story in the past we can use a variety of narrative tenses.

We use the past simple to talk about the main events of the story.
> The audience **watched** the live broadcast in horror.

We use the past continuous to describe other events and actions that were in progress at the time of the main events.
> A woman **was lying** on a surgical table.

We use the past perfect to show that a past action took place before another past action.
> Frida **had finished** school and was travelling home when her bus crashed.

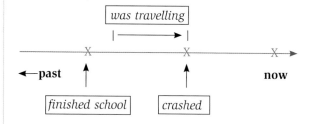

Past perfect continuous

We use the past perfect continuous to talk about actions or events that were in progress before or up to a certain point in the past.
> I returned to my chair and arranged myself as I **had been sitting** before.

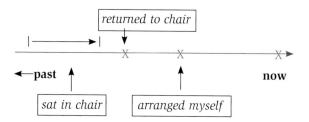

1 We do not use the past perfect continuous to talk about a completed action. We use the past perfect simple.
   He **had finished** the painting.
   (Not ~~he had been finishing~~ the painting.)
2 Stative verbs are not used in the past perfect continuous.
   She **had not been** with the family long.
   (Not She ~~had not been being~~ with the family long.)

Affirmative & Negative

subject			present participle
He/She/ They/etc.	had hadn't	been	doing/studying/ travelling etc.

Question

Had	he/she/ they/etc.	been	doing/studying/ travelling etc?

FUNCTIONAL LANGUAGE
Evaluating

Positive evaluations
It's a masterpiece.
It's extremely valuable.
It's priceless.
It's worth a fortune.

Negative evaluations
It has no redeeming features.
It's a load of rubbish.
It's absolutely worthless.
It's not worth anything at all.

WORD LIST

Art

abstract *adj* **	/ˈæbstrækt/
collection *n C* ***	/kəˈlekʃ(ə)n/
conceptual *adj*	/kənˈseptʃuəl/
dealer *n C* ***	/ˈdiːlə(r)/
exhibition *n C* ***	/ˌeksɪˈbɪʃ(ə)n/
figurative *adj*	/ˈfɪɡərətɪv/
landscape *n C* **	/ˈlæn(d)ˌskeɪp/
mural *n C*	/ˈmjʊərəl/
patron *n C* *	/ˈpeɪtrən/
portrait *n C* *	/ˈpɔː(r)trɪt/
sculpture *n C* **	/ˈskʌlptʃə(r)/
self-portrait *n C*	/ˈselfpɔː(r)trɪt/
still life *n C*	/stɪl laɪf/

-*ever* words

however ***	/haʊˈevə(r)/
whatever ***	/wɒtˈevə(r)/
whenever **	/wenˈevə(r)/
wherever **	/werˈevə(r)/
whoever **	/huːˈevə(r)/

Phrasal verbs

come up with	/kʌm ˈʌp wɪð/
live up to	/lɪv ˈʌp tuː/
put (sb/sth) off	/ˌpʊt ˈɒf/
set up	/ˌset ˈʌp/
take to	/ˈteɪk ˌtuː/
turn (sb) away	/ˌtɜː(r)n əˈweɪ/
turn (sb/sth) down	/ˌtɜː(r)n ˈdaʊn/
turn out	/ˌtɜː(r)n ˈaʊt/

Other words & phrases

ambiance *n U*	/ˈæmbiəns/
best-seller *n C*	/ˌbestˈselə(r)/
billionaire *n C*	/ˌbɪljəˈneə(r)/
boxed set *n C*	/ˌbɒkst ˈset/
brass *n U*	/brɑːs/
bring up *v*	/ˌbrɪŋ ˈʌp/
broadcast *n C* *	/ˈbrɔːdˌkɑːst/
campaigner *n C*	/kæmˈpeɪnə(r)/
candle *n C* **	/ˈkænd(ə)l/
catch up with *v*	/ˌkætʃ ʌp ˈwɪð/
charm *n U*	/tʃɑː(r)m/
chin *n C* **	/tʃɪn/
cloth *n C* **	/klɒθ/
clove *n C*	/kləʊv/
colossal *adj*	/kəˈlɒs(ə)l/
commission *n C*	/kəˈmɪʃ(ə)n/
commit suicide	/kəˌmɪt ˈsuːɪsaɪd/
comply *v*	/kəmˈplaɪ/
controversy *n C* **	/ˈkɒntrəvɜː(r)si; kənˈtrɒvə(r)si/
conviction *n U*	/kənˈvɪkʃ(ə)n/
cover *n C* ***	/ˈkʌvə(r)/
craze *n C*	/kreɪz/
curator *n C*	/kjʊˈreɪtə(r)/
dangle *v*	/ˈdæŋɡ(ə)l/
deafen *v*	/ˈdef(ə)n/
depression *n U* **	/dɪˈpreʃ(ə)n/
detention centre *n C*	/dɪˈtenʃ(ə)n ˌsentə(r)/
disbelief *n U*	/ˌdɪsbɪˈliːf/
elitist *adj*	/ɪˈliːtɪst/
exhibit *v* **	/ɪɡˈzɪbɪt/
faint *v* *	/feɪnt/
falter *v*	/ˈfɔːltə(r)/
farce *n C*	/fɑː(r)s/
focal point *n C*	/ˈfəʊk(ə)l ˌpɔɪnt/
forehead *n C* **	/ˈfɒrɪd; ˈfɔː(r)ˌhed/
fuel *v*	/ˈfjuːəl/
godsend *n s*	/ˈɡɒdˌsend/
grab *v*	/ɡræb/
greet *v* **	/ɡriːt/
hallway *n C*	/ˈhɔːlˌweɪ/
have an affair	/ˌhæv ən əˈfeə(r)/
honour *v*	/ˈɒnə(r)/
influential *adj*	/ˌɪnfluˈenʃ(ə)l/
jug *n C* *	/dʒʌɡ/
juvenile *adj*	/ˈdʒuːvənaɪl/
lie on *v*	/ˈlaɪ ˌɒn/
life-size *adj*	/ˈlaɪfˌsaɪz/
maid *n C*	/meɪd/
needle *n C* **	/ˈniːd(ə)l/
negotiate *v* **	/nɪˈɡəʊʃieɪt/
network *n C* ***	/ˈnetˌwɜː(r)k/
nominate *v* *	/ˈnɒmɪneɪt/
nosedive *v*	/ˈnəʊzˌdaɪv/
operating theatre *n C*	/ˈɒpəreɪtɪŋ ˌθɪətə(r)/
organic *adj* *	/ɔː(r)ˈɡænɪk/
overly *adv*	/ˈəʊvə(r)li/
overpowering *adj*	/ˌəʊvə(r)ˈpaʊərɪŋ/
perfectionist *n C*	/pə(r)ˈfekʃ(ə)nɪst/
prestigious *adj*	/preˈstɪdʒəs/
provoke *v*	/prəˈvəʊk/
put forward *v*	/ˌpʊt ˈfɔː(r)wə(r)d/
quote *n C*	/kwəʊt/
rate *n C* ***	/reɪt/
recover *v* ***	/rɪˈkʌvə(r)/
regime *n C*	/reɪˈʒiːm/
release *v* ***	/rɪˈliːs/
resemble (sb) *v* **	/rɪˈzemb(ə)l/
retire *v* **	/rɪˈtaɪə(r)/
sabre *n C*	/ˈseɪbə(r)/
satellite *n C* **	/ˈsætəlaɪt/
scandal *n C*	/ˈskænd(ə)l/
set about *v*	/ˌset əˈbaʊt/
single (sth/sb) out *v*	/ˈsɪŋɡ(ə)l aʊt/
siren *n C* *	/ˈsaɪrən/
slight *adj* ***	/slaɪt/
slip *v*	/slɪp/
slot *n C* *	/slɒt/
smarten (sth/sb) up *v*	/ˌsmɑː(r)t(ə)n ˈʌp/
stain *n C* *	/steɪn/
stardom *n U*	/ˈstɑː(r)dəm/
steel *n U* **	/stiːl/
stench *n U*	/stentʃ/
sting *v* *	/stɪŋ/
strict *adj* **	/strɪkt/
surgical *adj*	/ˈsɜː(r)dʒɪk(ə)l/
suspend *v*	/səˈspend/
take over *v*	/ˌteɪk ˈəʊvə(r)/
talented *adj* *	/ˈtæləntɪd/
tireless *adj*	/ˈtaɪə(r)ləs/
unveil *v*	/ʌnˈveɪl/
vending machine *n C*	/ˈvendɪŋ məˌʃiːn/
viewer *n C* **	/ˈvjuːə(r)/
worldwide *adj* *	/ˌwɜː(r)ldˈwaɪd/

6A | At the polls

SPEAKING

1 Work in pairs, A and B. Read the three stories and tell your partner about them.

A: Turn to page 140. B: Turn to page 143.

2 Discuss these questions.

- Which celebrities in your country have been involved in political or other protests?
- Do you think that celebrities should be involved in politics?
- Do celebrities have social responsibilities because of their fame?

READING

1 Work in pairs. How much do you know about Arnold Schwarzenegger? Use the topics in the box to help you.

family	education	sports
films	politics	future plans

2 Read a short biography which was written when Arnold first became governor of California. Which of the topics in exercise 1 are not mentioned?

3 Read the article again and put the events in the correct order.
Arnold ...

☐ got interested in weight lifting.
☐ got involved in politics.
☐ was cast in a series of action movies.
☐ won his first body building title.
☐ moved to the States.
☐ met his wife.
☐ became governor of California.
☐ became a millionaire.

4 Work in pairs. Discuss these questions.

- Has Arnold Schwarzenegger been in the news again since this biography was written? If yes, why?
- Do you think a former actor could become president in your country? Why or why not?

The many faces of ARNOLD SCHWARZENEGGER

Arnold Schwarzenegger: body builder, film star, millionaire, governor of the State of California. Will this man one day be president? If Arnie's fans have their way, he will. They are campaigning to amend the constitution so that a US citizen born outside
5 the United States can run for office. And provided they win, there's no doubt that Arnie will have his sights set on the White House.

Schwarzenegger is, to many, an embodiment of the American dream. He arrived in the States in 1968 at the age of 21 with no money to his name and barely speaking English, but in little over a year he was
10 a millionaire, running his own mail order firm selling body building equipment. Things were definitely going his way.

In the 1970s he was Mr Universe, in the 1980s he was the world's greatest action hero, starring in films like *Terminator, Predator* and *Total Recall*. In the 1990s he got involved with politics when President George
15 Bush senior appointed him as chairman to the President's Council on Physical Fitness. He is now governor of one of the largest states in the US.

But how did it all start? Arnie's dad wanted his son to become a footballer. Arnie
20 trained hard with his local team and showed promise. He would probably have become a professional footballer if his coach hadn't taken him to a gym one day. Arnie tried out the weights and fell in love
25 with body building. Five years later, Arnie won the 1966 Mr Europe title. He was on his way.

Arnie was committed to making a career for himself as an actor, and he was sure that his Mr Universe body
30 would get him there. He was right. He worked hard, he made the right contacts and became one of the US's biggest box office successes in the 80s and 90s.

And what about Arnie the politician? Many say he wouldn't be where he is today unless he'd met and married Maria Shriver (a member
35 of the influential Kennedy family). They may not share political views (Maria is a Democrat and Arnie has always stood under a Republican banner) but she always stands by him. And as all politicians know, a long stable relationship (he and Maria have been together for nearly 30 years) certainly helps win votes. So long as he can point to the happy
40 family photos (he and Maria have four children) he'll be able to fight off the Hollywood playboy image.

※ **This week**

And so, can family man Arnold Schwarzenegger, American citizen
45 since 1983, make American history and become the first president with a foreign accent? We'll have to wait and see. His fans may be able to change the constitution, but would Americans really vote for a president Schwarzenegger if
50 they had the chance? Stranger things have happened in the movies!

GRAMMAR: real & unreal conditions

1 Underline the conditional clauses in the sentences and answer the questions below.

1 He would probably have become a professional footballer if his coach hadn't taken him to a gym.
2 If Arnie's fans have their way, he'll be president.
3 So long as he can point to the photos, he'll be able to fight off the playboy image.
4 Provided they win, Arnie will have his sights set on the White House.
5 He wouldn't be where he is today unless he'd met Maria Shriver.

1 Do the conditions refer to a) the past, b) the present or c) the future? Do the results refer to a) the past, b) the present or c) the future?
2 Are the conditions real (possible or probable) or unreal (impossible or improbable)?
3 Replace *unless* with *if* in the last sentence and rewrite it.

2 Put the verbs in brackets into the correct tense.

1 I _____ (not / vote) for a celebrity politician unless I really liked his films.
2 I'd never vote for a politician if he _____ (not / be) born in my country.
3 I'll probably always vote for the same party unless they _____ (change) in a big way.
4 If I _____ (have) the chance, I'd love to be a politician.
5 I'd prefer it if there _____ (be) more women politicians.
6 If people had known what our prime minister was really like, they _____ (not / vote) for him/her.

3 Work in pairs. Discuss these questions.

1 Do you agree with the statements in exercise 2?
2 How many different ways can you complete the sentences below?

- Things in this country will get better so long as … .
- I'd never become a politician unless … .

Conditional sentences describe a situation (real or imaginary) and its probable consequences or results.
- We use these words to introduce the situation:

if,   on condition that,   provided/providing (that),   as/so long as,   unless

We use **real conditional sentences** to talk about real situations.
- Use a present tense to describe the **situation**.
- Use *will/may/might/can/must* + infinitive to describe the **result**.
  *Arnie **cannot stand** for president unless the law is changed.*
  *So long as he keeps a clean image, he **will remain** popular.*

We use **unreal conditional sentences** to talk about imaginary situations.
- Use a past tense to describe a **present or future situation.**
  *If he **wanted** to stop working … (= But he doesn't.)*
- Use *would/could/might* + infinitive to describe **a present or future result.**
  *… he **would have** enough money to live on.*
- Use the past perfect to describe a past situation.
  *If he **hadn't met** Maria Shriver … (= But he did.)*
- Use *would/might/could* + *have* + past participle to describe **a past result**.
  *… he **might** never **have got involved** in politics.*

A present situation can have a past result, and a past situation can have a present result.
  He wouldn't be where he is today, if he hadn't taken up bodybuilding.
  If he wasn't so stubborn, he would have given up at the first obstacle.

➤ SEE LANGUAGE REFERENCE PAGE 64

6B | Women in politics

SPEAKING & VOCABULARY: elections

1 Work in pairs. Discuss these questions.

- When was the last election held in your country?
- What was the result?
- Was it a surprise? Why or why not?

2 Read the text and match the words in bold to the definitions 1–7.

> **General elections** usually take place every four years in Britain. The country is divided into about 650 local **constituencies**, and each district elects one **Member of Parliament** (MP). Anyone can stand for election but voters choose only one **candidate** and most of the seats in parliament are won by the main political parties. Voting is not compulsory and the **turnout** is sometimes very low, especially in places that are considered to be safe seats for one of the big parties. The **polling stations** close at the end of the day, and the results are announced when the **ballot papers** have been counted.

1 a person competing in an election
2 a politician who has been elected to parliament
3 geographical areas that elect a representative to parliament
4 the number of voters in an election
5 the pieces of paper where the voters show their choice
6 the places where people go to vote
7 the process by which the national UK government is elected

3 Work in pairs. Discuss these questions.

- How are general elections organized in your country?
- What happens in the days around a general election in your country?
- Do you think that voting should be compulsory?

LISTENING

1 🔊 **1.35** Listen to the introduction of a radio programme about women in politics and answer the questions.

1 What was Grover Cleveland's attitude towards women in politics?
2 How has the political situation for women changed in the last one hundred years?
3 In what way is further progress needed?
4 What is the 'quota system'?

2 🔊 **1.35** Listen again. What do the numbers in the box refer to?

22nd	1905	91	50/50	1 in 3

3 🔊 **1.36** Listen to the second part of the programme. Which speaker supports the quota system? Which speaker is against the quota system?

4 Match the opinions a–g to the speakers, 1 or 2, in exercise 3.

a She thinks that 'positive action' is a better expression than 'positive discrimination'.
b She thinks that politicians should talk about equal pay and childcare.
c She thinks that excellence is the best way to fight discrimination.
d She thinks that the political world is changing because there are more women in it.
e She thinks that Denmark and Sweden are good examples.
f She thinks that there are many stupid men in politics.
g She thinks that we need to have people in positions of responsibility who are good at what they do.

5 🔊 **1.36** Listen to the recording again to check your answers.

6 Which speaker do you sympathize with more? Why?

GRAMMAR: *I wish* & *If only*

> - Use *wish* (+ *that*) or *if only* + simple past/past continuous to express regret about the present or the future.
>   *All the political parties* **wish they had** *more women.* (= But they don't have more women.)
>   **If only he wasn't** *a man!* (= But he is a man!)
> - Use *wish* (+ *that*) or *If only* + past perfect to express regret about the past.
>   *I* **wish that we'd introduced** *the system 100 years ago.* (= But we didn't introduce it then.)

⟩ SEE LANGUAGE REFERENCE PAGE 64

1 Choose the best verb form to complete the sentences.

1 If only they *introduced / 'd introduced / were introducing* the quota system earlier! It would have been so much better.
2 She must be wishing she *tells / 'd told / told* the truth at the start.
3 If only we *are able to / can / could* get more women interested in politics.
4 I wish I *am living / live / was living* in a country like Denmark.
5 I wish you *don't vote / didn't vote / hadn't voted* for her!
6 She's probably wishing she *is / were / had been* the prime minister.

2 Rewrite the sentences beginning with the words given.

1 I really regret eating so much.
  I wish _____.
2 I'd love to have more money.
  If only _____.
3 I'm sorry that I can't help you.
  I wish _____.
4 It's a shame you're not here.
  I wish _____.
5 It's a real pity that I listened to him.
  If only_____.

3 Look at the photos on page 140. What do you think the people are thinking? Write two sentences for each picture beginning *I wish* or *If only*. Then compare your ideas with a partner.

4 Work in pairs. Have you ever said or thought any of the things in exercise 2? If yes, what were the circumstances?

  What do you regret about your life now or in the past?

PRONUNCIATION: word stress in word families

1 Work in pairs. Read out the words below.

politics, political, politician

🔊 **1.37** Listen to check your pronunciation.

2 Count the syllables in the words below and mark the main stress in each word.

1 economy, economics, economist
2 philosophy, philosophical, philosopher
3 parliament, parliamentary
4 democracy, democratic, democrat
5 government, governmental, governing

🔊 **1.38** Listen to the recording to check your answers.

3 Work in pairs, A and B. Test your partner's memory and pronunciation.

A: Turn to page 140.   B: Turn to page 144.

DID YOU KNOW?

1 Work in pairs. Read the text and discuss the questions.

In 1893, New Zealand took the historic step of becoming the first country in the world to grant the vote to all adult women. The decision came after a fifteen-year campaign led by Kate Sheppard. Sheppard became a well-known historical figure in her own country where she can be seen on a ten-dollar bill. She also travelled to Canada, the United States and Britain where she met other suffragettes who were fighting for the right to vote. By the time of her death in 1934, women in nearly twenty countries around the world had won the right to vote. New Zealand had its first woman prime minister in 1997 and ten years later, women had been elected heads of state on all five continents.

- When were women granted the vote in your country?
- How much political power do women have in your country?
- Would the sex of a political candidate ever influence the way you vote?

6c | Politically incorrect

SPEAKING & VOCABULARY: embarrassment

1 Complete the sentences with a word from the box. If necessary, use a dictionary to help you.

> acutely   ashamed   bright   blush
> conscious   humiliating   squirmed

- ☐ a He ____ with embarrassment when his phone went off during the film.
- ☐ b She was ____ embarrassed every time her parents opened their mouths.
- ☐ c I always ____ when my tummy makes a funny noise.
- ☐ d He went ____ red when he realized he'd forgotten his wallet.
- ☐ e I find it really ____ that I can't find a job.
- ☐ f He's not ____ of making mistakes when he speaks other languages.
- ☐ g She's very self-____ about her haircut at the moment.

2 Put the situations in exercise 1 in order of embarrassment (1= most embarrassing → 7 = least embarrassing).

3 Do you know any other stories about embarrassing experiences?

READING

1 Work in pairs. Do you know of an embarrassing mistake made by a prominent politician? Tell your partner about it.

2 Read the two texts opposite. What mistakes did these two men make?

3 Read the stories and complete the sentences with (G) Gloystein or (P) Prescott.

1 _____ was attacked in public.
2 _____ reacted violently.
3 _____ resigned almost immediately.
4 _____ tried to bribe his way out of trouble.
5 _____ won the support of the general public.
6 _____ lost the support of his party.
7 _____ was taken to court.
8 _____ was not taken to court.

4 Work in pairs. Discuss these questions.

1 Who made the biggest mistakes?
2 What should he have done?
3 Which of these men should have been punished?

Gloystein

Peter Gloystein, the deputy leader of the German state of Bremen, caused acute embarrassment to the centre-
5 right Christian Democrat party when his attempt at a joke went disastrously wrong.

Gloystein, who was Bremen's finance minister at the time,
10 was attending the launch of the German Wine Week. Gloystein thought that it would be funny to pour a magnum of champagne over the head of a homeless man who was standing nearby. The audience watched in horror as an amused Gloystein emptied
15 the bottle over the man's head. 'Here's something for you to drink,' he said as he poured. Udo Oelschlager, the homeless man, was understandably less amused. But instead of getting angry, he asked Gloystein for an explanation of his humiliating experience. 'Who are you?'
20 he asked. 'Why are you doing this?'

A red-faced Gloystein made matters worse by attempting to be 'friends' with Mr Oelschlager. First of all, he offered his business card, then the money in his pocket, and finally his Mont Blanc pen worth £150. He shouldn't have
25 bothered.

A tearful Oelschlager refused the offer. 'I don't need his money,' said Oelschlager. 'I'm not going to be bribed. You offended me and wanted to make me look like an idiot.'

Oelschlager pressed charges and a Bremen ministry
30 spokesman confirmed that Gloystein had resigned from his various posts.

Prescott

With the government cruising to another victory, the general election campaign was of little interest to many people, until John Prescott, the Deputy Prime Minister, brought a spark of life to proceedings.

5   Prescott was visiting Rhyl in North Wales as part of the campaign when farmhand, Craig Evans, threw an egg at him from close range. The egg hit its target, breaking all over the politician's smart grey suit. But Prescott's reaction was not that of a typical, embarrassed politician.
10 Instead of brushing it off with a false smile, he wheeled around and promptly punched his assailant full in the face.

His reaction was criticized by opposition parties who said he should have kept his cool when provoked. The police, however, decided not to press charges against
15 either the Deputy Prime Minister or Craig Evans, his assailant, who was taking part in a protest about the government's lack of support for farmers and farm workers during an outbreak of foot and mouth disease.

Whilst the spin doctors of Prescott's party squirmed
20 with embarrassment, the opinion polls showed that Prescott's honest (though violent) response had actually won him a lot of sympathy and had possibly even won some extra votes for the ruling Labour Party.

GRAMMAR: *should have*

- Use *should/shouldn't have* + past participle to make criticisms of past actions.
  He **should have resigned** earlier.
  He **shouldn't have bothered**.

> SEE LANGUAGE REFERENCE PAGE 64

1 Complete the sentences with *should* or *shouldn't*.

1 He _____ have thought about the other man a little more.
2 He definitely _____ have done that. I mean, it wasn't strictly necessary, was it?
3 I think he got away with it. They _____ have locked him up.
4 It serves him right. He _____ have thrown the egg in the first place.
5 He really _____ have tried to make things better – he just made things worse.
6 What an idiot! He _____ have ignored it and let the police deal with it.

🔊 **1.39** Listen to check your answers.

2 Work in pairs. Match the statements in exercise 1 to the two stories about politicians. Which statements do you agree with?

3 Think of five small mistakes you have made in your life. Talk to a partner about them and say what you should or shouldn't have done.

6D | Politically correct

Vocabulary: -isms

1 Which words in the box suggest a prejudice against a certain group of people?

> ageism elitism idealism nationalism optimism pacifism
> pessimism racism realism sexism socialism

2 Change the words in the box in exercise 1 into adjectives.

3 Work in pairs. Explain which of the adjectives from exercise 2 you would use to describe yourself.

Think of three situations where a prejudice is shown against a particular group of people.

Have you ever felt that you were the victim of prejudice?

Listening

1 Work in pairs. Look at the advert and answer the question.

Why might this job ad cause offence?

> **Receptionist**
> required immediately in central Oxford. Suit young graduate.
> Good promotion prospects. The ideal candidate will have
> excellent secretarial skills, a good phone manner and a
> smart appearance. She should also be open, friendly and
> approachable. For more details and an application form
> please contact **b.whote@itsolutions.com**

2 🔘 1.40 Listen to two people discussing the advert. Answer these questions.

1 Who was responsible for writing the advert?
2 What problems has it caused?

3 Correct the five incorrect sentences.

1 Frank has always been sexist while working at this company.
2 Frank's boss approves of his attitude.
3 Frank's an accountant.
4 The two women discussing Frank think he's been treated fairly.
5 Frank's been with the company for a long time.
6 The two women feel Frank's generally incompetent in his work.
7 One of the women tries to defend Frank.
8 The two women believe the unions will back Frank's sacking.

4 Complete the sentences with a word. Then check your answers in tapescript 1.40 on page 156.

1 I'm surprised _____ didn't get rid of him sooner.
2 _____ asked him to write this advert ...
3 Someone complained to the government organization and _____ 're taking the whole thing very seriously.
4 Whoever asked him to write the ad should really have written it _____ or at the very least _____ should have asked to see it before it got sent off.
5 I don't think someone should lose _____ job for making an honest mistake.

5 Work in pairs. Draw up a list of reasons why Frank isn't very popular at work. Then discuss this question.

Do you think Frank deserved to lose his job?

FUNCTIONAL LANGUAGE: asking for & giving clarification

1 Look at the expressions in bold. Divide them into two groups, a or b.

a asking for clarification
b explaining what you mean

1 But **what are you suggesting**? That she's got rid of him because of his sexist comments?
2 The company could face massive fines. **What are you saying**?
3 It probably hasn't helped his case, but no, **that's not what I'm saying** …
4 A: … and then he goes and slips in a completely unnecessary 'she' …
   D: What do you mean? **I don't follow**.
5 So, **basically you're saying that** he's incompetent? That he can't actually do his job without someone overseeing everything he does …
6 **I mean**, it's not as if he did it on purpose … I feel quite sorry for him actually, …
7 I know, I know, but **what I meant to say was that** we all know what he's like, I mean, he's not the most articulate person we know, is he?
8 I'm not disputing that. But **my point is that** I don't think someone should lose their job for making an honest mistake.

"To avoid accusations of sexism, be a sweetie, Dalrymple, and make tea."

2 Complete the two dialogues below with expressions from exercise 1.

1
A: I think he should make a public apology.
B: (1) _____? That he should take sole responsibility for the situation?
A: No, (2) _____. The company is equally to blame. But he did make a very costly mistake and I think he should own up to it.

2
C: So (3) _____ it's my fault, are you?
D: No, not all. (4) _____ you shouldn't feel responsible for what happened. It was out of your hands.
C: What do you mean? (5) _____.
D: Well, (6) _____, you weren't to know that the hotel had been double-booked, were you?

🔘 **1.41–1.42** Listen and compare your answers with the recording.

SPEAKING

Roleplay

1 Work in two groups, A and B. Prepare to roleplay the meeting between Frank and his boss when she tells him he's been sacked.

Group A: You are Frank. Prepare your defence.
Group B: You are the boss. Prepare to explain your decision to Frank.

2 Work in pairs. Roleplay the meeting between Frank and his boss.

> ### Useful language
>
> *I understand that this may come as a bit of a shock …*
> *What you need to understand is …*
> *I'm afraid it's out of my hands …*
> *I'd like to put my side of the argument, if that's all right.*
> *I'm sorry, but I don't accept that at all.*
> *This is outrageous!*
> *You'll be hearing from my lawyer …*

GRAMMAR

Real & unreal conditions

Conditional sentences describe a situation (real or imaginary) and its probable consequences or results.

CONDITION   RESULT
  If it rains,   *we'll get wet.*
We can join the two parts of a conditional sentence with *if* and other conjunctions:

on condition (that) as long as so long as provided (that) providing (that)	= *if* (and **only** *if*)

Unless is used for saying that if something does not happen, something else will happen or be true as a result.

> *We'll miss the bus **unless** we hurry.*
> (= If we don't hurry.)
> *I'll stay here **unless** you call.*
> (= If you don't call.)

1   Real conditions

We use real conditional sentences to talk about real, possible or probable situations or conditions.
We use a present tense (simple, continuous, perfect) to describe the situation or condition. We use *will/may/ might/can/must* + infinitive to describe the result.

>   CONDITION   RESULT
> *If he says the right things, he**'ll** remain popular.*
> *If you've voted for him, you **may** regret it.*

We can also use a present tense in the result clause to show that something is true in general.

> *If you **don't eat**, you die.*

2   Unreal conditions

We use unreal conditional sentences to talk about imaginary, impossible or improbable situations.
We use a past tense (simple or continuous) to describe a present or future situation.

> *If we **had** more time, ...*
> (= But we don't have more time.)

We use the past perfect to describe a past situation.

> *If we **had arrived** earlier, ...*
> (= But we didn't arrive earlier.)

We use *would/could/might* + infinitive to describe a present or future result of our hypothesis.

> *If we had more time, we**'d sit** in the park/we **could visit** the museum.*

We use *would/might/could* + *have* + past participle to describe a past result of our hypothesis.

> *If we'd arrived earlier, we **would have paid** less/we **might have got** a better seat.*

(a) Conditional sentences can begin with either the condition or the result.

> *If I were you, I wouldn't do that.*
> *I wouldn't do that if I were you.*

(b) In unreal conditions, *was* and *were* are both used as the past form of *be*. Some people think that *were* is more correct.

> *If I were you/If she were here/If he were alive*

(c) A present situation can have a past result, and a past situation can have a present result.

> *If I had more money* (ie now/in general), *I wouldn't have walked* (ie in the past).
> *If she had tried harder* (ie in the past), *she wouldn't be where she is today.*

(d) Conditionals are sometimes described in the following way:
Type 1: *If* + simple present, *will* + infinitive
Type 2: *If* + simple past, *would* + infinitive
Type 3: *If* + past perfect, *would* + *have* + past participle
However, most conditional sentences in actual use do not fit into these three categories.

I wish & If only

We use *I wish* and *if only* to express regrets.
We use the simple past, past continuous or *could* + infinitive to express a regret about the present or the future.

> **I wish** (that) you were here. (= But you're not.)
> **If only** we were sitting on the beach! (= But we're not.)
> **I wish** I could see you. (= But I can't.)

We use the past perfect to express a regret about the past.

> *I wish* (that) you **hadn't said** that. (= But you did.)
> *If only I'd known!* (= But I didn't.)

We can also use *I wish* and *If only* followed by a subject and *would*. This does not express regret. It is used to show that we want someone to do something.

> **I wish** he would stop talking.
> **If only** they would go away!

Should have

We use *should/shouldn't have* +
past participle to make criticisms of
past actions.

> He **should have kept** quiet.
> (= But he didn't keep quiet.)
> We **shouldn't have** come.
> (= But we came.)

FUNCTIONAL LANGUAGE

Asking for clarification

What are you suggesting?
What are you saying?
Basically you're saying that …
I don't follow.

Clarifying

That's not what I'm saying …
What I meant to say was that …
My point is that …
I mean, …

WORD LIST

Elections

ballot paper *n C*	/ˈbælət ˌpeɪpə(r)/
candidate *n C* ***	/ˈkændɪdeɪt; ˈkændɪdət/
constituency *n C* **	/kənˈstɪtjʊənsi/
general election *n C*	/ˌdʒen(ə)rəl ɪˈlekʃ(ə)n/
Member of Parliament *n C* *	/ˌmembə(r) əv ˈpɑː(r)ləmənt/
polling station *n C*	/ˈpəʊlɪŋ ˌsteɪʃ(ə)n/
stand for *v*	/ˈstænd fɔː(r)/
turnout *n C*	/ˈtɜː(r)naʊt/

Embarrassment

acutely *adv*	/əˈkjuːtli/
ashamed *adj* **	/əˈʃeɪmd/
bright *adj* ***	/braɪt/
blush *v* *	/blʌʃ/
humiliating *adj*	/hjuːˈmɪliˌeɪtɪŋ/
self-conscious *adj*	/self ˈkɒnʃəs/
squirm *v*	/skwɜː(r)m/

-isms

ageism	/ˈeɪdʒɪz(ə)m/
elitism	/ɪˈliːˌtɪz(ə)m/
idealism	/aɪˈdɪəˌlɪz(ə)m/
nationalism *	/ˈnæʃ(ə)nəˌlɪz(ə)m/
optimism *	/ˈɒptɪˌmɪzəm/
pacifism	/ˈpæsɪˌfɪz(ə)m/
pessimism	/ˈpesəˌmɪz(ə)m/
racism *	/ˈreɪˌsɪz(ə)m/
realism *	/ˈrɪəˌlɪz(ə)m/
sexism	/ˈseksɪz(ə)m/
socialism **	/ˈsəʊʃəˌlɪz(ə)m/

Other words & phrases

action hero *n C*	/ˈækʃ(ə)n ˌhɪərəʊ/
ad *n C*	/æd/
alienate *v*	/ˈeɪliəneɪt/
amend *v* **	/əˈmend/
approachable *adj*	/əˈprəʊtʃəb(ə)l/
assailant *n C*	/əˈseɪlənt/
banner *n C*	/ˈbænə/
banter *n U*	/ˈbæntə(r)/
barely *adv* **	/ˈbeə(r)li/
big time	/ˈbɪg ˌtaɪm/
body builder *n C*	/ˈbɒdɪ ˌbɪldə(r)/
bribe *v*	/braɪb/
brush (sth) off *v*	/brʌʃ ˈɒf/
centre-right *adj*	/ˌsentə(r)ˈraɪt/
chancellor *n C*	/ˈtʃɑːnsələ(r)/
chairman *n C* ***	/ˈtʃeə(r)mən/
childcare *n U*	/ˈtʃaɪldˌkeə(r)/
close range	/ˌkləʊs ˈreɪndʒ/
commit to *v*	/kəˈmɪt tuː/
competent *adj* **	/ˈkɒmpɪtənt/
compulsory *adj* *	/kəmˈpʌlsəri/
condescending *adj*	/ˌkɒndɪˈsendɪŋ/
constitution *n C* ***	/ˌkɒnstɪˈtjuːʃ(ə)n/
cruise *v* *	/kruːz/
deputy leader *n C*	/ˌdepjʊti ˈliːdə(r)/
deserve *v* **	/dɪˈzɜː(r)v/
determine *v* **	/dɪˈtɜː(r)mɪn/
disagreement *n U* *	/ˌdɪsəˈgriːmənt/
disastrously *adv*	/dɪˈzɑːstrəsli/
discrimination *n U* **	/dɪˌskrɪmɪˈneɪʃ(ə)n/
dismissal *n C* **	/dɪsˈmɪs(ə)l/
dollar bill *n C*	/ˌdɒlə(r) ˈbɪl/
embodiment *n U*	/ɪmˈbɒdɪmənt/
engineer *n C* ***	/ˌendʒɪˈnɪə(r)/
fair *adj* ***	/feə(r)/
foot and mouth disease *n U*	/ˌfʊt ən ˈmaʊθ dɪˌziːz/
fuss *n U* *	/fʌs/
give (sb) the sack	/ˌgɪv ðə ˈsæk/
governor *n C* **	/ˈgʌvə(r)nə(r)/
graduate *n C* **	/ˈgrædʒuət/
grounds *n pl*	/graʊndz/
have your sights set on	/hæv ˈsaɪts set ɒn/
have (your) way	/hæv weɪ/
heel *n C* **	/hiːl/
horrified *adj*	/ˈhɒrɪfaɪd/
issue *n C* ***	/ˈɪʃuː/
laddish *adj*	/ˈlædɪʃ/
launch *n C* **	/lɔːntʃ/
liability *n U* **	/ˌlaɪəˈbɪləti/
macho *adj*	/ˈmætʃəʊ/
magnum *n C*	/ˈmægnəm/
make history	/meɪk ˈhɪst(ə)ri/
make matters worse	/ˌmeɪk mætə(r)z ˈwɜː(r)s/
memo *n C*	/ˈmeməʊ/
mess (sth) up	/ˌmes ˈʌp/
object to (sth) *v* *	/ɒbˈdʒekt tuː/
offensive *adj* *	/əˈfensɪv/
on purpose *adv*	/ɒn ˈpɜː(r)pəs/
outbreak *n C* *	/ˈaʊtˌbreɪk/
outcome *n C* ***	/ˈaʊtkʌm/
oversee *v*	/ˌəʊvə(r)ˈsiː/
pour *v* ***	/pɔː(r)/
press charges	/pres ˈtʃɑː(r)dʒəz/
proceedings *n pl*	/prəˈsiːdɪŋz/
promptly *adv*	/ˈprɒmptli/
prospect *n C* *	/ˈprɒspekt/
punch *v* *	/pʌntʃ/
quota system *n C*	/ˈkwəʊtə ˌsɪstəm/
red-faced *adj*	/ˌredˈfeɪst/
refer to (sth) *v* ***	/rɪˈfɜː(r) tuː/
resign *v* ***	/rɪˈzaɪn/
right *n C* ***	/raɪt/
run for office	/ˌrʌn fə ˈɒfɪs/
scribble *v*	/ˈskrɪb(ə)l/
secretarial *adj*	/ˌsekrəˈteəriəl/
show promise	/ˌʃəʊ ˈprɒmɪs/
spark *n C*	/spɑː(r)k/
spin doctor *n C*	/ˈspɪn ˌdɒktə(r)/
stable *adj* **	/ˈsteɪb(ə)l/
stand by (sb) *v*	/ˈstænd baɪ/
step aside *v*	/ˈstep əˈsaɪd/
suffragette *n C*	/ˌsʌfrəˈdʒet/
supervise *v* **	/ˈsuːpə(r)vaɪz/
sure as hell	/ˈʃɔː(r) əz ˈhel/
tackle *v* *	/ˈtæk(ə)l/
tearful *adj*	/ˈtɪə(r)f(ə)l/
un-PC *adj*	/ˌʌn piːˈsiː/
victory *n C* ***	/ˈvɪkt(ə)ri/
wheel around *v*	/ˌwiːl əˈraʊnd/

7A | Green issues

SPEAKING & VOCABULARY: the environment

1 Use the words in the box to complete the compound nouns in the sentences.

> farms   food   fumes   fuels
> gases   panels   change   warming

1   Diesel exhaust _____ may cause chronic asthma.
2   Fossil _____ currently account for about 85% of world energy consumption.
3   Global _____ could cause sea levels to rise dramatically over the next ten years.
4   Greenhouse _____, like CO_2, have become a serious cause for concern.
5   Europe is now the biggest market for organic _____ in the world, expanding by 25% a year over the past ten years.
6   Spain wants to take advantage of its sunshine by making solar _____ compulsory in new buildings.
7   Six of the world's top polluters met last week to promote clean energy as a way to deal with climate _____.
8   Wind _____ are best located in coastal areas where the wind is strong and reliable.

2 Put the compound nouns in exercise 1 into two groups: (a) problems and (b) solutions. Add two more items to each group.

3 Work in pairs. Look at the leaflet and discuss the questions.

1   How exactly do each of these actions benefit the environment?
2   Can you add three more tips to the leaflet?

Ten top tips to a greener lifestyle

* Walk or cycle to work/school
* Use public transport
* Buy organic food
* Re-use paper, envelopes, plastic carrier bags etc
* Take a shower instead of a bath
* Take your holidays close to home
* Buy things second-hand or used

4 Ask your classmates how many of the things in the leaflet they do regularly. Who has the greenest lifestyle?

READING

1 Read the webpage and match the photos A–F to the stories 1–6.

2 Read the webpage again and complete the stories 1–6 with the sentences a–f.

a   A series of underwater turbines are to be installed in the River Thames.
b   And none of these people was actually born there.
c   Even the car dealers are refusing to take them in part exchange.
d   I'm trying to cut down on my energy consumption.
e   The black carbon powder that is normally used is refined from pure oil and the end product costs more than vintage champagne.
f   This causes widescale water pollution, chronic illness in farmworkers and devastating effects on wildlife.

3 Match the highlighted words on the webpage to the definitions 1–5.

1   drinking very fast
2   falling very fast
3   machines that produce power
4   substances for changing the colour of something
5   thrown away

4 Work in pairs. Discuss these questions.

* Which story would you like to know more about? Why?
* Do you know of a story that could be posted on the Ecochat website?

SPEAKING

1 Work in pairs. You want to persuade your classmates to make some small changes to their lifestyle, but ones that will have a significant effect on the environment. Follow these steps.

1   Choose two lifestyle changes (turn to page 149 for ideas).

2   Prepare to explain why these changes are important.

2 Speak to other students in the class and try to persuade them to make the change.

3 Discuss these questions.

* Whose idea was the most practical?
* Do you think you will put it into practice?

ecochat

NEWS AND VIEWS FOR A GREENER WORLD

 How green is your T-shirt?

2 Cheap printer ink?

3 Victims of oil shortage

4 On her Majesty's service

5 It's an ill wind ...

6 A shaving query

1 Unless it's made with organic cotton – not very. Cotton is one of the most environmentally damaging crops grown in the world. In developing countries, more than 50% of all pesticides used in agriculture are sprayed onto cotton fields. (1) _____ In the USA, cancer rates in cotton-producing states are significantly higher than in neighbouring states. And as if that wasn't enough, the final fabric is bleached, dyed and sprayed with a fire retardant before it is converted into the fashion item you buy in the shops. Organic cotton is grown without using any chemical pesticides or fertilisers and the final cloth is unbleached and dyed with natural plant dyes. So make a difference this summer and wear a green T-shirt.

 CONTINUE READING ...   **(6) COMMENTS:**

2 All lovers of creative recycling will be happy to hear about a new use for used car tyres. A group of British inventors have found a way to extract the carbon from used car tyres to make printer ink. (2) _____ With more than one million tyres being dumped every year, this new system should open the way to cheaper, greener printer ink.

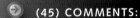 CONTINUE READING ...   **(45) COMMENTS:**

3 The much-loved American SUV (sports utility vehicle) is quickly losing its appeal. With petrol prices rising dramatically, more and more of these gas-guzzling four-wheelers are finding themselves out on the streets with a For Sale sign in their windows. But it seems that no one loves them anymore. (3) _____

CONTINUE READING ...   **(217) COMMENTS:**

4 Windsor Castle, the main residence of Elizabeth II, is to get a hydro-electric power system. (4) _____ The £1,000,000 project will provide the castle with one third of its electrical needs, resulting in a reduction of approximately 600 tonnes in CO_2 emissions every year. Engineers insist that the underwater turbines will have very little impact on the ecology and marine life of the river.

 CONTINUE READING ...   **(17) COMMENTS:**

5 Plans to erect a wind farm on the picturesque Island of Skye off the west coast of Scotland have provoked thousands of complaints from local residents. But who exactly is complaining? It seems that all the letters sent to the local Member of Parliament have been written by the same sixteen people. (5) _____ They are all wealthy second homeowners who don't want to see the value of their holiday property plummeting as the wind farm 'destroys the local landscape'. Local farmers, on the other hand, welcome the farm as it will help subsidize their lifestyles on this remote, but beautiful island.

 CONTINUE READING ...   **(8) COMMENTS:**

6 Q. Can anyone help me out with a problem? (6) _____ One of the things I want to get rid of is my electric razor. But what is the best alternative? What is the most eco-friendly way of shaving? Any advice you could offer will be greatly appreciated. Tom C

 CONTINUE READING ...   **(1) COMMENTS:**

A

B

C

D

E

F

LISTENING

1 Look at the book covers. Which of the phrases in the box would you expect to find in books like these?

> car tyres
> dust and rubble
> insulation
> sledgehammer
> wiring and plumbing
> flush the toilet
> double glazing

2 🔘 2.1 Listen to a conversation and tick the home improvements that are mentioned.

1 insulate the walls
2 replace the wiring system
3 build a rainwater collection tank
4 install a water recycling system
5 put in double glazing
6 buy an air filter
7 install solar panels
8 sand the floorboards

3 🔘 2.1 Listen again and answer the questions.

1 How are they going to get money from their local council?
2 What will they get if they win the competition?
3 What is Nell going to do in the kitchen?
4 What is a greywater tank?
5 How did Winston hurt himself?

4 How could you make your home more environmentally friendly?

GRAMMAR: futures review

1 Match the examples a–f to their uses 1–6.

1 to talk about a schedule
2 to talk about a definite arrangement
3 to talk about an intention
4 to talk about a decision made at the time of talking
5 to make a prediction
6 to make a prediction based on present evidence

a You're not going to win an ecological competition with all those old car tyres.
b We're going to make the whole house green.
c The judging doesn't start till next spring.
d We're doing the bathroom next week.
e With a bit of luck, we won't need any central heating.
f I'll just move this out of the way.

2 Choose the best verb forms to complete the dialogue.

Becky: Have you heard? Nell and Winston (1) *are going to / will* add an extension on to the back of their house. They (2) *'re starting / 'll start* work next week.
Tim: And I suppose they (3) *do / 're doing* it all themselves.
Becky: They're (4) *needing / going to need* some help to do the wiring. But they've said that this is the last job they (5) *do / 're going to do*. And they haven't got much time to do it in. They've entered some sort of eco-competition and it (6) *closes / is closing* at the end of the month.
Tim: They (7) *'re never finishing / 'll never finish* on time.
Becky: And it's (8) *going to / will* look awful. I saw Winston at work and he hasn't got a clue.
Tim: I (9) *'ll give / 'm giving* him a call and see if he needs a hand.

3 Work in pairs, A and B. Speak for thirty seconds. Your partner must guess what question you are answering. (Your partner will not be able to see your questions.)

A: Turn to page 148 for your list of questions.
B: Turn to page 146 for your list of questions.

Schedules

- Use the present simple to talk about schedules.

Plans, arrangements and decisions

- Use the present continuous + a future time expression to talk about definite arrangements.
- Use *going to* + infinitive to talk about intentions.
- The use of the present continuous and *going to* is very similar. You can always use *going to* instead of the present continuous, but you only use the present continuous to talk about a definite arrangement.
- Use *will* + infinitive to talk about a decision made at the time of talking (ie there has been no decision, plan or arrangement made previously).

Predictions

- Use both *going to* + infinitive and *will* + infinitive to make predictions about the future.
- When there is present evidence for the prediction we usually use *going to*.

⊙ SEE LANGUAGE REFERENCE PAGE 74

VOCABULARY: expressions with *make*

1 Look at tapescript 2.1 on page 157 and answer the questions.

1 What does Becky think makes sense?
2 What do Nell and Winston want to make the most of?
3 What will make a difference to their bills?
4 How do they make it easier to decide what else they need to do?

2 Complete the sentences 1–8 in column A with a phrase a–h in column B.

A
1 Governments should make it
2 In a greener world, we will all have to make do
3 It doesn't really make
4 There's not much that ordinary people can do to make
5 Instead of driving around in limousines, politicians should make
6 Schools should make
7 The next ten years will be make
8 With oil running out fast, we need to make

B
a a difference to the future of the planet.
b a point of using public transport.
c the most of it before it dries up completely.
d with less of everything.
e easier for people to be more green.
f or break for our planet.
g sense to be green if other countries are not green.
h time for ecology classes for all children.

3 Work in pairs. Do you agree with the statements in exercise 2?

PRONUNCIATION: pronouncing *o*

1 Work in pairs. Add the words in the box to the sounds 1–9.

hot	come	hook	shoe	world
sore	now	go	kind of	

1 /ɒ/ model, involve, offer, _____
2 /ʊ/ cook, wooden, look, _____
3 /ʌ/ front, double, doesn't, _____
4 /ə/ serious, neighbours, complain, _____
5 /ɔː/ door, orders, absorb, _____
6 /uː/ room, too, food, _____
7 /ɜː/ work, worse, worth, _____
8 /aʊ/ house, proud, downstairs, _____
9 /əʊ/ home, old, know, _____

🔊 2.2 Listen and check.

2 Underline all the words that contain the letter *o* in the speech bubble. Decide how each one pronounced. Which sound 1–9 from exercise 1 is missing from these words?

The government has announced new laws to encourage eco renovations. Solar panel grants, worth up to £3,000, will be made available. Local authorities will foot the bill to encourage householders to insulate their outside walls.

SPEAKING

1 Work in groups of three, A, B and C. You are judging a green lifestyle competition.

A: Turn to page 142.
B: Turn to page 141.
C: Turn to page 144.

2 Tell your partners about your product and decide which idea should win first, second and third place in the competition.

3 Work with a student from a different group. Compare your decisions and discuss these questions.

- Would you buy any of these products? Why or why not?

7c | Lifestyle changes

READING

1 Work in pairs. Discuss these questions.

- What would you like to change about yourself or the way you live? Why?
- How would you go about making the change?

2 Work in pairs, A and B.

A: Read the introduction and text A and answer the questions.
B: Read the introduction and text B and answer the questions.

1 What change does Ginny want to make?
2 Why did she approach a life coach?
3 How did she feel about the experience at the beginning?
4 Why did her opinion change?
5 When does she hope to achieve her final goal?

Compare your answers with your partner.

3 Read your partner's text then work in pairs. In which text, A or B, can you find the answer to the questions below? Sometimes the answers are given in both texts.

1 How long has Ginny been trying to give up smoking?
2 How long have Ginny and Brian been working together?
3 What did Brian and Ginny talk about in their first session?
4 What was the first step Ginny decided to take?
5 What will Ginny be telling Brian about at this week's session?
6 What is the next step going to be?
7 When do they think she'll have given up smoking?

4 Work in pairs. Discuss these questions.

- Do you know anyone who has given up, (or tried to give up) smoking? How did they do it?
- Do you think that going to a life coach is a good way to stop smoking?
- Have you ever made a significant change to your lifestyle? What was it? Did you find it difficult?

Close up: life coaching

Ever tried to make a change to your lifestyle? Get in shape? Change your job? But you've never had the time or energy? A life coach could be
5 the answer to your problems. Life coaches help people achieve their goals. They help them draw up realistic action plans and, more importantly, help them find the strength and the willpower to put them into action. Brian Moffat is a life coach. He helps people
10 change their lives for the better. Ginny is one of his clients.

A Brian's side of the story

Ginny was interested in giving up smoking but she was finding it hard to find the necessary strength. A mutual friend told her about me and she got in touch. In our first session we pinpointed the main barriers to her stopping and the reasons why, when she does stop,
15 she invariably starts up again. Of course, there were no surprises, but it helps to get things out into the open. It clears the air and allows you to work on moving on and looking to the future. That's what life coaching is all about. As a first step she declared her house a no-smoking zone. By the time we next speak, she'll have managed
20 to keep her house smoke free for over a month. We'll be talking about the next step in our next session. From what we talked about last time, it seems that she wants to work on her social smoking. We'll be exploring the options together but she's the one who'll be taking the decisions.
25 At the beginning, I think she was a bit frustrated by the coaching philosophy. She was looking for a 'quick fix', an overnight solution to her problem and she got quite angry when she realized that I wasn't going to give her the answers, and that she had to find them for herself. But now that's she's seen that she's getting results, and
30 getting them through her own strength and willpower, she's much happier.
I'm convinced she'll have reached her goal to stop smoking for good in another month's time at the most.

B Ginny's side of the story

I've been trying to give up smoking for the last five years. I've
35 managed it a couple of times, I even gave up for six months once, but then something happens – a stressful day at work, an argument with my boyfriend – and I start again. So when a friend mentioned life coaching I thought, why not? To start with, I thought it was a total waste of money and I almost gave up after the first session. I
40 wanted someone to give me answers, not ask me endless questions, but I'd committed myself to five sessions so I decided to see them through, and I'm glad I did.
We've been working together for just over three months now, and in that time I've given up smoking during my coffee breaks at work,
45 I've given up smoking in the house and in the next session we'll be tackling the hardest goal of all: not smoking when I'm out with my friends.

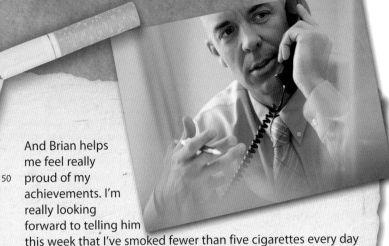

And Brian helps
me feel really
50 proud of my
achievements. I'm
really looking
forward to telling him
this week that I've smoked fewer than five cigarettes every day
55 this week. And it feels so good at the end of each session to be
able to say, OK, this week I'm going to do this and know that
by the end of the week I'll have achieved all the goals I've set
myself.
I'm convinced that with Brian's moral support I'll have given up
60 smoking by the end of the year. And this time it'll be for good.

GRAMMAR: future perfect & future continuous

- Use *will* + *be* + verb + *-ing* to form the future continuous.
  We'll be exploring the options together.
- Use the future continuous to talk about an action that
  will be in progress at a point in time in the future.
  We'll be talking about the next step in our next session.
- Use *will* + *have* + past participle to form the future
  perfect.
  I'll have achieved all the goals I've set myself.
- Use the future perfect to talk about an action that will be
  completed before a point in time in the future.
  I'll have given up smoking by the end of the year.

Expressions often used with the future perfect:
*By this time (next week), by then, by one o'clock, by the time
(we next meet)*

❯ SEE LANGUAGE REFERENCE PAGE 74

1 Choose the correct verb forms to complete the text.

I'll (1) *be speaking / have spoken* to Clare again next
week. By that time she'll (2) *be going / have been* to the
gym at least three times, she'll (3) *be running / have run*
a distance of over ten miles at least once and she'll
(4) *be thinking / have thought* about increasing her
distance to fifteen miles or more over the following week.
At the meeting we'll (5) *be talking / have talked* about
how she can find time in her busy schedule to do more
running and she'll (6) *be telling / have told* me about the
problems and frustrations she's been suffering over the
last ten days.

What goal do you think Clare is preparing herself for?

2 Write the verbs in brackets in the correct form,
future perfect or future continuous.

Bill wants to change his job. Brian is helping
him. In their next session they (1) _____ (*talk*)
about how Bill can improve his CV. By this
time tomorrow, Bill (2) _____ (*hand*) in his
resignation. By this time next week, he
(3) _____ (*apply*) for at least five jobs and he
and Brian (4) _____ (*work*) on preparing him
for his first job interviews. In a month's time
he (5) _____ (*find*) a new job and this time
next year he (6) _____ (*aim*) for promotion in
his new job.

3 Complete the sentences to make predictions for
you and your classmates.

1 This time tomorrow, we'll all be _____.
2 By this time next week, some of us will have
   _____.
3 This time next year, most of us will be _____.
4 By this time next year, one or two of us will have
   _____.
5 Five years from now, only one of us will have
   _____.
6 In ten years' time, none of us will be _____.

Talk to your classmates and find out whose
predictions are most similar to yours.

SPEAKING

Roleplay

1 You are going to prepare for a roleplay. Work in
   two groups, A and B.

   Group A: Turn to page 142.
   Group B: Turn to page 146.

2 Work in pairs with one student from Group A and
   one student from Group B. Roleplay the coaching
   session.

3 Change pairs, so that each client is talking to a new
   coach, and each coach is dealing with a new problem.

4 Change pairs again as above.

5 Work in your original groups, A and B. Discuss
   these questions and report back to the class.
   Group A: Which client was most difficult to help?
   Why?
   Group B: Which coach gave the best support and
   guidance?

7D | Trends

LISTENING

1 Work in pairs. Make a list of three changes you expect to take place in the next 20 years for each of the three topics.

a What we'll be wearing
b What we'll be doing in our free time
c What we'll be eating

2 ⊙ **2.3–2.5** Listen to three lifestyle experts and match the experts 1–3 to topics a–c in exercise 1. Were the experts' predictions similar to yours?

3 ⊙ **2.3–2.5** Listen again and complete the predictions.

1 The next twenty years will be marked by ever-decreasing sizes. _____ will be more and more fashionable.
2 Advances in packaging technology will mean that we will be able to keep food _____ out of the fridge for much longer.
3 Watch out for a huge increase in the consumption of _____.
4 As always, there'll be a whole host of new _____.
5 A whole range of clothes will be developed that can integrate _____ with fabrics.
6 Heat-sensitive fabrics will also be coming into their own with a _____ different uses.
7 Virtual reality will have revolutionized _____.
8 We'll still be _____ to keep fit, but in virtual scenery that our present-day dreams are made of.

4 Work in pairs. Discuss these questions.

- Which of the innovations do you think are most likely to be developed in the next 20 years?
- Which do you think would be the most useful? Why?
- And which would be the most enjoyable?

FUNCTIONAL LANGUAGE: giving examples

Use one of the expressions below to show that you are giving an example of something.

for example/for instance
For example/For instance, *men will be wearing skirts to work.*

such as/like (only use before a noun phrase)
Health foods, **such as/like** *low fat spreads, will be replaced by new products.*

in particular (to highlight a special example)
Chocolate, **in particular**, *will be sold in smaller bars.*

among other things (to talk about one or more things out of a larger number)
VR options will include, **among other things**, *the possibility to change your seat at any time.*

to name but two/a few (to talk about two or more examples of a larger group)
Microchips will perform hundreds of household chores, cleaning the oven, hoovering the hall or watering the plants, **to name but a few**.

❯ SEE LANGUAGE REFERENCE PAGE 74

1 Choose the correct expressions to complete the text. On one occasion, both expressions are possible.

The 21st-century Kitchen

We can expect to see major changes in the home, too, and some rooms will look rather different. The kitchen and the bathroom, (1) *like / to name but two*, will be unrecognizable. In the kitchen, (2) *for example / to name but two*, hi-tech appliances will be revolutionized. Automatic waste disposal and a water purification system, (3) *among other things / such as*, will become standard features of most kitchens. The new intelli-kitchen is already making our lives easier by looking after some of the dirtier jobs. Self-cleaning ovens, (4) *for instance / in particular*, are already available in some shops. Cooking accidents, (5) *such as / to name but a few* burnt toast or undercooked pasta, will be a thing of the past with self-timing appliances. And with a fridge that orders food direct from online home-delivery companies, you'll never run out of essentials (6) *such as / like* milk or orange juice. The changes will transform the lives of everyone, housewives (7) *among other things / in particular*. In the bathroom of the future, …

2 Work in pairs. Read the notes and answer the questions below.

The 21st-century Bathroom

Digital mirrors
- make you look ten years younger
- help you apply make-up

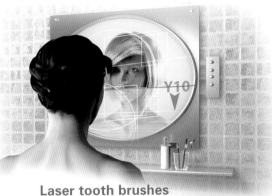

Laser tooth brushes
- kill germs
- run simple blood tests

Video tiles in the shower/bath
- watch the news in the shower
- watch your favourite film in the bath

- Can you think of an extra use for each appliance?
- Which would you prefer to have in your bathroom and why?

3 Write three sentences describing your future bathroom. Use as many expressions from exercise 1 as you can.

VOCABULARY: nouns & prepositions

1 Complete the sentences below with *for*, *in* or *of*.

1 The drive _____ a perfect body will push forward the limits of cosmetic surgery.
2 Growing interest _____ saving energy at home will result in a range of new kitchen appliances.
3 Children will develop a taste _____ more and more complicated computer games.
4 Fears of health problems will increase the demand _____ new and better sun protection.
5 An increase _____ global temperatures will affect people's holiday choices.
6 Advances _____ genetically-modified food will revolutionize our diet.
7 Changes to air travel will drastically reduce the production _____ carbon dioxide.
8 There will be no shortage _____ new sports.

2 Work in pairs. Do you agree with the predictions in exercise 1?

DID YOU KNOW?

1 Work in pairs. Read the text and discuss the questions.

Millions of middle-class Americans look to one person to tell them how to live their lives: how to throw a party, how to dress, how to decorate their homes, and even how to bring up their children. Martha Stewart is that person. She is a lifestyle guide and an American icon. Her magazines, *Martha Stewart Living*, *Martha Stewart Weddings*, *Martha Stewart Kids* and *Martha Stewart Baby*, are read by millions. She has won numerous awards for her TV programmes and her shopping website and lifestyle merchandise have made her a millionaire several times over. She was born, one of six children, to a middle-class Polish-American family, and, true to the American dream, she has grown to be one of the States' wealthiest and most successful businesswomen.

- Are there any famous self-made millionaires in your country? How did they make their money?
- Are they looked up to as lifestyle role models?
- Who or what has the greatest influence on your lifestyle choices (TV, magazines, friends and family, shops, celebrities)?
- Is the same true for your parents and your grandparents?
- Do you feel that there is any pressure on you to conform to a particular lifestyle? If yes, who or what exerts that pressure?

Grammar

Futures

English does not have one future tense. There are many possible ways of expressing the future. Our choice of verb form depends on the aspect of future time that we want to emphasize.

Schedules

We use the present simple to talk about schedules and timetables.
> We **leave** at midnight.
> What time **does** the train **arrive?**

Future time clauses

We also use the present simple in future time clauses that begin with *if/when/as soon as*, etc.
> **If** it snows, we'll go to the mountains.
> She'll hire a car **when** she gets there.

Plans, arrangements and decisions

We use the present continuous to talk about definite arrangements (eg we have bought a ticket for something or written something in a diary).
> We**'re meeting** at six.

We use *am/is/are going to* + infinitive to talk about intentions (ie plans or decisions that have been made before the moment of speaking).
> They**'re going to buy** a new car.

The use of the present continuous and *going to* is very similar. You can always use *going to* instead of the present continuous, but you only use the present continuous to talk about a definite arrangement.

We use *'ll* + infinitive to talk about a decision made at the time of talking (ie there has been no decision, plan or arrangement made previously).
> OK. I**'ll give** you a call next week.

Predictions

We use both *going to* + infinitive and *will* + infinitive to make predictions about the future. Sometimes both forms are possible.
> They**'re not going to win.**
> I don't think they**'ll win.**

When there is present evidence for the prediction we usually use *going to*.
> Look at the clouds. It's **going to** rain.

We often use *will* after phrases like I (*don't*) *think/I expect/I'm* (*not*) *sure/I reckon/I guess.*
> I expect you**'ll** understand.

We often use *will* with an adverb of probability: *definitely/maybe/perhaps/possibly/probably.*
> They **definitely won't** win.

We can use *may* and *might* in place of *will* to make our prediction less certain.
> It **might** be sunny later on.

Future continuous

We use the future continuous to talk about an action that will be in progress at a point of time in the future.

> At 9.15 tomorrow, we**'ll be watching** the match.

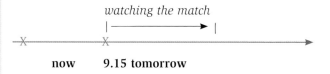

subject	will won't		present participle
he/she/they /etc.	will won't	be	making/watching /working/etc.

Future perfect

We use the future perfect to talk about an action that will be completed before a point in time in the future.

> By 10.00 tomorrow, the match **will have finished**.

We often use the future perfect with expressions with *by*.

> **by** then/tomorrow
> one/two o'clock
> (this time) next Monday/week
> the time we arrive/we've finished

subject	will won't		present participle
he/she/they /etc.	will won't	have	made/watched /worked/etc.

FUNCTIONAL LANGUAGE

Giving examples

among other things
for example
for instance
in particular
like
such as
to name but two/a few

WORD LIST

The environment

climate change *n U*	/ˈklaɪmət ˌtʃeɪndʒ/
exhaust fume *n C*	/ɪgˈzɔːst ˌfjuːm/
fossil fuel *n C*	/ˈfɒs(ə)l ˌfjuːəl/
global	/ˈgləʊb(ə)l ˈwɔː(r)mɪŋ/
warming *n U* *	
greenhouse gas *n C*	/ˈgriːnhaʊs ˈgæs/
organic food *n U*	/ɔː(r)ˌgænɪk ˈfuːd/
solar panel *n C*	/ˌsəʊlə(r) ˈpæn(ə)l/
wind farm *n C*	/ˈwɪnd ˌfɑː(r)m/

Expressions with *make*

make a difference	/meɪk ə ˈdɪfrəns/
make a point of	/meɪk ə ˌpɔɪnt əv
(doing) (sth)	ˈduːɪŋ/
make it easier	/meɪk ɪt ˈiːziə(r)/
make sense	/meɪk ˈsens/
make the most of	/meɪk ðə məʊst
(sth)	əv/
make time for (sth)	/meɪk ˈtaɪm fə(r)/
make or break	/meɪk ɔː ˈbreɪk/

Nouns & prepositions

advances in	/ədˈvaːnsəz ɪn/
consumption of	/kənˈsʌmpʃ(ə)n ˌəv/
demand for	/dɪˈmaːnd fɔː/
drive for	/draɪv fɔː/
increase in	/ˈɪnkriːs ˌɪn/
interest in	/ˈɪntrəst ˌɪn/
shortage of	/ˈʃɔː(r)tɪdʒ əv/
taste for	/teɪst fɔː/

Other words & phrases

account for *v*	/əˈkaʊnt fɔː/
a host of	/ə ˈhəʊst əv/
all the rage	/ˌɔːl ðə ˈreɪdʒ/
appliance *n C* *	/əˈplaɪəns/
approve *v* ***	/əˈpruːv/
asthma *n U* *	/ˈæsmə/
backpack *n C*	/ˈbæk,pæk/
bare bones	/ˌbeə(r) ˈbəʊnz/
barrier *n C* **	/ˈbæriə(r)/
beachwear *n U*	/ˈbiːtʃˌweə(r)/

blanket *n C* **	/ˈblæŋkɪt/
bleach *v*	/bliːtʃ/
bleed *v* *	/bliːd/
block *v* **	/blɒk/
breeze *n C* **	/briːz/
carbon *n U*	/ˈkɑː(r)bən/
charger *n C*	/ˈtʃɑː(r)dʒə(r)/
charming *adj* **	/ˈtʃɑː(r)mɪŋ/
chronic *adj* *	/ˈkrɒnɪk/
cooker *n C* *	/ˈkʊkə(r)/
crop *n C* *	/krɒp/
cut down on *v*	/ˌkʌt daʊn ɒn/
damp *adj* **	/dæmp/
darling *n C* **	/ˈdɑː(r)lɪŋ/
decorate *v* **	/ˈdekəreɪt/
delightful *adj* *	/dɪˈlaɪtf(ə)l/
devastating *adj*	/ˈdevəˌsteɪtɪŋ/
diesel *n U* *	/ˈdiːz(ə)l/
double glazing *n U*	/ˌdʌb(ə)l ˈgleɪzɪŋ/
drill *n C* *	/drɪl/
dump *v* **	/dʌmp/
dust *n U* **	/dʌst/
dye *n C/v*	/daɪ/
emission *n C* **	/ɪˈmɪʃ(ə)n/
erect *v* *	/ɪˈrekt/
exert *v* *	/ɪgˈzɜː(r)t/
extract *v* **	/ɪkˈstrækt/
fabric *n C* **	/ˈfæbrɪk/
fancy *v* **	/ˈfænsi/
fertiliser *n C*	/ˈfɜː(r)təˌlaɪzə(r)/
fittings *n pl* *	/ˈfɪtɪŋz/
floorboard *n C*	/ˈflɔː(r)ˌbɔː(r)d/
flush *v*	/flʌʃ/
foot the bill	/ˌfʊt ðə ˈbɪl/
four wheeler *n C*	/ˌfɔː(r) ˈwiːlə(r)/
frustrated *adj* *	/frʌˈstreɪtɪd/
furnishings *n pl*	/ˈfɜː(r)nɪʃɪŋz/
genetically modified	/dʒəˌnetɪkli
food *n U*	ˌmɒdɪfaɪd ˈfuːd/
germ *n C*	/dʒɜː(r)m/
get in shape	/ˌget ɪn ˈʃeɪp/
glove *n C* **	/glʌv/
greywater tank *n C*	/ˈgreɪwɔːtə(r) ˌtæŋk/
guided tour *n C*	/ˌgaɪdɪd ˈtʊə(r)/
guzzle *v*	/ˈgʌz(ə)l/
heat-sensitive *adj*	/ˈhiːtˌsensətɪv/
helmet *n C* *	/ˈhelmɪt/
hire *v* **	/ˈhaɪə(r)/
hydro electric *adj*	/ˌhaɪdrəʊˈilektrɪk/
icon *n C*	/ˈaɪkɒn/
ink *n C* *	/ɪŋk/
insulation *n U*	/ˌɪnsjʊˈleɪʃ(ə)n/
integrate *v* **	/ˈɪntɪˌgreɪt/
invariably *adv* *	/ɪnˈveəriəbli/
kick *n C* **	/kɪk/
kid *v*	/kɪd/
kilt *n C*	/kɪlt/
laptop *n C*	/ˈlæpˌtɒp/
layer *n C* ***	/ˈleɪə(r)/
life coach *n C*	/ˈlaɪf ˌkəʊtʃ/
lifestyle *n U* **	/ˈlaɪfˌstaɪl/
marine *adj* *	/məˈriːn/
merchandise *n U*	/ˈmɜː(r)tʃ(ə)ndaɪz /

moral support *n U*	/ˌmɒrəl səˈpɔː(r)t/
mutual *adj* *	/ˈmjuːtʃuəl/
neighbouring *adj* *	/ˈneɪbərɪŋ/
packaging *n U* *	/ˈpækɪdʒɪŋ/
palm *n C* **	/pɑːm/
pathway *n C*	/ˈpɑːθˌweɪ/
pesticide *n C*	/ˈpestɪsaɪd/
pinpoint *v*	/ˈpɪnˌpɔɪnt/
plumbing *n U*	/ˈplʌmɪŋ/
plummet *v*	/ˈplʌmɪt/
pop in *v*	/ˈpɒp ɪn/
portion *n C* **	/ˈpɔː(r)ʃ(ə)n/
power up *v*	/ˌpaʊə(r) ˈʌp/
PVC *n U*	/ˌpiː viː ˈsiː/
razor *n C* *	/ˈreɪzə(r)/
recycle *v* *	/riːˈsaɪk(ə)l/
refine *v*	/rɪˈfaɪn/
remote *adj* **	/rɪˈməʊt/
retardant *n C*	/rɪˈtɑː(r)d(ə)nt/
rubble *n U*	/ˈrʌb(ə)l/
sanding machine *n C*	/ˈsændɪŋ məˈʃiːn/
sarong *n C*	/səˈrɒŋ/
seaweed *n C*	/ˈsiːˌwiːd/
self-cleaning *adj*	/ˌselfˈkliːnɪŋ/
shave *v* *	/ʃeɪv/
sledgehammer *n C*	/ˈsledʒˌhæmə(r)/
smash up *v*	/ˌsmæʃ ˈʌp/
spray *v* *	/spreɪ/
step-by-step *adj*	/ˌstepbaɪˈstep/
strip *v* **	/strɪp/
subsidize *v*	/ˈsʌbsɪdaɪz/
supplement *n C* **	/ˈsʌplɪmənt/
SUV *n C*	/ˌes juː ˈviː/
take (sth) to pieces	/ˌteɪk tə ˈpiːsəz/
tank *n C* ***	/tæŋk/
tasty *adj* *	/ˈteɪsti/
thermos bag *n C*	/ˈθɜː(r)məs ˌbæg/
throw a party	/ˌθrəʊ ə ˈpɑː(r)ti/
tile *n C*	/taɪl/
tip *n C*	/tɪp/
truck *n C* **	/trʌk/
tunnel *n C* **	/ˈtʌn(ə)l/
turbine *n C*	/ˈtɜː(r)baɪn/
tyre *n C* **	/ˈtaɪə(r)/
underwater *adj*	/ˌʌndə(r)ˈwɔːtə(r)/
watch out for *v*	/ˌwɒtʃ ˈaʊt fɔː(r)/
widescale *adj*	/ˈwaɪdskeɪl/
willpower *n U*	/ˈwɪlˌpaʊə(r)/
wiring *n U*	/ˈwaɪərɪŋ/

8A | Cold comfort

Speaking & vocabulary: symptoms

1 Complete the sentences with words from the box.

aches	hacking	rash	run-down	runny
stiff	temperature	throat	throbbing	upset

1 All my muscles feel really _____ and my back _____.
2 I woke up with a high _____ and a _____ headache and it won't go away.
3 I've got a _____ cough and a very sore _____ that hurts when I speak.
4 I've had a really _____ nose for the last few days and I feel generally _____.
5 I've had an _____ stomach and a strange _____ on my face since we went to that restaurant.

2 Work in pairs. Discuss these questions.

- Which of the ten symptoms in the box in exercise 1 would you go to the doctor for?
- What would you do or take to treat the other symptoms?
- What are the possible causes of the symptoms in exercise 1?
- Can you add three more symptoms to the list?

3 Work in pairs. Match the sentences 1–9 to the situations a–c.

a calling in sick   c at the doctor's
b at the chemist

1 What exactly seems to be the problem?
2 I'm sorry, I don't think I'm going to make it in today.
3 Have you got anything for a sore throat?
4 Take it easy and let us know if you're coming in tomorrow.
5 Take two of these after meals, and if you're not feeling any better, see a doctor.
6 I've been having these terrible pains.
7 Sorry to hear that. I hope it's nothing too serious.
8 OK, lie down over there and I'll have a look.
9 I need something for this swelling on my arm.

4 Work in pairs, A and B. Roleplay the three situations in exercise 3.

A: Turn to page 142. B: Turn to page 146.

How to ... have a heavy cold

There are colds and heavy colds, but only heavy colds are worth talking about. It is only with a heavy cold that you can claim to be ill. People are not always totally sympathetic, so it's important
5 to describe your suffering in great detail. With other illnesses, you can ask people to feel your forehead to see if you have a temperature, but with a heavy cold, it's not a good idea to ask other people to feel your nose and ask how runny it is.

10 To have a truly heavy cold you need more than just a runny nose. The standard supplementary symptoms are a headache, sore throat, temperature, sickness, achiness and a cough. Once you've got three out of six you can call the boss and skip work. Loud,
15 repeated sniffing is good on the phone, but don't try to communicate general achiness or you may come across as a bit too melodramatic. Your cough must sound as though you're starting an old car in cold weather, and you must cough at least three times on
20 the phone during any conversation with work. Saying you've just got a temperature isn't good enough; you've got to have a raging fever of 45°.

Stage two is bed. A heavy cold requires bed rest and you need to make sure you've got all the right equipment. A large box of tissues is vital, as is the little collection of used tissues around the bin where you haven't quite got the energy to throw them in. You'll also need some paracetamol to cope with the symptoms of your cold. One of the nastiest is the headache and vomiting shortly after having the hot toddy specially prepared for you by someone who claims to love you.

You normally lose your appetite and go off your food when you are ill, so if you find yourself eating a lot of cake and ice cream you're more likely to be pregnant. There's a saying 'feed a cold, starve a fever', or 'starve a cold, feed a fever'. Neither makes much sense. These sayings are used by elderly relatives as an excuse to give you the country soup they make by feeding left-over vegetables into a blender and which 'will have you on your feet in no time'. You'll certainly be on your feet, but you'll just be running quickly for the lavatory.

The final phase of the heavy cold is the hacking cough, where you feel much better but you still sound like death. Use this time to get maximum attention and pampering from your loved ones and to make more deathbed phone calls to work. Finally, go back to work fit and ready, and realize that the people you thought were doing your work for you while you were away have also been off with … a heavy cold.

READING

1 Read the article. Choose the main purpose of the article 1–5.

1 To describe the symptoms
2 To suggest remedies
3 To prescribe medicine
4 To explain the origin of heavy colds
5 To amuse the reader

2 Read the article again. Which of the following bits of advice are not given?

1 Be careful to avoid giving your germs to other people.
2 Talk at length about your symptoms.
3 Try not to make too much noise when you sneeze.
4 Don't leave too many tissues stuffed up your sleeve.
5 Sound very ill when you call your boss.
6 Exaggerate your symptoms.
7 Get everything you need before you go to bed.
8 Don't confuse being ill and expecting a baby.

3 Match the highlighted words or expressions in the text to the definitions 1–7.

1 not go to work or school
2 toilet
3 a warm drink, often including alcohol
4 tender loving care
5 a machine for mixing food
6 a very high temperature
7 not give food to

4 Work in pairs. Discuss these questions.

- When did you last have a cold?
- Did you take time off work/school?
- How long did it take you to get over it?

8B Bill of health

SPEAKING & VOCABULARY: health idioms

1 Rearrange the phrases in the correct order to make a short story.

- ☐ I was feeling a bit under the
- ☐ *bill of health*. 'Hypochondria is your only problem,' he said.
- ☐ *door*. Once more, the doctor *gave me a clean*
- ☐ *down with something*. The doctor told me I was fine, but I got a splitting
- ☐ headache that afternoon. My back was also *killing me*, so I went back to the doctor's. But again, he told me I was *in good*
- ☐ *round*, so I thought I was *going*
- ☐ *shape*. The next day I was even worse and thought I was *at death's*
- ☐ weather and I knew *there was a bug going*

2 Replace the words in italics in exercise 1 with the phrases below.

1	extremely ill	4	lots of people had
2	extremely painful		the same illness
3	falling ill	5	said I was not ill
		6	well

3 Work in pairs. Turn to page 143 and do the quiz.

4 For the quiz in exercise 3, what sort of people give (1) mostly (a) answers, (2) mostly (b) answers, (3) mostly (c) answers? Do you know anyone like this?

LISTENING

1 Match the words in the box to the definitions 1–5.

> compensation   stroke   diagnosis
> migraine   consultation

1 a meeting with a professional person (eg a doctor) in order to get advice or discuss a problem
2 a serious medical condition that can make someone suddenly unable to speak or move
3 a statement about what disease someone has, based on examining them
4 a very severe headache
5 money that someone receives because something bad has happened to them

2 🔘 2.6 Listen to the recording and explain its connection with the words in exercise 1.

3 🔘 2.6 Listen again and complete the sentences.

1 Some American doctors do not want to _____ because they cannot afford the insurance policies.
2 The British government is putting aside nearly _____ in order to cover compensation claims.
3 Adrian Bowe will receive compensation which could be _____ of pounds.
4 Critics say that more _____ are inevitable.
5 It is _____ for doctors to make correct diagnoses all the time.
6 Online databases of symptoms and diseases can cause healthy people to start _____ nothing.

4 Work in pairs. Discuss these questions.

Do you think that doctors should be punished if they make mistakes? Why or why not?

GRAMMAR: modals of speculation

1 Look at examples 1–6 and answer the questions.

1 *Insurance costs for doctors **could rise** further.*
2 *He **must be suffering** from a migraine attack.*
3 *The stroke **might have been** avoided.*
4 *The increase in compensation claims **cannot be** the result of more medical errors.*
5 *His symptoms **could have been** caused by a heavy cold.*
6 *A patient who is feeling under the weather **may be going down** with a virus.*

1 In which sentences is the speaker speculating about (a) the future, (b) the present and (c) the past?
2 In which sentences is the speaker (a) sure and (b) less sure of what he or she is saying?

2 Read the story and then choose the best verb form to complete the sentences 1–8.

Mystery Bug at the Royale
Twenty people were brought into the Heath Infirmary last night suffering from acute stomach problems. The health authorities have ruled out food poisoning. All the patients had been to the late show at the Royale Cinema but none of them had bought anything to eat at the cinema shop. Some of the patients claim they smelt gas, but no traces of gas were found. It was later discovered that all twenty patients had drunk from the water fountain using the plastic cups provided.

1 It *must / can't* have been food poisoning.
2 The cinema *might / must* be having problems with its air-conditioning.
3 The popcorn in the cinema kiosk *can't / could* be the source of the problem.
4 Their symptoms *can't / must* have been caused by a gas leak.
5 It *could / must* be either the water or the cups.
6 The cups *might / can't* have been dirty.
7 Or the water fountain itself *may / must* be in need of maintenance.
8 Whatever the answer, it *can't / must* have something to do with the water they drank.

3 Work in pairs. Look at the picture. Why do you think these people are sitting in a hospital waiting room?

- Use *must, may, might, could* and *can't* to speculate about events in the present, past or future.
  You **may** come across as a bit too melodramatic.
- Use modal verb + infinitive/*be* + *-ing* to speculate about the present or future.
  He **must be suffering** from a migraine.
- Use modal verb + *have* + past participle to speculate about the past.
  Their doctor **may have made** a mistake.
- Use *must* when you're very sure that something is true.
- Use *may, might* or *could* when you're less sure that something is true.
- Use *can't* when you are sure that something isn't true or didn't happen.

> SEE LANGUAGE REFERENCE PAGE 84

PRONUNCIATION: weak forms & contractions

1 🌐 **2.7** Listen to the conversation. Notice the pronunciation of the verbs in bold. What happens to the auxiliary verbs *have* and *been*?

A: Where can he be?
B: I don't know! Anything **could have** happened to him!
C: Yes, he **might have** been *stopped by the police*!
A: Or he **could have** been *in a car accident*!
C: On the other hand, he **may have** *got caught in the traffic*.
A: No, it **can't have** been any of those things. He wasn't in his car.

2 Work in groups of three. Think of three alternatives to replace the phrases in italics. Read your alternative versions out loud, changing roles each time.

DID YOU KNOW?

1 Work in pairs. Read the information and discuss these questions.

Australia is the sixth largest country in the world, but there are fewer than two million people living in the vast Australian outback, or bush, as it's called. Before the 1920s people in the bush had little or no access to doctors. The nearest one was often weeks away. Then, in 1928, John Flynn became the outback's first flying doctor and began the medical service, which still exists today. The Royal Flying Doctors Service (RFDS) supplies medical care to outback residents. It has 45 aircraft and offers 24-hour emergency service in very isolated communities. Each aircraft carries a doctor, a nurse and their equipment. The pilots sometimes have to land on roads or unpaved tracks.

- Where are the remotest areas in your country? How far are they from a large town or hospital?
- Does everyone in your country receive good medical care?
- What is the reputation of doctors in your country?
- When you have needed treatment, were you well looked after?

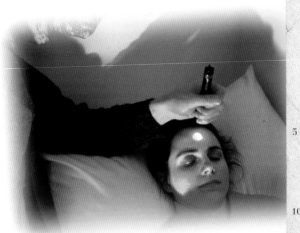

READING

1 Work in pairs. Look at the box and discuss the questions.

> acupuncture   aromatherapy
> colour therapy   hypnosis
> reflexology   Tai Chi

- What do you know about these therapies?
- Do you know anyone who has tried an alternative therapy?

2 You are going to read an article about alternative therapies in the workplace. Answer these questions.

1 Which therapies are mentioned?
2 What conditions are they treating?

3 Complete the text with the extracts a–g.

a Colour wasn't her only concern
b they obviously hadn't been decorated in a long time
c These simple changes have made a world of difference to the office and to the staff
d repetitive stress injuries and other workplace-related illnesses,
e and one in five adults in the UK suffer from chronic back pain
f and relieve the tensions on their backs.
g 'and green, as well as fighting irritability, also has a healing effect on the body'

4 Work in pairs. Discuss these questions.

- Which changes sound like good ideas?
- Which changes do you think made the biggest difference? Why?

The Office Doctors: an alternative approach to fighting stress

With stress-related illness on the increase, and workers starting to sue their companies for chronic back pain, (1) _____ more and more companies are turning to alternative therapies to help reduce the levels of stress in their workplace. The Office Doctors is one of a growing number of companies which claim they can reduce work related stress by making workplaces healthier and happier. They talked us through one of their makeovers.

A small accountancy firm had been experiencing problems with staff illness and low morale. When a new office manager was appointed she decided to call in the Office Doctors. The offices were housed in an old building, (2) _____ and there were a number of basic stress factors that needed immediate attention: the light, the colour scheme, the furniture.

'There was an enormous amount of work to do. But we had to make sure that we didn't disrupt the day to day work of the office.' The only solution was to work at weekends. 'It meant we had to work fast but it also meant we could work in peace and we didn't have to worry about getting in the way of the staff.'

The colour therapist, Liz, was the first in. She chose a range of calming blues and greens for the offices and reception area. 'Blue is a particularly calming colour and ideal in counterbalancing high levels of stress,' she explained, '(3) _____. In the staff rest area she decided to use colours that stimulate and energize. 'Yellow heightens motivation and orange stimulates creativity. The rest area doesn't just provide a break from work, but helps the staff go back to their desks with renewed energy and enthusiasm.'

(4)_____. Being an old building the windows were small and let in very little natural light. As she couldn't install new windows, Liz installed full spectrum fluorescent lights instead. 'Full spectrum lights have all the colours and wavelengths of natural light and studies show that they have a very positive effect in fighting stress and depression.'

Next came the aromatherapist, Jules. 'Chosen with care, essential oils can reduce stress and boost immunity,' he explained. He chose a blend of lemon, bergamot and lavender for the central diffusion system. 'Recent tests have shown that the use of lemon can reduce typing errors by more than 50%, so we're not only fighting stress and promoting health, we're also increasing productivity.'

Finally Clara, our massage expert, came in and assessed the ergonomics of each work station. 'These people have to sit at their desks for up to eight hours a day. Very often they aren't allowed to get up except for short coffee breaks. So they really must make sure that they are looking after their backs as well as they possibly can.' Back pain is the second most common reason for visits to the doctor (5) _____. She helped each member of staff find the correct desk and chair height, and showed them the best position for their computer screen. She also persuaded the company to invest in ergonomic keyboards and cordless mouses as well as cordless phones. The phones mean that staff don't have to take their phone calls at their desks. Now they can get up and stretch their legs (6) _____. In addition, each member of staff can request a massage at their desks once a week. 'Everybody should have regular massage sessions. Not only does it help ease back pains, it also relieves built up tensions and revitalizes.'

'The changes have made a huge difference,' said the Managing Director, '(7) _____. Absenteeism has gone down by a staggering 30% and everyone seems to be much happier.'

3 🔊 **2.8** Listen to a story about an alternative therapist. Make notes about (1) the main events of the story and (2) any key words. If necessary, listen a second time.

4 Work in groups of three and write the story.

5 Compare your version to the one in tapescript 2.8 on page 158. Did you use the same modal verbs and expressions?

Permission
- Use *can* or *is/are allowed to* in the present and *could* or *was/were allowed to* in the past.

Obligation
- Use *must* or *have to* in the present and *had to* in the past.

Lack of obligation
- Use *don't have to* or *don't need to* in the present and *didn't have to* or *didn't need to* in the past.

Prohibition
- Use *can't, mustn't* or *isn't/aren't allowed to* in the present and *couldn't* or *wasn't/weren't allowed to* in the past.

❯ SEE LANGUAGE REFERENCE PAGE 84

GRAMMAR: modals (permission, obligation & prohibition)

1 Rewrite the phrases in bold using an appropriate form of the verbs in the box.

> be allowed to   can   could
> have to   must   need to

1 we **were obliged to** work fast
2 we **were allowed to** work in peace
3 we **didn't have to** worry about getting in the way of the staff
4 she **wasn't allowed to** install new windows
5 they **can't** get up except for short coffee breaks
6 they really **have to** make sure that they are looking after their backs
7 staff **don't need to** take their phone calls at their desks
8 staff **are allowed to** request a massage at their desks once a week

2 Match sentences 1–8 in exercise 1 to the uses a–d.

a permission   c prohibition
b obligation   d lack of prohibition

SPEAKING

1 Work in groups. Decide what changes you would make to your school to make it a healthier place to study in. Consider the factors in the box.

> colour   aromas   furniture
> artwork   plants   music

2 Tell your class about your plans. Decide whose makeover is …

- the most realistic.
- the most imaginative.

Useful language

We need to do something about the (light) …
The main problem here is …
The only solution is to …
Another thing we could do is …
One idea would be to …

8D | Back pain

LISTENING

1 Look at the photo and discuss these questions.

- What is the man's problem?
- What might have caused this problem?

2 🔘 **2.9–2.13** Listen to the conversations 1–5. Who is Bob talking to each time? Write a number next to the person or people he's talking to a–e.

a	a friend	d	a colleague
b	a group of friends	e	his wife
c	a doctor's receptionist		

3 🔘 **2.9–2.13** Listen again and answer the questions.
1 What solutions do they suggest?
2 Whose advice does he decide to take? Why?

4 Work in pairs. Discuss these questions.

- Do you know anyone who suffers (or has suffered) from back pain?
- What do they do to ease or relieve it?

FUNCTIONAL LANGUAGE: changing the subject

1 Work in pairs. Find the expressions 1–6 in tapescripts 2.9–2.13 on page 158 and answer the question.

1	that reminds me ...	4	come to think of it ...
2	anyway, as I was saying, ...	5	talking of ...
3	by the way, ...	6	as for ...

What expressions does the speaker use to ...
a talk about something completely different?
b pick up on a small detail?
c return to what they were talking about earlier in the conversation?

2 Complete the dialogues with expressions from exercise 1.

1 **A:** I'm just going out to meet up with Ken.
   B: (a) _____, can you take this book with you? I've been meaning to give it back to him for ages. Thanks!
2 **A:** Then we went out for a drink at the Hare and Hounds. A quiet evening, but nice enough.
   B: (b) _____ the Hare and Hounds, did you know Ann's booked it for her 30th birthday party?
3 **A:** Meet you at the car then. At 4 o'clock.
   B: Yeah, fine. Oh, (c) _____, did I tell you your mother called?
4 **A:** And another thing, it's not urgent, but I think some of the figures may be wrong.
   B: OK, so we need to go back and look at them again then?
   A: Yes, I think so and (d) _____ there's no rush, we've got plenty of time to get it all done by the end of the month.
5 **A:** Did you get the tickets for the concert?
   B: Yeah, I did, they were pretty expensive, but it's worth it. Hey, (e) _____, Frank hasn't paid me back for the last time, yet.
6 Right John, it's time you were doing your homework. And (f) _____ you, young lady, you should be in bed by now!

🔘 **2.14** Listen to compare your answers with the recording.

3 🔘 Work in groups of three. You are going to play a game.

A: Turn to page 143.   C: Turn to page 147.
B: Turn to page 145.

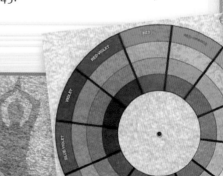

VOCABULARY: phrasal verbs with objects

1 Match the phrasal verbs in bold in the sentences 1–6 to their meanings a–f.

1 I need to call him. I'd promised I'd **get back to** him today.
2 It'll **sort** itself **out**. It always does.
3 I don't know how Linda **puts up with** you!
4 How long are you going to keep **putting** it **off**?
5 So it was your idea was it? You **put** him **up to** it.
6 Even little Jo was **telling** me **off** the other day.

a accept an annoying situation without complaining
b avoid doing something you don't want to do
c contact someone at a later time
d criticize someone for doing something wrong
e encourage someone to do something
f find a solution for a problem

2 Underline the objects of the phrasal verbs in exercise 1. Then add these phrasal verbs to the categories of phrasal verbs 1–3 in the grammar box.

> 1 **Inseparable phrasal verbs**: the verb and the particle must always come together.
> eg *look after **your back**/look after **it**/*
> (1)_____ /(2) _____
>
> 2 **Separable verbs**: the verb and particle can be separated by an object. If the object is a pronoun it must come between the verb and particle,
> eg *call **the Office Doctors** in/call **them** in/*
> (3)_____ /(4) _____ (5) _____
>
> 3 **Phrasal verbs with two objects**: one of the objects goes after the verb and the other goes after the particle or particles,
> eg *talk **us** through **the makeover**/*
> *talk **us** through **it** /*(6)_____

3 Insert the object in brackets in the correct position in the sentences.

1 You've only got one body, and I think it's important to look after properly. That's why I try to do some sort of exercise every day. (*it*)
2 I smoke about 40 cigarettes a day. I know it's bad for me, but I have no intention of giving up. (*it*)
3 I don't eat meat or dairy products. I order a box of fruit and vegetables from a local organic farm once a week. They drop off at my house every Friday. (*it*)
4 I know I should do some sort of exercise, but I keep on putting off – I'd much prefer to be curled up on the sofa watching TV. (*it*)
5 My mother was telling off the other day because I always eat fast food and microwave dinners. But I just haven't got time to cook! (*me*)
6 I refuse to enter a room where someone's smoking. I really don't see why I should have to put up with. (*it*)

4 Do you know anyone like the people in exercise 3?

SPEAKING

1 Work in pairs. Match the people 1–6 in Vocabulary exercise 3 to the labels a–f.

a an anti-smoker		b a chain smoker	
c a fitness freak		d a couch potato	
e a vegan		f a junk food addict	

2 Imagine a discussion between each pair in exercise 1. What would they say to defend their positions?

1 Make a list of the arguments that the people a, c and e in exercise 1 could use in order to persuade the people b, d and f to change their lifestyle.
2 Make a list of the counter-arguments that the people b, d and f could use.

3 Work in pairs. Decide what you think is an acceptable happy medium for each pair of positions. Compare your answers with the rest of the class.

GRAMMAR

Modals of speculation

We use the modal verbs *must, may, might, could* and *can't* to speculate about events in the present, past or future.
The choice of modal verb reflects your degree of certainty when speculating.

certain	less certain	certain
must	*may* *might* *could*	can't

We use a modal verb + infinitive or *be* + -*ing* to speculate about the present or future.
> It **could be** dangerous.
> You **must be** joking.

We use a modal verb + *have* + past participle to speculate about the past.
> She **can't have been** very well.
> He **may not have understood**.

We can also use a phrase instead of a modal verb:
> It's   certain/sure
>   likely/probable/possible   that ...
>   unlikely/improbable
>   impossible

> **It's certain that** she wasn't very well.
> **It's possible that** he didn't understand.

Modals of permission, obligation & prohibition

Modal verbs (*can, could, will, must*) are followed by an infinitive without *to*. Other modal expressions (*have to, are allowed to, are permitted to*) include *to*, and are also followed by an infinitive.

language function	present	past	future
permission This is permitted/possible.	*can* *is/are allowed to*	*could* *was/were allowed to*	*can* *will be allowed to*
obligation This is necessary/obligatory.	*must* *have to* *have got to* *need to*	*had to* *needed to*	*must* *will have to* *will need to*
lack of obligation This is permitted, but not necessary.	*don't have to* *don't need to* *needn't*	*didn't have to* *didn't need to*	*won't have to* *won't need to*
prohibition This is not permitted/not possible.	*can't* *mustn't* *isn't/aren't allowed to*	*couldn't* *wasn't/weren't allowed to*	*can't* *won't be allowed to*

We can use *may/might* for permission when we want to be more formal.
> **May** I borrow your pen, please?

Have got to is similar in meaning to *must* and *have to*, but it is more informal.
> Sorry, I**'ve got to** go.

Need not/needn't is followed by an infinitive without *to*.
> You **needn't worry**.

FUNCTIONAL LANGUAGE

Changing the subject

Anyway, as I was saying, ...
As for ...
By the way, ...
Come to think of it, ...
Talking of ...
That reminds me ...

Word list

Symptoms

ache v *	/eɪk/
backache n C	/'bækeɪk/
hacking cough n C	/'hækɪŋ 'kɒf/
high temperature n C	/haɪ 'temprɪtʃə(r)/
rash n C	/ræʃ/
run-down adj	/rʌn'daʊn/
runny nose n C	/rʌni 'nəʊz/
sore throat n C	/sɔː(r) 'θrəʊt/
stiff muscles n C	/ˌstɪf 'mʌsl(ə)z/
throbbing headache n C	/ˌθrɒbɪŋ 'hedeɪk/
upset stomach n C	/ˌʌpset 'stʌmək/

Health idioms

at death's door	/ət ˌdeθs 'dɔː(r)/
there's a bug going around	/ˌðeə(r)z ə 'bʌg ˌgəʊɪŋ ə'raʊnd/
give (sb) a clean bill of health	/ˌgɪv ə ˌkliːn bɪl əv 'helθ/
go down with (sth)	/gəʊ ˌdaʊn wɪð/
in good shape	/ɪn ˌgʊd 'ʃeɪp/
my back was killing me	/maɪ ˌbæk wəz 'kɪlɪŋ miː/

Phrasal verbs with objects

get back to (sb)	/get 'bæk tə/
put up with (sb/sth)	/ˌpʊt ʌp 'wɪð/
put (sth) off	/ˌpʊt 'ɒf/
put (sb) up to (sth)	/ˌpʊt ʌp tə/
sort (sth) out	/ˌsɔː(r)t 'aʊt/
tell (sb) off	/ˌtel 'ɒf/

Other words & phrases

absenteeism n U	/ˌæbs(ə)n'tiːˌɪz(ə)m/
achiness n U	/'eɪkɪnəs/
acupuncture n U	/'ækjʊˌpʌŋktʃə(r)/
alarmed adj	/ə'lɑː(r)md/
anti-smoker n C	/ˌænti'sməʊkə(r)/
aromatherapist n C	/əˌrəʊmə'θerəpɪst/
aromatherapy n U	/əˌrəʊmə'θerəpi/
bed rest n U	/bed rest/
bergamot n U	/'bɜːgəmɒt/
blend n C	/blend/
blender n C	/'blendə(r)/
boost v	/buːst/
calm v **	/kɑːm/
chain smoker n C	/'tʃeɪn ˌsməʊkə(r)/
chronic adj *	/'krɒnɪk/
claim n C	/kleɪm/
clinical adj	/'klɪnɪk(ə)l/
collapse v **	/kə'læps/
colour therapy n U	/'kʌlə(r) ˌθerəpi/
come across v	/kʌm ə'krɒs/
concern n C	/kən'sɜː(r)n/
compensation n U **	/ˌkɒmpən'seɪʃ(ə)n/
consultation n C **	/ˌkɒns(ə)l'teɪʃ(ə)n/
cordless adj	/'kɔː(r)dləs/
couch potato n C	/ˌkaʊtʃ pə'teɪtəʊ/
counter-argument n C	/'kaʊntə(r) ˌɑː(r)gjʊmənt/
counterbalance v	/'kaʊntə(r)ˌbæləns/
cure v *	/kjʊə(r)/
deathbed n C	/'deθˌbed/
deliver a baby	/dɪˌlɪvə(r) ə 'beɪbi/
diagnosis n C **	/daɪəg'nəʊsɪs/
disrupt v *	/dɪs'rʌpt/
ease v	/iːz/
energize v	/'enə(r)dʒaɪz/
entitled adj	/ɪn'taɪt(ə)ld/
ergonomics n pl	/ˌɜː(r)gə'nɒmɪks/
essential oil n C	/ɪ'senʃ(ə)l ɔɪl/
fitness freak n C	/'fɪtnəs ˌfriːk/
flu n U *	/fluː/
fluorescent adj	/flɔː'res(ə)nt/
fly off the handle	/ˌflaɪ ɒf ðə 'hænd(ə)l/
go off (your) food	/ˌgəʊ ɒf fuːd/
GP n C	/ˌdʒiː 'piː/
grumble v	/'grʌmb(ə)l/
happy medium n s	/ˌhæpi 'miːdiəm/
healing adj	/'hiːlɪŋ/
heighten v	/'haɪt(ə)n/
hot toddy n C	/ˌhɒt 'tɒdi/
house v	/haʊz/
hypnosis n U	/hɪp'nəʊsɪs/
hypochondria n U	/ˌhaɪpəʊ'kɒndriə/
hypochondriac n C	/ˌhaɪpəʊ'kɒndriæk/
immunity n U	/ɪ'mjuːnəti/
insurance policy n C	/ɪn'ʃʊərəns 'pɒləsi/
irritable adj	/'ɪrɪtəb(ə)l/
junk food addict n C	/'dʒʌŋk fuːd ˌædɪkt/
lavatory n C	/'lævətri/
leftover adj	/'leftˌəʊvə(r)/
melodramatic adj	/ˌmelədrə'mætɪk/
migraine n C	/'miːgreɪn; 'maɪgreɪn/
moan v *	/məʊn/
moody adj	/'muːdi/
morale n U *	/mə'rɑːl/
negligence n U	/'neglɪdʒ(ə)ns/
osteopath n C	/'ɒstiəʊˌpæθ/
painkiller n C	/'peɪnˌkɪlə(r)/
pampering n U	/'pæmpə(r)ɪŋ/
paracetamol n C/U	/ˌpærə'siːtəmɒl/
physiotherapist n C	/ˌfɪziəʊ'θerəpɪst/
prescribe v **	/prɪ'skraɪb/
put aside v	/ˌpʊt ə'saɪd/
raging fever n U	/ˌreɪdʒɪŋ 'fiːvə(r)/
reflexology n U	/ˌriːflek'sɒlədʒi/
renewed adj	/rɪ'njuːd/
repetitive stress injury n C	/rɪ'petətɪv stres 'ɪndʒəri/
revitalize v	/riː'vaɪtəlaɪz/
sickness n U **	/'sɪknəs/
skip v *	/skɪp/
snap v **	/snæp/
sneeze v	/sniːz/
sniff v *	/snɪf/
spectrum n C **	/'spektrəm/
spinal adj	/'spaɪn(ə)l/
splitting headache n C	/ˌsplɪtɪŋ 'hedeɪk/
staggering adj	/'stægərɪŋ/
starve v *	/stɑː(r)v/
stress-related adj	/'stresrɪˌleɪtɪd/
stroke n C **	/strəʊk/
t'ai chi n U	/taɪ'tʃiː/
tetchy adj	/'tetʃi/
the bush n U	/ðə bʊʃ/
the outback n U	/ðiː 'aʊtˌbæk/
tissue n C	/'tɪsjuː/
trace n C	/treɪs/
under-fire adj	/ˌʌndə(r)ˌfaɪə(r)/
under the weather	/ˌʌndə(r) ðə 'weðə(r)/
vegan n C	/'viːgən/
wavelength n C	/'weɪvˌleŋθ/
wheelchair n C	/'wiːlˌtʃeə(r)/
workload n U *	/'wɜː(r)kˌləʊd/
work-related adj	/'wɜː(r)krɪˌleɪtɪd/

9A | Celebrity heroes

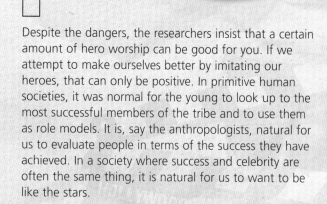

SPEAKING

1 Work in pairs. Discuss these questions.

- Who are the most popular film, music and sports stars in your country?
- What do you think of them?
- Which of these people are the best and worst role models for young people?

2 Use the questions below to interview other members of your class. If someone answers 'yes' to a question, ask for more details.

Have you ever …
- seen a film or bought a CD because you really liked the actor or singer?
- had a conversation with friends about someone you admire?
- visited a website that is devoted to a famous person?
- used a picture of someone you really like as a screensaver or to decorate your bedroom wall?
- bought something (an item of clothing, for example) which has the name of someone you really like on it?
- changed your appearance so that you look like someone you really admire?

READING

1 Read the article and choose the best title 1–3.

1 The dangers of hero worship
2 The harmless fun of hero worship
3 The heroes and heroines of *Star Wars*

2 Read the article again and put the paragraphs in the correct order.

3 Match the highlighted words in the text to the definitions a–f.

a   a shiny material
b   considering something or someone as important in an extreme way
c   extremely small
d   extremely ugly or strange
e   telling personal secrets
f   with similar opinions and interests

4 What advice would you give to someone with Celebrity Worship Syndrome?

☐

Despite the dangers, the researchers insist that a certain amount of hero worship can be good for you. If we attempt to make ourselves better by imitating our heroes, that can only be positive. In primitive human societies, it was normal for the young to look up to the most successful members of the tribe and to use them as role models. It is, say the anthropologists, natural for us to evaluate people in terms of the success they have achieved. In a society where success and celebrity are often the same thing, it is natural for us to want to be like the stars.

☐

The syndrome is unquestionably fuelled by the media's own obsession with celebrities. Gossip magazines and TV shows parade the stars before us, and reality TV shows create more overnight stars for us to admire and emulate. It almost seems as if Andy Warhol's prediction that, in the future, everyone will be famous for fifteen minutes, is coming true. But at a price.

☐

For some, like Tilly Kimber who had travelled from Sunderland for the event, it was the highlight of the year. Tilly, who was dressed as her heroine, Queen Amidala, in a gorgeous, red satin dress and strange gold headdress, runs two websites in her spare time, one devoted to *Star Wars* and the other to Natalie Portman, who plays the role of Queen Amidala. 'It's just great to be with other people who are as obsessed as me,' she said. Sharing the experience with a large like-minded crowd made up a little for the fact that Portman herself was not there.

Like everything else, it is a question of finding a healthy balance. For the great majority of people, there's nothing wrong with an interest in the love lives of well-known American film stars. But when hero worship turns into an all-consuming passion, it can be an addiction as dangerous as any other.

There was a handful of people wearing grotesque brown rubber Yoda masks, at least six Darth Vaders and any number of Jedi Knights in the crowd of over 1,300 packed into a huge widescreen cinema in London's Leicester Square. They had arrived at seven in the morning and had watched the first five *Star Wars* movies before the highlight of the day – the chance to be the first fans in the country to see the sixth and final instalment of the *Star Wars* series.

Tilly would probably describe her obsession as a bit of harmless fun. But for many others who suffer from Celebrity Worship Syndrome, such obsessions can be extremely unhealthy and even dangerous. When an impressionable young adolescent believes that his or her celebrity hero is their 'soulmate', there is serious cause for concern. Scientists who have studied the syndrome say that celebrity worshippers tend to be anxious and depressive. Some spend hours on the internet discussing minute personal details of the stars' lives; others write long confessional letters to their heroes. In a small number of cases, some are even ready to hurt themselves in the name of their hero.

GRAMMAR: adjective order

When you have two or more adjectives together, adjectives of opinion come before adjectives of description.
> *an exciting new movie*   *a brilliant young actor*

- Use adjectives of description in the following order: size / age / colour / origin / material
  a long, white plastic light-sabre
  adolescent British film fans
  Other descriptive adjectives come immediately before the noun.

> SEE LANGUAGE REFERENCE PAGE 94

1 Rearrange the words in the correct order.

1 headdress   strange   gold   a
2 a   cinema   huge   widescreen
3 crowd   a   large   like-minded
4 a   red   gorgeous   dress   satin
5 American   film stars   well-known
6 an   adolescent   impressionable   young
7 brown   grotesque   Yoda masks   rubber
8 confessional   letters   long
9 details   minute   personal

Check your answers in the article.

2 Think of three well-known film, music or sports stars. You have three minutes to write as many adjectives as possible that you can use to describe these people.

3 Work in small groups. Describe the celebrities to the other students in your group but do not mention their names.

He's a short, ageing, bald British rock star.
She's a fantastic young blonde tennis player.

The other students in your group must guess the name of the person you are describing.

9B | Local hero

LISTENING

1 Look at the photo and the newspaper headlines and answer the questions.

1 Who is the man in the picture? Describe him.
2 What is he doing? What do you think he is going to do?

2 🔘 **2.15** Listen to the news item and check your answers in exercise 1.

3 🔘 **2.15** Listen again and tick the information 1–8 that is mentioned.

1 Darren Hasell would like to see a perfect Tunbridge Wells.
2 Monkey Man has helped various people carry their shopping.
3 He has rescued a young woman in the town centre.
4 He rides an Italjet Dragster moped.
5 He will soon reveal the meaning of the letter 'O' on his suit.
6 National newspapers are trying to find the identity of the masked man.
7 The local mayor supports Monkey Man.
8 The photo was taken by a Polish tourist.

4 Work in pairs. Discuss these questions.

1 Why does the man hide his identity?
2 What do you think he does when he is not dressed as a superhero?

5 🔘 **2.16** Listen to a second news item and find out if your answers were correct in exercise 4.

6 🔘 **2.16** Listen again and replace the words in italics with the words you hear.

1 We turn to *the latest news* on the story of the Tunbridge Wells superhero.
2 It seems that the press has *made an embarrassing mistake*.
3 The three friends *invented it all* from the start.
4 National newspapers were *really keen* on publishing the story.
5 It was interesting to see how the press could be *made to believe such nonsense*.

7 Work in pairs. Discuss these questions.

- Do you think that what Matt Lees and his friends did was funny or irresponsible?
- Do you know of any other untrue stories that have been printed in the newspapers?

88

VOCABULARY: adjectives with prepositions

1 Match the adjectives 1–10 to the prepositions from the box that follow them.

for from in of on to
to to to with

1	aware	6	intent
2	connected	7	involved
3	devoted	8	responsible
4	familiar	9	restricted
5	free	10	sympathetic

2 Check your answers in tapescripts 2.15–2.16 on page 159.

3 Complete the sentences with an adjective and preposition from exercise 1.

1 Tunbridge Wells is generally _____ serious crime.
2 Some parts of the town are _____ pedestrians.
3 The town mayor is _____ many important decisions.
4 Many people in the town were not _____ the newspaper reports.
5 Three people were _____ the Monkey Man joke.
6 The jokers were _____ making more newspapers report the story.
7 An experienced journalist is usually _____ joke letters of this kind.

4 Work in pairs. Choose combinations of words from the boxes A and B and ask your partner to complete the sentences honestly.

A	*I can't understand people who are …* *I have never been …* *I would never want to be …* *I'd love to be …*
B	*aware connected devoted familiar free intent involved responsible restricted sympathetic*

SPEAKING

1 Work in pairs. Discuss these questions.

- Which of the powers of a superhero (in the box) would you most like to have? Why?

super hearing   super intelligence   super speed super strength   super vision   the ability to fly the ability to read other people's minds X-ray vision   immortality

- How would your life change if you had one of these powers?
- Are there any of these superhuman powers that you would not like to have? Why?

2 Work in small groups. Use seven of the phrases in the box to make a story about a superhero.

a black belt in karate   the mayor   rubber tyres a hairdresser   a moped   a rubbish bin a masked man   orange-suited   underpants

3 Compare your story with other groups.

DID YOU KNOW?

1 Work in pairs. Read the information and discuss these questions.

The most well-known American woman superhero often wears a bikini in the design of the Stars and Stripes. But Wonder Woman isn't American at all. Her real name is Diana and she has been sent by her Amazon tribe as an ambassador to the world. She is beautiful and has a woman's sensitivity and she is also strong and intelligent. She possesses superhuman skills, including the ability to fly, and she is a member of the Justice League of America. Wonder Woman was created by William Marston, a Harvard psychologist, who wanted an alternative to the macho world of superheroes.

- What other superheroes do you know about? (eg Batman, Superman, …)
- Who are the greatest heroines in your country (alive or dead, real or fictional)?
- How were their lives heroic? What did they do?

Reading

1 Work in pairs. What do you know about the screen villains below?

1 Count Dracula in *Dracula*
2 Cruella De Vil in *101 Dalmatians*
3 Darth Vader in *The Empire Strikes Back*
4 Dr Hannibal Lecter in *The Silence of the Lambs*
5 The Joker in *Batman*
6 The Queen in *Snow White and the Seven Dwarfs*
7 The Shark in *Jaws*
8 The Wicked Witch of the West in *The Wizard of Oz*

Can you think of anyone else to add to the list? In what way were they villains?

2 Read the competition opposite. Then work in pairs, and put the five villains in order of 'pure nastiness' (1 = most nasty → 5 = least nasty).

3 Find words or expressions in the text that match the definitions 1–8.

1 no longer active or alive (Blofeld)
2 close supporter of a powerful person (Saruman)
3 extremely frightening (Saruman)
4 long piece of wood (Captain Hook)
5 persuade someone to do something by making it seem attractive (Captain Hook)
6 promising (The Sheriff of Nottingham)
7 good-looking in an exciting way (The Sheriff of Nottingham)
8 without any reason or pattern (Alex de Large)

4 Work in pairs. Discuss these questions.

• Why are men usually the villains in movies?
• Can you think of any other women villains?

WIN 100 DVDS
VOTE FOR YOUR FAVOURITE SCREEN VILLAIN IN OUR WICKED DVD COMPETITION

How B-A-A-A-A-D can you get?
We've picked five of the worst British screen villains of all time. Put them in order of pure nastiness from 1 (totally poisonous) to 5 (pretty unpleasant).
Call now 0946 400400 (calls cost 85p/min)
Five lucky winners will receive 100 absolutely fabulous DVDs of their choice.

BLOFELD

(You only live twice)
– Donald Pleasance
Blofeld is the terrifying, scar-faced head of SPECTRE, an evil organization that is attempting to push the world's superpowers into a nuclear war. From his command centre in an extinct volcano, Blofeld hijacks Russian and American spacecraft. With a helping hand from Kissie Suzuki, his extremely attractive Japanese colleague, James Bond comes to the rescue.

SARUMAN

(Lord of the Rings trilogy) – Christopher Lee
Saruman is the henchman of Sauron, the lord of the rings and the lord of death. Powerful, power-mad and extremely dangerous, he hates the wise wizard, Gandalf, and despises the hobbits. He casts powerful spells with his magic staff and his spine-chilling voice has convinced thousands to follow him. The world of men and elves will never be completely free from his evil until the towers at the castle of Isengard have been destroyed

CAPTAIN HOOK

(Peter Pan) – Jason Isaacs
With an iron hook in place of one hand that was cut off by Peter Pan and swallowed by a hungry crocodile, Captain Hook is totally consumed with hatred for Peter and his Lost Boys, and dreams of making them all walk the plank off his pirate ship. He kidnaps Wendy, Peter's sweetheart, and uses every trick in the book to lure Peter to a painful death. His life ends when the rest of his body joins the hand in the crocodile's stomach. Tick tock, tick tock.

THE SHERIFF OF NOTTINGHAM

(Robin Hood: Prince of Thieves)
– Alan Rickman
The Sheriff of Nottingham has murdered Robin's father, and Robin returns to England vowing vengeance. In an all-American cast, the Sheriff's cutting British accent marks him out as the perfect villain. He wants to force the king's cousin, a horrified Maid Marian, to marry him. Absolutely furious when the dashing Robin of Locksley stands in his way, the sheriff's cruelty knows no bounds.

ALEX DE LARGE

(A Clockwork Orange) – Malcolm McDowell
Every night, Alex and his gang go on the rampage, beating and murdering. The violence is meaningless and random, and is as incomprehensible as the language that Alex speaks. He carries out his acts of brutality with

enthusiasm and pleasure, to the accompaniment of a Beethoven symphony. The whole film is a disturbing vision of a future Britain gone totally wrong.

GRAMMAR: adjectives & modifying adverbs

- **Gradable** adjectives (eg *attractive, painful, unpleasant*) can be made **stronger** or **weaker** with a modifying adverb.

  | *a bit* | *pretty* | *very* | *a little* |
  | *quite* | *really* | *extremely* | *slightly* |

  quite *painful*   **very** *painful*   **extremely** *painful*

- **Ungradable** adjectives (*furious, horrified, terrifying*) cannot be made weaker, but they can be made stronger with a modifying adverb.

  | *absolutely* | *completely* | *really* | *totally* |

  absolutely *furious*   **totally** *horrified*

  Not ~~**absolutely** attractive~~

- Some ungradable adjectives do not collocate with some intensifying adverbs.

  absolutely *fabulous* Not ~~**completely** fabulous~~

- Some adjectives (eg *random*) can be gradable or ungradable.

  slightly random   *totally random*

> SEE LANGUAGE REFERENCE PAGE 94

1 Find and correct the four incorrect phrases in italics.

1 His behaviour was a *little cynical*.
2 I think that Alan Rickman is *absolutely attractive*.
3 Jason Isaacs was *very perfect* in the role.
4 Maid Marion is a *completely pleasant* princess, but too nice to be believable.
5 Saruman is a *very typical* British villain.
6 Most villains are *really mean*.
7 The volcano was *slightly extinct*.
8 We got the answer *a bit wrong*.

2 Complete the beginnings of the sentences with a modifying adverb. More than one answer is possible.

1 He felt _____ frightened and …
2 It was _____ amazing, so he …
3 He was _____ cruel when he …
4 She was _____ exhausted because …
5 She didn't realize it was _____ illegal until …
6 She was _____ horrified when …

3 Work in pairs. Complete the sentences in exercise 2 with your own ideas.

SPEAKING & VOCABULARY: crimes

1 Work in pairs. Put the crimes in order of seriousness (1 = most serious → 8 = least serious).

	armed robbery		mugging
	assault		murder
	hijacking		vandalism
	kidnapping		smuggling

2 Match the crimes in exercise 1 to a punishment 1–5.

1 a prison sentence of X years
2 a fine of X pounds
3 a suspended prison sentence of X years
4 X months of community service
5 a caution

3 Which crimes are a problem in your town? Which crimes have been in the news recently?

9D | Hate list

SPEAKING & VOCABULARY: compound nouns (jobs)

"Sorry kid, but rules are rules!"

1 Complete the beginning of the compound nouns 1–9 in column A with an ending a–i in column B. Then add three more compound nouns (jobs) to the list.

A		B	
1	disc	a	agents
2	estate	b	bouncers
3	fire	c	couriers
4	motorcycle	d	fighters
5	nightclub	e	inspectors
6	rescue	f	jockeys
7	tax	g	reps
8	telesales	h	wardens
9	traffic	i	workers

2 Work in pairs. Look at the list of jobs from exercise 1 and answer the questions.

1 Which of these jobs are the best/worst paid?
2 Which of these jobs are most/least often done by women? Why do you think this is so?
3 Which of these jobs would you like/hate to do? Why?

3 Work in pairs. Decide what you would say in the following situations.

1 You are celebrating your birthday with some friends and you are refused entry to a club.
2 You stop your car for two minutes to buy some stamps at the post office. When you return to your car, you are about to get a parking ticket.
3 In the middle of a romantic dinner, your telephone rings. Someone wants to sell you some insurance.
4 You are one day late with your annual tax declaration. You receive a phone call and learn that you must pay a fine of £150.

4 Which of these situations would you find the most annoying?

LISTENING

1 🔘 **2.17** Listen to the results of a survey about different jobs. Answer the questions.

1 Which of the jobs in Speaking & vocabulary exercise 1 are mentioned?
2 Which is the most hated profession?
3 Do people hate or respect these professions?

2 🔘 **2.17** Listen again and tick the things that are mentioned.

1 The presenter had a bad experience with a traffic warden.
2 Traffic wardens claim that they do not deserve their reputation.
3 Fewer and fewer people want to become traffic wardens.
4 Phone companies are sometimes responsible for cold-calling.
5 The survey was probably carried out in a city.
6 Football players are more popular with men than with women.
7 The presenter has a poor opinion of politicians.
8 People's attitudes towards the police are changing.

3 Look at the expressions 1–6. Which job or jobs are they referring to? Check your answers in tapescript 2.17 on page 159.

1 a necessary evil
2 they're only doing their job
3 they often behave like pigs
4 famous for being famous
5 the professional liars
6 the flip side

4 Work in pairs. Discuss these questions.

• Would the results of the survey be the same in your country?
• What are the professions you most love to hate?

FUNCTIONAL LANGUAGE: contrast

- *Use although, even though, despite* and *in spite of* to link two pieces of contrasting information.
  She was writing out the ticket, **even though** *I said I was going to move my car.*
  Despite *all the stories to the contrary, they are not vindictive.*
- Use *although* and *even though* with a clause.
  Although/Even though *I know they're only doing their job, I absolutely hate being disturbed by cold callers.*
- Use *despite* and *in spite of* with a noun, a noun phrase or verb + -ing.
  Despite *admitting that traffic wardens are a necessary evil, there was still no doubt in people's minds that they are the number one high street villains.*
  In spite of *their special hero status, they can be arrogant, obnoxious thugs at times.*
- NB Use *despite/in spite of the fact (that)* with a clause.
  Despite the fact that *they're paid like gods, they often behave like pigs.*

> SEE LANGUAGE REFERENCE PAGE 94

1 Replace *but* with the linker in bold and rewrite the sentences.

1 Fire fighters are very well-respected *but* they are extremely badly-paid.
in spite of

2 There are more and more traffic wardens on the streets *but* drivers continue to park badly.
even though

3 The paparazzi are very unpopular *but* they were not on the list.
in spite of

4 Members of the armed forces are highly respected *but* recruitment is at an all-time low.
although

5 Estate agents have a very bad reputation *but* they perform an extremely useful service.
despite

6 Some people love footballers *but* others hate them.
although

2 Work in groups of three, A, B, and C. You are going to match sentence openers 1–6 with the sentence endings a–f in the information.

A: Turn to page 144.
B: Turn to page 148.
C: Turn to page 138.

3 Complete the story with your own ideas.

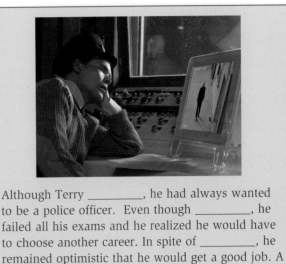

Although Terry _____, he had always wanted to be a police officer. Even though _____, he failed all his exams and he realized he would have to choose another career. In spite of _____, he remained optimistic that he would get a good job. A careers adviser suggested that he become a security guard, although _____. After six interviews, he finally got a job, despite _____. Even though _____, he still dreams of being a police officer.

4 Work in pairs. Compare your stories.

PRONUNCIATION: intonation (completion & non-completion)

We use intonation to show that we have finished saying something. Our voice goes down to show that we have finished. Our voice goes up to show that we have more to say.

1 2.18 Listen to the phrases below. Which are the beginnings and which are the ends of sentences?

1 although it all turned out OK in the end
2 despite all our efforts
3 in spite of everything he'd done for her
4 even though we needed the money

2 2.19 Listen to the complete sentences and repeat them from memory.

3 Work in pairs. Take it in turns to read out the following sentences. Your partner must decide if the sentence is complete or not, judging by your intonation. If the sentence is not complete, he/she must complete it with an appropriate ending.

1 although I didn't really enjoy it
2 even though she'd studied medicine
3 despite being incredibly wealthy
4 in spite of the high levels of stress

GRAMMAR

Adjective order

When we use two or more adjectives together, adjectives of opinion (subjective) come before adjectives of description (objective or factual).
a brave new world   an attractive English actress

The order of objective (or factual) adjectives will depend on the word which we want to stress, but the diagram below provides a useful guide.

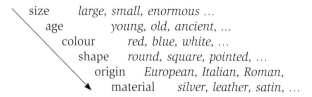

size   *large, small, enormous …*
age   *young, old, ancient, …*
colour   *red, blue, white, …*
shape   *round, square, pointed, …*
origin   *European, Italian, Roman,*
material   *silver, leather, satin, …*

a big, black, plastic ball
a new, wide Japanese screen
vintage red Rioja wine
short pink woollen socks

Adjectives & modifying adverbs

Adjectives in English are gradable or ungradable. We can make gradable adjectives (*big, dangerous, strange*) stronger or weaker. Here are some common adverbs that we can use to modify the adjectives.

weaker	⟶		stronger
a bit	pretty	very	
a little	quite	really	extremely
slightly	rather		
quite big	very dangerous		extremely strange

We cannot make ungradable adjectives weaker. But we can make them stronger with a modifying adverb. Here are the four most frequent:
absolutely   completely   really   totally
absolutely *fabulous*   **totally** *spine-chilling*
Not ~~slightly~~ *fabulous*

Common ungradable adjectives		
amazing	exhausted	impossible
awful	fantastic	marvellous
boiling	fascinating	perfect
brilliant	freezing	terrible
disastrous	furious	vital
enormous	horrified	wonderful
excellent	huge	

1 We can use *really* with all ungradable adjectives. Some collocations of *absolutely, completely* and *totally* are more common than others.
   absolutely *brilliant/certain/clear/correct/delighted/ essential/necessary/right/sure/true*
   completely *different/free/new/separate/wrong*
   totally *different/new/opposed/unacceptable/wrong*

2 Many adjectives (eg *different, poisonous, primitive, random, unpleasant*) can be gradable or ungradable.
   a little *primitive*   **absolutely** *primitive*

3 We can use *quite* with gradable adjectives to mean 'fairly but not very'.
   The weather's **quite** *nice.* **Quite** *warm, actually.*
   We can also use *quite* with some ungradable adjectives to mean 'completely'.
   Are you **quite** *certain about it? Yes, it's* **quite** *impossible.*

4 We often use *rather* instead of *pretty* or *quite* to express negative ideas.
   The film was **rather** *long and the plot was* **rather** *complicated.*

FUNCTIONAL LANGUAGE

Contrast

We use *though, although, even though, despite* and *in spite of* to link two pieces of contrasting information.
   There was already a long queue, **even though** *we tried to arrive early.*
   Despite *our attempt to arrive early, there was already a long queue.*

We use *though, although* and *even though* with a clause.
   Though/Although/Even though *it was very expensive, we were happy to pay.*
Though is less formal than *although* and *even though.* We use *even though* when we want to make the information in the main clause very surprising.

We use *despite* and *in spite of* with a noun, a noun phrase or verb + -ing.
   Despite beginning *the journey very late, we arrived on time.*
   In spite of the late start *to our journey, we arrived on time.*

We can also use *despite* and *in spite of* with *the fact that* to introduce a clause.
   Despite/In spite of the fact that *we started late, we arrived on time.*

WORD LIST

Adjectives with prepositions

aware of	/ə'weə(r) əv/
connected to	/kə'nektɪd ˌtu:/
devoted to	/dɪ'vəʊtɪd ˌtu:/
familiar with	/fə'mɪliə(r) ˌwɪð/
free from	/'fri: ˌfrɒm/
intent on	/ɪn'tent ɒn/
involved in	/ɪn'vɒlvd ɪn/
responsible for	/rɪ'spɒnsəb(ə)l fɔ:(r)/
restricted to	/rɪ'strɪktɪd ˌtu:/
sympathetic to	/ˌsɪmpə'θetɪk ˌtu:/

Crimes

armed robbery n C	/ˌɑː(r)md 'rɒbəri/
assault n C **	/ə'sɔ:lt/
hijacking n U	/'haɪˌdʒækɪŋ/
kidnapping n U	/'kɪdnæpɪŋ/
mugging n U	/'mʌgɪŋ/
murder n U ***	/'mɜː(r)də(r)/
smuggling n U	/'smʌg(ə)lɪŋ/
vandalism n U	/'vændəˌlɪz(ə)m/

Compound nouns (jobs)

disc jockey	/'dɪsk ˌdʒɒki/
estate agent	/ɪ'steɪt ˌeɪdʒ(ə)nt/
firefighter	/'faɪə(r)ˌfaɪtə(r)/
motorcycle courier	/'məʊtə(r)ˌsaɪk(ə)l ˌkʊriə(r)/
nightclub bouncer	/'naɪtklʌb ˌbaʊnsə(r)/
rescue worker	/'reskju: ˌwɜː(r)kə(r)/
tax inspector	/'tæks ɪnˌspektə(r)/
telesales rep	/'teliseɪlz ˌrep/
traffic warden	/'træfɪk ˌwɔː(r)d(ə)n/

Other words & phrases

all-consuming adj	/ɔ:lkən'sju:mɪŋ/
an all-time low	/ən ɔ:l'taɪm ləʊ/
anthropologist n C	/ˌænθrə'pɒlədʒɪst/
baddy n C	/'bædi/
bigoted adj	/'bɪgətɪd/
book (sb) v **	/'bʊk/
cape n C	/keɪp/
caped adj	/keɪpt/
cast n C *	/kɑːst/
citizenship n U *	/'sɪtɪz(ə)nʃɪp/
cold caller n C	/'kəʊld ˌkɔ:lə(r)/
cold-calling n U	/'kəʊld'kɔ:lɪŋ/
comic n C *	/'kɒmɪk/
community-minded adj	/kə'mju:nəti'maɪndɪd/
confessional adj	/kən'feʃ(ə)nəl/
crusader n C	/kru:'seɪdə(r)/
cutting adj	/'kʌtɪŋ/
dashing adj	/'dæʃɪŋ/
dazzling adj	/'dæzlɪŋ/
despise v	/dɪ'spaɪz/
dungeon n C	/'dʌndʒ(ə)n/
dutifully adv	/'dju:tɪf(ə)li/
elf/elves n C	/elf/elvz/
emulate v	/'emjʊleɪt/
extinct adj *	/ɪk'stɪŋkt/
flip side n U	/'flɪp ˌsaɪd/
fuel v	/'fju:əl/
gossip n U	/'gɒsɪp/
grotesque adj	/grəʊ'tesk/
gullible adj	/'gʌləb(ə)l/
handful n C	/'hæn(d)fʊl/
hatred n U *	/'heɪtrɪd/
have egg on (sb's) face	/hæv 'eg ɒn feɪs/
headdress n C	/'hedˌdres/
henchman n C	/'hentʃmən/
hero worship n U	/'hɪərəʊ ˌwɜː(r)ʃɪp/
highlight n C *	/'haɪˌlaɪt/
hook n C **	/'hʊk/
immortality n U	/ˌɪmɔ:(r)'tæləti/
impressionable adj	/ɪm'preʃ(ə)nəb(ə)l/
in store	/ɪn 'stɔ:(r)/
instalment n C	/ɪn'stɔ:lmənt/
know no bounds	/ˌnəʊ nəʊ 'baʊndz/
liar n C	/'laɪə(r)/
like-minded adj	/ˌlaɪk'maɪndɪd/
look up to v	/lʊk ʌp tə/
lure v	/'ljʊə(r)/
macho adj	/'mætʃəʊ/
make (sth) up	/ˌmeɪk 'ʌp/
masked adj	/mɑːskt/
meaningless adj *	/'mi:nɪŋləs/
menace n C	/'menəs/
minute adj	/maɪ'nju:t/
moped n C	/'məʊped/
nastiness n U	/'nɑ:stinəs/
obnoxious adj	/əb'nɒkʃəs/
obsessed adj *	/əb'sest/
on the rampage	/ɒn ðə 'ræmpeɪdʒ/
parade v	/pə'reɪd/
parking ticket n C	/'pɑ:(r)kɪŋ 'tɪkɪt/
patrol v *	/pə'trəʊl/
perk n C	/pɜː(r)k/
plank n C	/plæŋk/
power-mad adj	/'paʊə(r)ˌmæd/
prankster n C	/'præŋkstə(r)/
purse n C *	/pɜː(r)s/
random adj **	/'rændəm/
role model n C **	/'rəʊl ˌmɒd(ə)l/
satin adj	/'sætɪn/
scar-faced adj	/'skɑ:(r)ˌfeɪst/
sight v	/saɪt/
sighting n C	/'saɪtɪŋ/
soulmate n C	/'səʊlˌmeɪt/
slimy adj	/'slaɪmi/
spacecraft n C	/'speɪsˌkrɑːft/
spine-chilling adj	/'spaɪnˌtʃɪlɪŋ/
spit v *	/spɪt/
staff n C	/stɑːf/
stressed out adj	/'strest aʊt/
superhero n C	/'su:pə(r)ˌhɪərəʊ/
superhuman adj	/ˌsu:pə(r)'hju:mən/
tax declaration n C	/tæks ˌdeklə'reɪʃ(ə)n/
thug n C	/θʌg/
tick tock n s	/'tɪk tɒk/
trick n C **	/trɪk/
triumph v	/'traɪʌmf/
tyre n C	/'taɪə(r)/
underpants n pl	/'ʌndə(r)ˌpænts/
unquestionably adv	/ʌn'kwestʃ(ə)nəbli/
update n C *	/ʌp'deɪt/
vengeance n U	/'vendʒ(ə)ns/
villain n C *	/'vɪlən/
vindictive adj	/vɪn'dɪktɪv/
vow v	/vaʊ/
walk the plank	/ˌwɔ:k ðə 'plæŋk/

10A | Good deeds

SPEAKING

1 Work in pairs. Read the information about Howard Drew and Li Ka-Shing and decide which man is more generous. Explain your reasons.

Howard Drew
Since becoming a blood donor in the 1940s, Drew has donated over 130 litres of blood, enough to save the lives of countless numbers of people. Drew's own life was saved after a blood transfusion.

Li Ka-Shing
One of the most generous philanthropists in the world, Li Ka-Shing has given over $140 million to educational causes in East Asia and millions more to help victims of the tsunami in 2004.

2 Work in small groups. How many different examples of altruistic behaviour can you think of?

altruism /ˈæltruˌɪz(ə)m/ noun [U] a way of thinking or behaving that shows you care about other people and their interests more than you care about yourself

altruistic /ˌæltruˈɪstɪk/ adj thinking or behaving in a way that shows you care about other people and their interests more than you care about yourself

3 Work in pairs. Discuss these questions.

- What is the most altruistic thing that a person can do?
- Have you ever made a sacrifice for another person? If so, explain what happened.
- Would you ever make a sacrifice for someone you did not know? If so, in what circumstances?

Why are humans good?

READING

1 Look at the title of the article. Imagine that a visitor from outer space asked you this question. How would you answer?

2 Now read the article and choose the best summary 1–3.

1 Human beings have altruistic genes.
2 Human beings are much less selfish than other animals.
3 Human beings have evolved to behave in an altruistic way.

3 Read the article again and complete it with the sentences 1–6 in the spaces a–f.

1 Genes are no excuse for immorality.
2 Most famously of all, insects like bees and ants will spend their whole lives working for the good of the colony.
3 On the international stage, we honour altruistic individuals like Nelson Mandela, Aung San Suu Kyi or Mother Teresa who sacrifice their freedom or comfort in order to improve the lives of those around them.
4 The puzzle shows that there is a conflict between what is good for the individual and what is good for the group.
5 There are, in other words, very good reasons for us to act in an unselfish way.
6 Why are we ready to help others whose genes we do not share?

4 Do you agree with the arguments in the text? Can you remember your last three good deeds?

Human beings, as a species, like to consider themselves different from other animals. We use words for animals – dog, pig or monkey, for example – as insults, and we pride ourselves on those aspects of our behaviour and culture that set us apart from the rest of the animal kingdom. Unlike other animals, we attach great importance to moral values, and we respect those members of our race who distinguish themselves by devoting their lives to the benefit of others. (a) _____

But recent research into our genetic make-up has shown that human beings and animals are not so different. We share more than 90% of our genes with chimpanzees, and even 60% of chicken genes are very similar to our own. What is more, there is increasing evidence that many animals also share our capacity to behave in an altruistic way. Some birds will help other birds to feed their young and to protect the nest. Some species of monkeys give alarm calls to other members of their troop to warn of danger, even though they endanger themselves in the process. (b) _____

Biologists have known for some time that many animals, including humans, are prepared to sacrifice themselves for their family, especially their young. By doing so, they give the genes that they share with their family a better chance to survive and reproduce. We can expect animals to behave in a way that increases their own genes' chances of survival, but this does not explain why altruistic behaviour is common in humans and other animals. (c) _____

In an attempt to provide answers to this question, scientists have turned to a puzzle known as 'The Prisoner's Dilemma' (see right). In the puzzle, the best move for both prisoners is to give evidence against the other because they do not know what the other will do. But this is only the case when the puzzle is considered from the point of view of the individual prisoner. If we ask ourselves which behaviour is best for the group (the group of two prisoners), the answer is very different. From the point of view of the group, it is better for both prisoners to remain silent because the total amount of time in prison will only be one year (2 x six months). (d) _____

It was Charles Darwin who first suggested that the process of natural selection in evolution works at the level of the group. Selfish individuals have a better chance of surviving than altruistic individuals, and they will benefit from the altruism of the others. But altruistic groups have a much better chance of survival than selfish groups, because, in the long run, selfish groups destroy themselves. It is for this reason, suggest evolutionists, that societies that adopt cooperative behaviour are likely to last longer than those where it is every man for himself. (e) _____

Evolutionary theory can therefore provide at least a partial explanation of why humans and other animals are capable of doing good deeds. Evolutionary biologists offer a genetic explanation for the way we act, but they do not suggest that we have genes for good behaviour and genes for bad behaviour. Our genes do not pre-programme us to behave in a particular way, even though they have contributed to the evolution of our society. (f) _____

The Prisoner's Dilemma

Two criminals are arrested by the police. At first, the two criminals remain silent, but the police have enough evidence to send both of them to prison for six months. The police then speak to each of the criminals and offer them a deal.

If one prisoner agrees to give evidence against the other, he will go free. The other will spend ten years in prison.

If both prisoners give evidence against each other, they will both spend two years in prison. Neither prisoner knows what the other will decide to do. What would you decide?

VOCABULARY: reflexive verbs

1 Look at the article again. How many reflexive verbs can you find?

endanger themselves

2 Complete the sentences with a word from the box.

adapt	content	deceive
express	pride	remind

1 We often _____ ourselves about our real reasons for doing something.
2 People should _____ themselves on their appearance.
3 People _____ themselves through their actions more than their words.
4 We should _____ ourselves with what we have and not expect more.
5 At some point in their life, everybody has to _____ themselves to new circumstances.
6 It's a good idea to _____ yourself from time to time that life is short.

3 Work in pairs. Do you agree with the sentences in exercise 2?

10B | Giving

SPEAKING

1 Work in small groups. Read the situation below and decide what you would do.

A well-dressed woman stops you in the street and asks you, in a foreign accent, for £5. She explains that she has been robbed. Her coat, money and telephone have been stolen. She needs the money to get home. If you decide to give her the money, turn to card #1 on page 144. If you decide not to give her the money, turn to card #2 on page 147.

2 Work with students from other groups. Compare your stories.

LISTENING

1 🔘 **2.20** Listen to a conversation between a woman who works in a charity shop and her husband. Answer the questions.

1 What did the three visitors to her shop want?
2 What happened to the coat in the end?
3 How much money did the shop make from the coat?

2 🔘 **2.20** Listen again and complete the sentences.

1 The shop assistants were pleased to get £500 for the coat because _____.
2 The man's ex-girlfriend had put the coat in the bin because _____.
3 Moira took the man's phone number so that _____.
4 The shop assistants found the coat again a few weeks later while _____.
5 They found the envelope in the pocket of the coat while _____.
6 Moira took the money to the bank because _____.
7 The second man didn't like the coat because _____.
8 The shop assistant didn't admit that she had seen the coat because _____.

3 Work in pairs. Discuss these questions.

• What do you think Moira said to her friend?
• Do you think the shop should return the money to the man who had left it in the pocket?

GRAMMAR: reporting

1 Correct the mistakes in the sentences.

1 She said she has seen it in the window.
2 She asked how much did it cost.
3 We hadn't thought how much should we ask for it.
4 We couldn't help wondering what he is doing.
5 He asked us we had any black leather coats.
6 She told him that we sold a nice one the day before.
7 He explained that his ex-girlfriend put the coat in the bin.
8 He wanted to know was there any way to get it back.

2 Change the sentences in exercise 1 to direct speech or direct thought.

3 Put the sentences into reported speech.

1 'An extraordinary thing happened at work today,' she told her husband.
2 'Did Moira arrive on time?' he asked her.
3 'He could probably have bought the whole shop if he'd wanted to,' she said.
4 'What are you going to do?' he asked.
5 'I'll take it to the bank on my way,' she said.
6 'Has Moira gone out for lunch?' she wondered.

4 Work in pairs. Imagine the telephone conversation between the woman in the recording and her friend, Moira.

5 Now work with another pair of students. Tell them what Moira and her friend said.

When we report someone's words or thoughts, the verb forms often move into the past.

'It's a bit risky.'
She said it **was** a bit risky.
'I may give him a call.'
She thought she **might** give him a call.
Use the normal word order of statements in reported questions (ie do not use the auxiliaries *do* or *did* in the present and past tense).
He asked what I was doing.
(Not *He asked what was I doing.*)
He asked what it looked like.
(Not *He asked what did it look like?*)
Introduce reported *yes/no* questions with *if* or *whether*.
*He asked **if** we had any black leather coats.*
We do not need to change the verb form into the past (1) if we report something that is still true or relevant now, or (2) if the reporting verb is in the present tense.
'Will you lend me your phone?'
She asks if you will lend her your phone.

> ❯ SEE LANGUAGE REFERENCE PAGE 104

VOCABULARY: collocations with *give*

1 Look at tapescript 2.20 on page 160. Find and underline examples of the word *give* and the objects of the verb.

2 Choose the best way to complete the sentences below.

1 Hard work often gives me *consideration / a headache*.
2 I don't give a *damn / speech* what other people think of me.
3 I don't give a *lot of thought / piece of my mind* to my future.
4 I like new experiences and I'll give anything a *try / warning* once.
5 I sometimes give people *permission / the impression* that I'm older than I am.
6 If I'm not sure about someone, I always give them *a lecture / the benefit* of the doubt.
7 People often ask me to give them *a hand / problems* with their work.
8 When I'm on holiday, I give my friends a *call / priority* every few days.

3 Work in pairs. Are the sentences in exercise 2 true for you? For each sentence, give some extra information.

No, it's not true for me. I often enjoy doing hard work.

DID YOU KNOW?

1 Work in pairs. Read the information and discuss the questions.

More than 30 million red poppy badges are sold in Britain every year to raise money for people who have been injured or lost their lives serving the country. At other times of the year, you will see people wearing pink geranium flower badges (for the blind), red ribbons (for Aids) or yellow bracelets (for cancer). About two-thirds of people in Britain regularly give money to charities, and each year about £7 million is collected. Volunteers collect donations at train stations, in streets and pubs and at work. Throughout the year, thousands of charity events are organized and, at Christmas time, people buy Christmas cards from their favourite charities.
The most popular charities are those that fund medical research or provide help for children and young people. Charities that rescue or look after animals are also well-supported.

- Is charity-giving popular in your country?
- How do people raise money for charity?
- What are the most popular charities?
- Are there any charities that you support? Why?

Rainforest Protection Agency

Positions vacant

Can you help us
stop the clock?
Click here for more
information

COMMUNICATIONS COORDINATOR

CENTRAL AMERICA

SPEAKING & VOCABULARY: job responsibilities

1 Work in pairs. Look at the advert and answer these questions.

1 What job is being advertised?
2 What do you think the job might involve?

2 Read the job description and check your answers to question 2 of exercise 1.

Post: Communications Coordinator Central America

The Rainforest Protection Agency (RPA) is an international non-profit organization dedicated to protecting ecosystems and the people and wildlife that depend on them.

The Communication Coordinator will
- **promote** the RPA's work in Central America.
- **liaise** between local projects and the central organization.
- **oversee** translation to and from Spanish of written materials as needed.
- **participate** in conferences both nationally and internationally.
- **coordinate** the work of local volunteers.
- visit local projects periodically to **track** developments.
- **seek out** and actively encourage potential projects in the region.
- **facilitate** applications for grants.

3 Match the words in bold in the job description to the definitions 1–8.

1 follow the progress of something
2 create a link between two groups
3 look for something
4 take part in something
5 draw people's attention to something
6 organize the various parts of a job
7 check something is done correctly
8 help people do something

4 Work in pairs. Look at the main responsibilities of the job described in exercise 2 and decide which would be …

a the most interesting.
b the most time-consuming.
c the hardest work.

Justify your answers.

5 Work in pairs. Tell your partner about your job or the job of someone you know well. Explain what the job is and what the main responsibilities are.

READING

1 Read an article about a communications coordinator's day-to-day life. Answer the questions.

1 Which of the tasks in the job description are mentioned in the article?
2 What other tasks are mentioned?

2 Read the article again and correct the statements.

1 John spends about a third of his time travelling.
2 He can only access his email when he's at home.
3 He spends most of his time preparing promotional materials.
4 He doesn't enjoy this aspect of his work.
5 He prefers writing to travelling.
6 He likes being able to tell people what to do.
7 He finds it difficult to find volunteers.
8 He's going to stay in his job for the foreseeable future.

3 Which aspect of John's job would you find most interesting? Why?

A DAY IN THE LIFE OF …

John Betterman, Communications Coordinator for the Rainforest Protection Agency, Central America.

Days always start early, at about 6am. It's great waking up to a tropical sunrise and it's also the coolest time of day. The first thing I do is make a
5 coffee and go out onto my veranda to check my email and find out what's been happening in the news. Of course, seven mornings out of ten I'm not at home, but that doesn't
10 disrupt my routine. With satellite phones and my faithful laptop, I can surf the web and catch up on the news wherever I am. That's a very important part of my job. I need to know what's happening, not only on a national level, but on an international level too. People are counting on me to tell them what's going on. For
15 example, this morning there was a story from Norway warning coffee growers not to sell their beans to the big multinationals. I need to find out more about that and pass the information on.

My time is shared more or less equally between sitting in front of my laptop, writing press releases and articles, and travelling
20 around Central America, visiting projects and helping the local people access and administer the grants that are available to them. I love both sides of my job. The writing and translating is stimulating – and challenging. Promoting the RPA's work is easy, the hardest part is encouraging big businesses to see the error of
25 their ways and change their business practices. It's easy enough to persuade them to give money to sponsor specific projects, but it's very difficult to convince them to make changes if they can't see the profits.

But much as I enjoy the writing, my favourite part of the job is
30 at grassroots, coordinating the local volunteers and meeting the people who live in and around the rainforest. The day before yesterday I visited a farmers' cooperative in the North. They've just been awarded an RPA grant. The village elders held a meeting to decide what to do with the money. They invited me to take
35 part. My role in these meetings is to observe and facilitate. I'm not there to tell them what to do, but I do want to help them make informed decisions. One of the elders proposed spending the money on seeds, whilst others suggested inviting a consultant to visit the farm and help them make the right choice. I promised to
40 find someone who'd do it free of charge. My job now is to seek out the right person, and then to persuade them to come and help out. Neither thing should be too difficult, there are a lot of people out there who are very happy to help out, they just need to know how to do it.

45 Today I'm meeting a delegation of journalists from Indonesia who are here to compare the conservation work here in Central America with their projects back home. They're only here for three days and I've agreed to show them as much as I can in the short time they've got. It'll be interesting from a personal point of view
50 as well, as I'm leaving my job here in Central America at the end of the year and joining the team in South-East Asia.

GRAMMAR: reporting verbs & patterns

Reporting verbs are followed by a number of different verb constructions. Here are three common patterns.

1 **Reporting verb + verb + -*ing***
   They **mentioned wanting** to visit our model farm.
   (also: *deny, admit*, (1)___ (2)___)

2 **Reporting verb + *to* + infinitive**
   They **offered to sponsor** one of our projects.
   (also: *refuse, threaten* (3)___ (4)___)

3 **Reporting verb + object + *to* + infinitive**
   I **advised them to ask** a consultant to help them.
   (also: *tell, ask*, (5)___ (6)___ (7)___ (8)___ (9)___)
   NB In negatives *not* comes before the verb.
   He told me **not** to worry.
   She suggested **not** telling him until the next day.

> SEE LANGUAGE REFERENCE PAGE 104

1 Look at the highlighted verbs in the article, underline the verb that follows them and then add them to the appropriate list of verbs, 1, 2 or 3, in the grammar box.

2 Report the direct speech using verbs from the grammar box.

1 'Honestly, it wasn't me. I didn't have anything to do with it.'
2 'Go on, have another one. There's plenty of time.'
3 'Listen, I know it's late but I'll definitely have it done by the end of the day.'
4 'Why don't we just leave it till tomorrow?'
5 'Would you like to join us?'
6 'Watch out! Don't cross, there's a car coming!'
7 'Don't worry. I'm sure you'll do much better next time!'
8 'No, I'm sorry, but I just won't do it. I don't think it's fair.'

3 Work in pairs. Look at the reported speech in exercise 2 and answer these questions.

1 Who's speaking to who?
   Number 1 could be a pupil talking to a teacher.
2 Have you said any of these things recently?
3 Has anyone said any of them to you?

10D | A good job

SPEAKING

1 Work in pairs. Discuss this situation. A friend is worried about a job interview they have next week and needs some help preparing for it. What advice would you give him/her?

2 Read the advice sheet below and answer the questions.

1 Do you think the advice is helpful?
2 Which question would you find most difficult to answer? Why?
3 Think of three more questions an interviewer might ask.
4 Have you, or anyone you know, been interviewed for a job recently?
5 What was the job? What questions did the interviewer ask? Did you (or they) get the job?

LISTENING

1 ● **2.21** Listen to Annette being interviewed for John Betterman's job as Communication Coordinator for the RPA. Did she follow the tips in the advice sheet?

2 ● **2.21** Listen again. Complete the questions that the interviewer asks Annette.

1 Can you tell _____?
2 Why are _____?
3 And what do _____?
4 What do _____?
5 What about _____?
6 Are there _____?

3 ● **2.21** Listen again and make notes about Annette's answers to the questions in exercise 2.

4 Work in pairs. Discuss these questions.

- Which question did Annette answer best?
- What mistake did she make?
- Do you think she has a good chance of getting through to the next stage in the recruitment process?

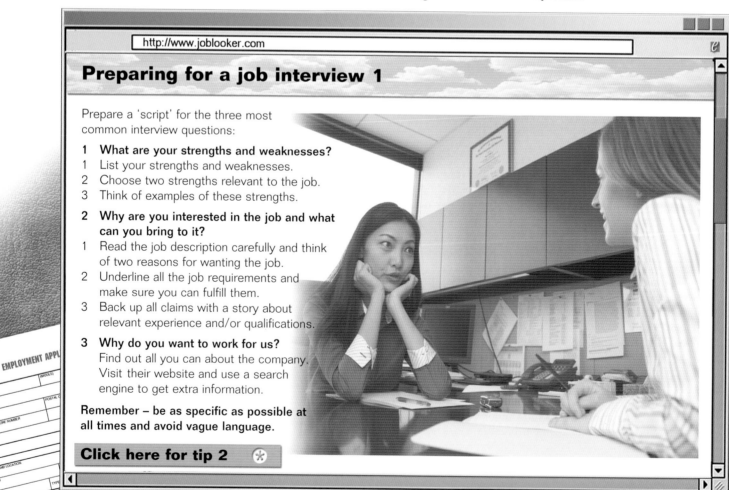

http://www.joblooker.com

Preparing for a job interview 1

Prepare a 'script' for the three most common interview questions:

1 What are your strengths and weaknesses?
1 List your strengths and weaknesses.
2 Choose two strengths relevant to the job.
3 Think of examples of these strengths.

2 Why are you interested in the job and what can you bring to it?
1 Read the job description carefully and think of two reasons for wanting the job.
2 Underline all the job requirements and make sure you can fulfill them.
3 Back up all claims with a story about relevant experience and/or qualifications.

3 Why do you want to work for us?
Find out all you can about the company. Visit their website and use a search engine to get extra information.

Remember – be as specific as possible at all times and avoid vague language.

Click here for tip 2 ✻

FUNCTIONAL LANGUAGE: job interviews

1 Complete the sentences 1–8 with the phrases a–h. Check your answers in tapescript 2.21 on pages 160–161.

A

1 I've been working in
2 To start with I worked as
3 The job involves
4 I'm usually good at
5 I've worked on various projects where
6 I take pride in my ability to
7 I think this post would give me the chance to
8 I know I have a tendency to

B

a get carried away sometimes.
b meet tight schedules and deadlines.
c a volunteer at a local radio station.
d develop my skills in this area.
e the communications sector since I left university.
f attending conferences and giving talks.
g I had to coordinate the work of small groups of volunteer workers.
h setting priorities.

2 Match the sentences in exercise 1 to the categories a–d.

a the job she has applied for
b past experience
c her present job
d strengths and weaknesses

3 Use expressions from exercise 1 to write five sentences about yourself, your past experience and your strengths and weaknesses.

4 Work in pairs. Show your sentences to your partner. Ask him/her to advise you on what kind of job would be best for you.

5 Look at tapescript 2.21 on pages 160–161 again and underline any other language that might be useful in a job interview.

PRONUNCIATION: intonation (questions & statements)

1 🔘 2.22 Read the information and listen to the examples.

We can turn a statement into a question by using rising intonation.
So you know something about our work out there already?
Your level of Spanish is pretty good?

2 🔘 2.23 Listen to the sentences below. Are they statements or questions? Insert a full stop or question mark.

1 It's the first time you've applied to work for us ___
2 You don't mind us contacting your referees ___
3 You've already seen the details about pay and conditions ___
4 You're happy with the salary ___
5 You would be free to start at the beginning of next week ___
6 You'd like some time to think about it ___

3 Work in pairs. Take it in turns to say the phrases from exercise 2. Your partner must decide if you are asking a question or making a statement.

SPEAKING

Roleplay

1 Work in two groups. You are going to prepare for a job interview.

Group A: Turn to page 145. Group B: Turn to page 149.

2 Work in pairs, with one student from Group A and one student from Group B. Roleplay the job interview.

3 Return to your original groups. Discuss these questions.
● Which question was the most difficult to answer?
● Which was the easiest?
● How many of the candidates would progress to the next stage of the recruiting process?

"I'm looking for a workaholic who feels the great job he does is compensation enough."

GRAMMAR

Reporting

When we report someone's words or thoughts, the verb forms often move into the past.

direct speech/ thought	reported speech/ thought
simple present *I do it.*	**simple past** *He said he did it.*
present continuous *I'm doing it.*	**past continuous** *He said he was doing it.*
present perfect *I've done it.*	**past perfect** *He said he'd done it.*
simple past *I did it.*	**past perfect** *He said he'd done it.*
past continuous *I was doing it.*	**past perfect continuous** *He said he'd been doing it.*
past perfect *I'd done it.*	**past perfect** *He said he'd done it.*
will/would *I'll/I'd do it.*	**would** *He said he'd do it.*
can/could *I can/could do it.*	**could** *He said he could do it.*
must/have to *I must/have to do it.*	**had to** *He said he had to do it.*
am going to *I'm going to do it.*	**was going to** *He said he was going to do it.*

When we report questions, we use the normal word order of statements (ie we do not invert the subject and the verb and we do not use the auxiliaries *do* or *did*).
> *He asked what I did for a living.*
> (Not *He asked what ~~did I do~~ for a living.*)
> *He asked what I was doing.*
> (Not *He asked what ~~was I~~ doing.*)

We introduce reported *yes/no* questions with *if* or *whether*.
> *He asked **if I** had done it.*

We do not need to change the verb form into the past (1) if we report something that is still true or relevant now, or (2) if the reporting verb is in the present tense.
> *He said he's done it.*
> *He says he's doing it.*

When the reporting takes place some time after the direct speech, we may need to change expressions of time and position or place.
Here are some examples:

today	*that day*
yesterday	*the day before*
tomorrow	*the following day*
here	*there*
this	*that*
these	*those*

Reporting verbs and patterns

Reporting verbs are followed by a number of different verb constructions. Here are three common patterns.

1 reporting verb + verb + *-ing*
> *She **admitted** being wrong.*

admit, deny, mention, recommend, suggest
Some verbs need a preposition before the verb + *-ing*.
> *He was blamed **for losing** the match.*

accuse someone **of**, blame someone **for**, congratulate someone **on**, insist **on**

2 reporting verb + *to* + infinitive
> *They **refused to give up**.*

agree, decide, offer, promise, refuse, threaten, warn

3 reporting verb + object + *to* + infinitive
> *She **told him (not) to see** a doctor.*

advise, ask, beg, invite, persuade, recommend, tell, warn

Functional language

Job interviews

*I know I have a tendency to +
infinitive*
*I take pride in my ability to +
infinitive*
*I think this job would give me the
chance to + infinitive*
*I'm usually good at + noun/-ing
form*
I've been working in …
*I've worked on various projects
where …*
The job involves + noun/-ing form
To start with, I worked as …

a volunteer at …
attend conferences
coordinate the work of …
develop (your) skills in …
get carried away
give talks
meet a deadline/a schedule
set priorities
the communications sector

Word list

Reflexive verbs

adapt yourself	/ə'dæpt/
content yourself	/kən'tent/
deceive yourself	/dɪ'siːv/
destroy yourself	/dɪ'strɔɪ/
distinguish yourself	/dɪ'stɪŋgwɪʃ/
endanger yourself	/ɪn'deɪndʒə(r)/
express yourself	/ɪk'spres/
pride yourself	/praɪd/
remind yourself	/rɪ'maɪnd/
sacrifice yourself	/'sækrɪfaɪs/

Collocations with *give*

give (sb) a call	/gɪv ə 'kɔːl/
give (sth) a clean	/gɪv ə 'kliːn/
give a damn	/gɪv ə 'dæm/
give (sb) a hand	/gɪv ə 'hænd/
give (sb) a headache	/gɪv ə 'hedeɪk/
give (sb) problems	/gɪv 'prɒbləmz /
give a lecture	/gɪv ə 'lektʃə(r)/
give a lot of thought	/gɪv ə ˌlɒt əv 'θɔːt/
give (sb) a piece of your mind	/gɪv ə ˌpiːs əv jə(r) 'maɪnd/

give (sb) a second	/gɪv ə 'sekənd/
give a speech	/gɪv ə 'spiːtʃ/
give (sth) a try	/gɪv ə 'traɪ/
give a warning	/gɪv ə 'wɔː(r)nɪŋ/
give consideration	/gɪv kənˌsɪdə'reɪʃ(ə)n/
give permission	/gɪv pə(r)'mɪʃ(ə)n/
give priority	/gɪv praɪ'ɒrəti/
give (sb) the benefit of the doubt	/gɪv ðə ˌbenɪfɪt əv ðə 'daʊt/
give the impression	/gɪv ði ɪm'preʃ(ə)n/

Job responsibilities

coordinate *v* *	/kəʊˈɔː(r)dɪneɪt/
facilitate *v* *	/fə'sɪləteɪt/
liaise *v*	/li'eɪz/
oversee *v*	/ˌəʊvə(r)'siː/
participate *v* **	/pɑː(r)'tɪsɪpeɪt/
promote *v* ***	/prə'məʊt/
seek out *v*	/ˌsiːk 'aʊt/
track *v* *	/træk/

Other words & phrases

access *v*	/'ækses/
administer *v*	/əd'mɪnɪstə(r)/
aid *n U* **	/eɪd/
altruism *n U*	/'æltruˌɪz(ə)m/
altruistic *adj*	/ˌæltru'ɪstɪk/
ambassador *n C* *	/æm'bæsədə(r)/
attach importance to (sth)	/ə'tætʃ ɪm'pɔː(r)t(ə)ns tuː/
bean *n C* **	/biːn/
beg *v* **	/beg/
blood transfusion *n C*	/blʌd 'trænsˌfjuːʒ(ə)n/
bracelet *n C*	/'breɪslət/
case study *n C*	/keɪs 'stʌdi/
charity shop *n C*	/'tʃærəti ˌʃɒp/
City *adj*	/'sɪti/
countless *adj* *	/'kaʊntləs/
delegation *n C* **	/ˌdelə'geɪʃ(ə)n/
detriment *n C*	/'detrɪmənt/
do good deeds	/ˌduː ˌgʊd 'diːdz/
donate *v* *	/dəʊ'neɪt/
donor *n C* *	/'dəʊnə(r)/
ecosystem *n C*	/'iːkəʊˌsɪstəm/
elders *n pl* *	/'eldə(r)z/
film crew *n C*	/'fɪlm ˌkruː/
fluff *n*	/flʌf/
foreseeable *adj*	/fɔː(r)'siːəb(ə)l/
fund *v/n C* ***	/fʌnd/
fur *n U* *	/fɜː(r)/
geranium *n C*	/dʒə'reɪniəm/
grant *n C* ***	/grɑːnt/
grassroots *n pl*	/ˌgrɑːs'ruːts/
grower *n C*	/'grəʊə(r)/
hang up *v*	/ˌhæŋ 'ʌp/
homeless *adj* *	/'həʊmləs/
honour *v* **	/'ɒnə(r)/
in a flash	/ˌɪn ə 'flæʃ/
innit	/'ɪnɪt/

juggle *v*	/'dʒʌg(ə)l/
knock over *v*	/ˌnɒk 'əʊvə(r)/
light up *v*	/laɪt 'ʌp/
limousine *n C*	/'lɪməˌziːn/
make-up *n U* *	/'meɪkʌp/
merchant banker *n C*	/'mɜː(r)tʃ(ə)nt 'bæŋkə(r)/
microphone *n C* *	/'maɪkrəˌfəʊn/
nest *n C* **	/nest/
non-profit *adj* *	/nɒn'prɒfɪt/
partial *adj* **	/'pɑː(r)ʃ(ə)l/
periodically *adv*	/ˌpɪəri'ɒdɪkli/
philanthropist *n C*	/fɪ'lænθrəpɪst/
poppy *n C*	/'pɒpi/
press release *n C*	/pres rɪ'liːs/
quid *n C* *	/kwɪd/
rainforest *n C* *	/'reɪnˌfɒrɪst/
raise money *v*	/ˌreɪz 'mʌni/
ribbon *n C* *	/'rɪbən/
rollerblades *n pl*	/'rəʊlə(r)ˌbleɪdz/
seed *n C* ***	/siːd/
self-help *n U*	/ˌself'help/
set (sb) apart from	/ˌset ə'pɑː(r)t frɒm/
shiver *v* *	/'ʃɪvə(r)/
single-handed *adv*	/ˌsɪŋg(ə)l'hændɪd/
tear *v* **	/teə(r)/
troop *n C* ***	/truːp/
veranda *n C*	/və'rændə/
well-supported *adj*	/ˌwelˌsə'pɔː(r)tɪd/
worried sick *adj*	/ˌwʌrid 'sɪk/

11A | Globe-trotting

VOCABULARY: geographical features

1 Complete the phrases with a word from the box.

Bay	Canal	Cape	Desert	Falls
Gulf	Mount	Ocean	Peninsula	Straits

1 _____ Everest
2 Niagara _____
3 the _____ of Bengal
4 the _____ of Gibraltar
5 the _____ of Good Hope
6 the Pacific _____
7 the Persian _____
8 the Sahara _____
9 the Sinai _____
10 the Suez _____

2 Work in pairs. Discuss these questions.

- How many more examples can you find for the words in the box in exercise 1?
- Which of these places have you visited? Which would you like to visit?

READING

1 Work in pairs. Look at the map (drawn in 1507) and answer the questions.

1 How many mistakes can you find on it?
2 If you wanted to sail a ship around the world, what would be the shortest route to take?
3 How would the route have been different for ships in the 16th century?

2 Read the article about the Chinese explorer, Zheng He, and answer the questions.

1 What is the connection between Zheng He and Christopher Columbus?
2 In what ways was Zheng He's achievement more impressive than that of Columbus?
3 What was so special about Zheng He's ships?
4 What evidence does Gavin Menzies have to support his claims?
5 Why is there so little evidence of Zheng He's voyages?

3 The author of the article uses a variety of words and expressions in order to avoid repeating the word *sailed*. How many can you find?

made the long, dangerous journey; travelled, …

4 Work in pairs. Discuss these questions.
- Why do you think this book is so controversial?
- Do you know of any other claims about explorers reaching America before Columbus?

GRAMMAR: *the* & geographical names

1 Underline all the geographical names in the article about Zheng He. Add one more for each example in the grammar box.

> Do not use *the* before the names of countries, continents or cities unless the name includes the word *states, republic, kingdom* or *union.*
> America, Europe, China, (1) _____.
> the EU, the UK, (2) _____.
> There are a few exceptions: *the Sudan, the Gambia.*
> Use *the* before the names of oceans, seas, rivers, deserts and groups of mountains or islands.
> *the Pacific, the Thames, the Sahara, the Philippines,* (3) _____.
> Do not use *the* before the names of individual mountains, islands or lakes.
> *Tenerife,* (4) _____.

> ❯ SEE LANGUAGE REFERENCE PAGE 114

2 Look at the highlighted place names. Add *the* where necessary.

> Join us on a tall ship adventure. Sail from Azores to Menorca in two action-packed weeks. Enjoy open sea-sailing across Atlantic from San Miguel to mainland Europe. Follow the coast of southern Portugal and south-west Spain to Cadiz, the oldest city on Mediterranean. Set foot on dry land for the first time in five days and enjoy a special Spanish welcome. Enter Med through Straits of Gibraltar, with incredible views of Rif Mountains in Morocco on one side and the unspoilt beaches of western Andalusia on the other. Dock at Gibraltar for a few days of well-earned rest before continuing to Balearic Islands. Your trip will end at Mahon, Menorca's world famous natural harbour – the second deepest in the world.

3 Work in pairs. Imagine you have won a two-week holiday on a luxury cruise ship. Draw up an itinerary for your cruise.

1421
THE YEAR CHINA DISCOVERED AMERICA?

Is it possible that a fleet of Chinese ships made the long, dangerous journey across the Atlantic to land on the American continent seventy years before Christopher Columbus did? Gavin Menzies, a retired British submarine commander, claims to have found clear evidence that they did. Menzies also suggests that the Chinese supplied Columbus with the maps that made his later journey possible.

Nobody disputes the Chinese fleets' capacity for long sea voyages at that time. The famous Chinese explorer, Zheng He, and his dragon ships travelled on more than one occasion from China as far as the east coast of
5 Africa. His early voyages are well documented. History books tell how his ships set sail from Nanjing on the River Yangtze, cruised through the Japanese Sea to Canton and Thailand, before sailing on to Malaysia where there was a supply post. Chinese artefacts and
10 settlements in Sri Lanka and the east coast of Africa support claims that he sailed across the Indian Ocean, calling in at Calicut in South India before reaching Mogadishu in Somalia.

Zheng He's ships were huge, larger than many modern
15 warships, and some of them carried over 1,000 people. They took everything that they thought they would need to start new colonies and to trade with other nations. There were interpreters in seventeen different languages, skilled craftsmen and hundreds of women to populate
20 the new settlements. There was also a wide variety of Chinese plants and flowers, animals for breeding and parts of the ship could be flooded to create giant fish tanks.

On his sixth voyage, Zheng He took his fleet even
25 further, according to Menzies. In his controversial book, *1421, The Year China Discovered The World*, Menzies describes how Zheng He's fleet rounded the Cape of Good Hope, set course westwards across the Atlantic and reached the coast of Brazil sometime in December
30 1421. The starting point for his theory is a 1424 map of Europe and the Atlantic that he says shows both Puerto Rico and Guadeloupe nearly 70 years before 1492, when Columbus first landed in America. Menzies argues that the 1424 map was drawn up by Zheng He and
35 was later used by Columbus on his voyages across the Atlantic. Menzies used reconstructions of 15th-century night skies to plot Zheng He's course across the Atlantic and he gives evidence of Chinese settlements on both the east and west coast of the United States.

40 Menzies' claims do not stop there. His book goes on to describe how the dragon fleets continued their voyage, sailing south along the coast of Argentina and navigating the Straits of Magellan almost a hundred years before Magellan himself did. From there Zheng He headed
45 West, discovering Antarctica and New Zealand and reaching Australia 350 years before Captain Cook.

Unfortunately, when Zheng He returned from his voyage, the political climate in China had changed. Long sea voyages were now seen as an unnecessary
50 luxury and the building of ocean going vessels had become a crime punishable by death. All papers relating to Zheng's voyage were destroyed and there is no direct historical evidence of it ever having happened.

However, this does not deter Menzies and his followers.
55 They claim that ancient maps, Chinese artefacts and computer simulations all help to support their theory. They are adamant that Zheng He's fleet not only sailed to America but also circumnavigated the globe almost 100 years before their European counterparts.

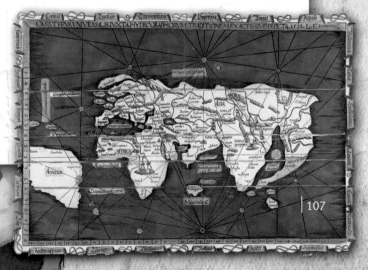

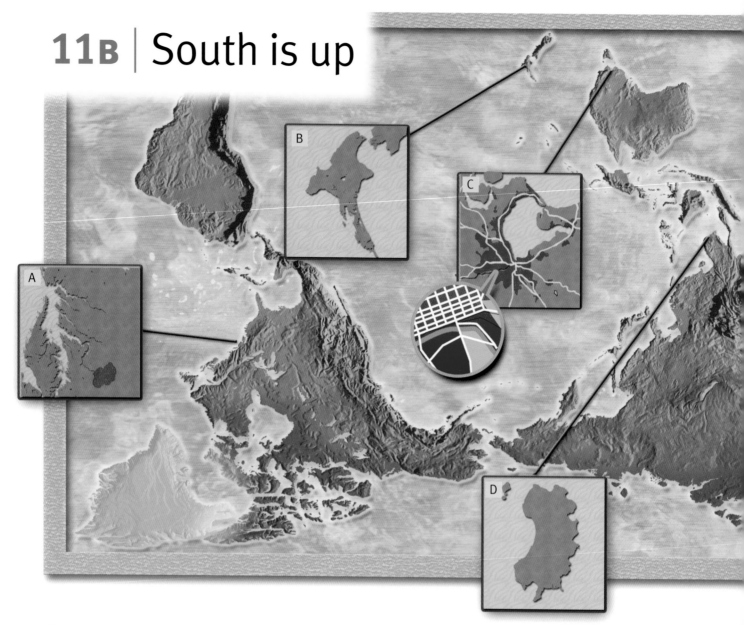

LISTENING

1 Work in pairs. Look at the map and discuss this question.

In what ways is this map different from a traditional world map?

2 🌐 **2.24** Listen to two friends discussing the map. Match the five magnified areas A–E to the reasons why they've been highlighted.

1 he went on holiday there
2 he'd like to go on holiday there
3 his in-laws live there
4 his wife's there at the moment
5 it's where Gavin's mother lives

3 💿 **2.24** Listen again and choose the correct answers.

1 Gavin got the map *in London / on the internet.*
2 Mark tries to *change his prejudices / turn the map around in his head.*
3 Stuart McArthur's geography teacher told him to *change / publish* the map.
4 Gavin's mother lives *in Melbourne / on Koh Tao.*
5 Gavin went to Thailand *on his own / with some friends.*
6 Gavin thinks that the Algarve is a *bad / good* place for a holiday.
7 Gavin's wife, Bel, is coming home for a couple of *days / weeks.*
8 Gavin *does not plan / plans* to visit New Zealand very soon.

4 Work in pairs. Discuss these questions.

• What maps have you got at home (atlases, road maps, wall maps, street maps etc)?
• How often do you use them? What do you use them for?

VOCABULARY: binomials

1 Find the following expressions in tapescript 2.24 on page 161 and explain what they mean.

1 sick and tired
2 bits and pieces
3 pick and choose
4 to and fro
5 short and sweet

2 Complete the binomial expressions with a word from the box.

blood	bred	forget	hard
now	out	tested	white

1 I was born and _____ in this country.
2 I always put my own flesh and _____ before my friends.
3 I prefer black and _____ explanations and I don't like ambiguity.
4 I always want to deal with problems here and _____.
5 I always buy things that are tried and _____.
6 I know that I'll never be down and _____
7 I find it difficult to forgive and _____.
8 I think about things long and _____ before I make decisions.

3 Work in pairs. Are the sentences in exercise 2 true for you?

FUNCTIONAL LANGUAGE: vague language

1 Find and underline ten vague expressions in the text.

> My girlfriend's really into, like, mountain climbing and stuff like that, so every year she spends, you know, a couple of weeks or so in the Alps or somewhere. And for six months, more or less, before she goes, she goes running and lifts weights and so on. It kind of worries me when she's up a mountain or something, but I'm sort of getting used to it now.

2 Complete the text with expressions from exercise 1. More than one answer is possible.

Her favourite place is called, (1) _____, Mount McKinley (2) _____, where she went a couple of years ago (3) _____. It's in Canada or Alaska (4) _____ – I've always been (5) _____ hopeless at remembering names of mountains and places (6) _____. I (7) _____ enjoy looking at her photos, (8) _____, and listening to her stories, (9) _____, but it's (10) _____ all she talks about.

🔘 2.25 Listen to the recording to compare your answers.

3 Work in pairs. How much can you remember about the conversation between Gavin and Mark? Use the vague expressions from exercise 1 to help you.

SPEAKING

1 Look at the map and choose five areas that you would like to magnify and circle them.

2 Work in groups. Explain your choices to the others in your group.

11c | Positive psychology

READING

1 Work in pairs. Discuss these questions.

- Would you describe the people in your country as generally happy or unhappy?
- What are they happy or unhappy about?
- In which countries in the world are the people happiest? Why?

2 Read the article and choose the best title 1–3.

1 In search of happiness
2 It's a wonderful world
3 The growing difference between rich and poor

3 Match the summary sentences 1–7 to the paragraphs A–E. Two of the summaries are not needed.

1 Colombia and Mexico are good places to go on holiday.
2 People want to buy happiness when they're on holiday.
3 Some people are getting richer but this doesn't make them happier.
4 Some politicians have tried to learn more about happiness.
5 The information in the World Database of Happiness is not very useful.
6 There are other factors that contribute to happiness.
7 Wealth and happiness are sometimes, but not always, the same thing.

4 Find words in the text that match the definitions 1–7.

1 rich enough to buy things for pleasure (*paragraph A*)
2 ways of understanding or thinking about something (*paragraph A*)
3 a connection or relationship between two or more things that is not caused by chance (*paragraph B*)
4 extremely important because it has a major effect on the result of something (*paragraph C*)
5 attractive, exciting and fashionable (*paragraph D*)
6 extremely happy (*paragraph D*)
7 make an attempt to deal with a problem (*paragraph E*)

5 Work in pairs. Discuss this question.

- In what ways could the government of your country improve the happiness of the people? Choose the three most important ways.

A For the last 50 years, the world's richest countries have grown wealthier and wealthier. Average salaries have more than doubled, but although we are much more affluent, it seems that we are not necessarily any happier than we were before. A new survey, published by the World Database of Happiness, gives statistical information, in the form of league tables, about people's perceptions of their own happiness in different countries around the world.

B By and large, there is usually a correlation between a nation's wealth and the happiness of its people. The United States and members of the European Union score higher than most countries in the Developing World, but money is not the only deciding factor. The Colombians and Mexicans, for example, are much happier than the populations of many European countries that are much richer than them. Among the richer nations, some, like the Danes and the Swiss, are much happier than others, like the Greeks or the Belgians, but in almost all of these countries that are getting richer and richer, people are no more satisfied with their lives now than they were two generations ago.

C For politicians, understanding what it is that makes us happy is crucial. The statistical information in the World Database of Happiness is a useful starting point and the new science of positive psychology (the science of happiness) is also helping our leaders decide how best to shape the future of our countries. What is clear from the research is that financial security is only important up to a certain point. After that, the most important factors are health, our families and a sense of belonging to a community. The danger for societies where material possessions and work are of paramount importance is that the other factors that contribute to happiness suffer. In Britain, for example, stress-related illnesses are a major problem and thirteen million prescriptions for anti-depressants are written every year. At the same time, family values and a sense of community disappear.

D Unable to find happiness at home, it is not surprising that many people look to find it elsewhere. The advertisements of national tourist boards, on TV and in glossy magazines, show pictures of happy, smiling faces, pretty resorts and euphoric carnivals. Cheap travel has made it possible for most people in rich countries to buy a week or two of happiness each year, but it is only a very temporary solution. Returning to our jobs and our worries after a fortnight in the sun, our lack of happiness may be felt even more acutely. Happiness, after all, is relative.

E In an attempt to tackle the 'happiness' problem, world leaders at the recent World Economic Forum in Davos took part in a workshop which explored the meaning of happiness. Various factors were discussed, and there were contributions from business leaders, university professors and pop singers. Unfortunately, the workshop failed to reach any practical conclusions. They did, however, agree on one thing: although governments will find it very difficult, if not impossible, to create happiness, they can remove some of the obstacles that stand in its way. But, even if they hadn't found the key to true happiness, there were plenty of smiling faces at the end of the day. It seems that the participants had all enjoyed taking part in the search.

GRAMMAR: articles

> Use *the* before a noun when it is clear what is being referred to, because
> - it is defined immediately afterwards.
>   (1) _____
> - it has already been mentioned.
>   *It is not surprising to learn from the survey ...*
> - it is unique. (2) _____
>
> Use *a/an* before a singular countable noun when it is not immediately clear what is being referred to, because
> - it is mentioned for the first time. (3) _____
> - it is not important which particular thing is being referred to. (4) _____
>
> When talking about things in general
> - do not use an article with plural and uncountable nouns. (5) _____
>
> ❯ SEE LANGUAGE REFERENCE PAGE 114

1 Complete the examples 1–5 in the grammar box with the highlighted phrases in the text.

2 Choose the best way to complete the sentences.

1 Happiness is *the* / Ø memory of *a* / *the* good times you have spent with *the* / Ø friends.
2 Happiness is drinking *a* / *the* glass of *the* / Ø champagne on *a* / Ø hot summer afternoon.
3 Happiness is reading *the* / Ø book you have been waiting to read *the* / Ø whole day.
4 Happiness is getting *a* / *the* good score in *an* / Ø important exam.
5 Happiness is having *a* / Ø fridge full of *the* / Ø food and *the* / Ø drink.
6 Happiness is *an* / Ø understanding look from *the* / Ø person you love.

3 Work in pairs. Do you agree with the sentences in exercise 2? Make up six more sentences that begin 'Happiness is ...'

PRONUNCIATION: *the*

1 🔘 **2.26** Listen to the recording. What is the difference between the pronunciation of the word *the* in groups A and B?

A	B
the database	the advertisements
the reasons	the EU
the research	the importance
the survey	the other factors
the world	the United States

2 Look at the words in the box for twenty seconds, then close your book. Work in pairs and try to remember as many of the phrases as possible.

the Americans	the Estonians	the Portuguese
the Argentinians	the French	the Slovenians
the Austrians	the Germans	the Spanish
the Brazilians	the Hungarians	the Swiss
the Czechs	the Indians	the Thais
the Dutch	the Irish	the Ukrainians
the Egyptians	the Italians	the Uruguayans

3 What generalizations can you make about the likes and dislikes of the nationality groups in exercise 2?

The Americans enjoy baseball.
The Argentinians like football.

SPEAKING

1 Work in groups. How important are the following for your own personal happiness? Put them in order from 1 (most important) → 7 (least important).

☐ family relations   ☐ social activities
☐ job satisfaction   ☐ health
☐ political freedom   ☐ social & gender
☐ security in your country   equality in your country

2 Choose three countries where you would all like to live. Consider the categories in exercise 1 and share what you know about these countries. Where do you think you would be happiest?

11D | Perfect locations

SPEAKING & VOCABULARY: describing landscape

1 Match the phrases 1–7 to the photos A–D.

1   a bare rocky ridge
2   a deep narrow gorge
3   a fertile wooded valley
4   gentle rolling hills
5   a jagged snowy peak
6   a sheltered sandy cove
7   a tall steep cliff

2 Which of the adjectives in exercise 1 can you use to describe the landscape features a–e?

a   estuary   d   plain
b   field   e   mountain
c   forest

3 Work in pairs. Discuss these questions.

1   Which country do you think the photos were taken in? Why?
2   What kind of film do you think could be made in these locations?

4 Work in pairs. Choose three different locations in your country to make each of the following films.

1   a science fiction film set on a distant planet
2   a horror film set in a very isolated place
3   a romantic comedy set in a beautiful location
4   a *James Bond* film

5 Work in groups. Compare your ideas and explain the reasons for your choice. Choose the best ideas and present them to the rest of the class.

LISTENING

1 🔘 **2.27** Listen to an interview with a location scout. Put the topics in the order that she discusses them.

☐   her current project
☐   her future plans
☐   how she does her research
☐   the Azores
☐   the work of a location scout

2 🔘 **2.27** Listen again and choose the best way to complete the sentences.

1   It is *more / less* stressful to be a location manager than a location scout.
2   She does a lot of research at home *after / before* travelling to the different places.
3   For the film of *Gulliver's Travels*, she needs to find *one area / four different areas*.
4   The ideal location is often *quite close to / a long way from* a town.
5   Cappadocia *has hardly changed / has changed a lot* since *Star Wars* was filmed there.
6   The *Lord of the Rings* films have helped the *film / tourist* industry in New Zealand.
7   The Azores is a good location because *the islands have a wide variety of landscapes / they are good for sailing*.
8   The Canary Islands are not suitable because *they don't have the same variety as the Azores / they are too well-known*.

3 Look at the phrases in tapescript 2.27 on page 162. What do the words in bold refer to?

1   **That side of the job** is so stressful
2   **That** sounds like a tall order
3   **It**'s not too important.
4   We think the Azores will give us all **that**
5   If the director goes for **it**

4 Would you like to work as a location scout? Why or why not?

GRAMMAR: *so & such*

1 Look at tapescript 2.27 on page 162 and complete the examples in the grammar box.

> Use *so* and *such* to make adjectives, adverbs and nouns more emphatic.
> Use *so* with an adjective or an adverb.
> With an adjective: *so* (1) _____.
> With an adverb: *everything has to be done so* (2) _____.
>
> Use *so* + *much, many, few* or *little* with nouns.
> so much: *There's so much* (3) _____.
> so many: (4) _____
> so few: (5) _____
> so little: (6) _____
>
> Use *such* with a noun phrase. Notice the position of *a/an* with a singular noun.
> *such a/an* (7) _____
>
> You can also use *such* with uncountable and plural nouns.
> With an uncountable noun: *it's such hard* (8) _____
> With a plural noun: *such awful people*
> Use *so/such ... that* to express a consequence.
> *So* (9) _____ *visit the islands that they're practically unknown.*

> **●** SEE LANGUAGE REFERENCE PAGE 114

2 Complete the text with *so* or *such*.

It was (1) _____ important to find the right location, and the director was delighted that the scouts had found (2) _____ a perfect spot. It took over a month to get everything ready because (3) _____ many people were involved, and everybody could hardly wait to get started after (4) _____ a long wait. But on the day that filming started, it began to rain. In fact, it rained (5) _____ much that thousands of dollars of equipment were washed away in the water. It was (6) _____ a shock because it never normally rains in the Almeria desert, but everybody had worked (7) _____ hard for nothing.

3 Rewrite the sentences so that the meaning stays the same.

1 It was such a remote location that they had to be flown in by helicopter.
   The location was _____ that _____.
2 The spot is so beautiful, it would be perfect for a film set.
   It's _____ that _____.
3 There were such a lot of people working on the set and they had to rent an entire ski resort to house them.
   There were so _____ that _____.
4 They were so surprised when the owner turned up and said they couldn't film there.
   It was _____ when _____.
5 Hardly any tickets had been sold for the film's first night, so they cancelled the showing.
   So _____ that _____.

4 Choose the correct word to complete the phrases.

1 I was *so / such* surprised ...
2 It was *so / such* a relief ...
3 I'd never seen *so / such* many people ...
4 I had *so / such* little time, I thought I'd never make it ...

5 Work in pairs. Choose one of the phrases in exercise 4 and tell your partner about something that happened to you recently starting with that phrase.

DID YOU KNOW?

1 Work in pairs. Read the information and discuss these questions.

Only 150 years ago, the San Fernando Valley in North Hollywood was a rural farming area, but it is now home to some of the world's most famous film studios: Walt Disney, NBC TV, Warner Brothers and Universal. California's year-round good weather, natural light and a wide variety of locations made it ideal for early film-makers. As a result, the scenery of Los Angeles and Southern California is better-known than anywhere else in the world. Universal Studios has become a major tourist attraction, although some of the other studios give a better idea of how films are made.

- What are the most well-known film or TV studios in your country? Where are they?
- Have you ever visited a film studio or film set? What did you see and do there? If not, would you like to visit one? Why or why not?

GRAMMAR

Articles

We use *the* before a noun when it is clear what is being referred to, because:
- it is defined immediately afterwards.
  The location they chose was very remote.
- it has already been mentioned.
  The researchers carried out a survey of job satisfaction … It is not surprising to learn from the survey, …
- it is unique.
  She works closely with the director and the producer.

We use *a/an* before a singular countable noun when it is not immediately clear what is being referred to, because:
- it is mentioned for the first time.
  I'm going to tell you a story about a little girl and three brown bears.
- it is not important which particular thing is being referred to.
  Police officers arrested a demonstrator outside the World Economic Forum.

When talking about things in general
- do not use an article with plural and uncountable nouns.
  ~~the women live longer than the men~~
  ~~the time is precious~~

the & geographical names

We do not use *the* before the names of countries, continents or cities unless the name includes the word *states, republic, kingdom* or *union.*
  America, Europe, China, Britain
  the USA, the EU, the People's Republic of China, the UK
There are a few exceptions: **the** *Netherlands,* **the** *Hague,* **the** *Vatican,* **the** *Gambia*

We use *the* before the names of oceans, seas, rivers, deserts and groups of mountains or islands:
  the *Pacific,* **the** *Mediterranean,* **the** *Thames,* **the** *Sahara,* **the** *Himalayas,* **the** *Canaries,* **the** *Philippines*

We do not use *the* before the names of individual mountains, islands or lakes.
  Mount Kilimanjaro, Tenerife, Lake Constance

so & such

We use *so* and *such* to make adjectives, adverbs and nouns stronger or more emphatic.

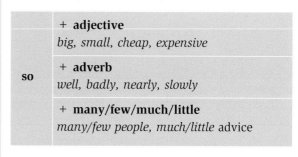

so	**+ adjective** *big, small, cheap, expensive*
	+ adverb *well, badly, nearly, slowly*
	+ many/few/much/little *many/few people, much/little advice*

| such | **+ (a/an) noun**
a pity, luck, friends |
| | **+ (a/an) adjective + noun**
a nice day, happy memories |

If we want to express a consequence, we follow the *so/such* phrase with *that* + clause. We can omit *that* in informal situations.
  *They were so cheap (**that**) I bought ten.*
  (= I bought ten because they were very cheap.)
  *He drives so slowly (**that**) we'll never get there.*
  *It was such a nice day (**that**) we decided to go to the beach.*

FUNCTIONAL LANGUAGE

Vague language

kind of/sort of
like
you know
more or less
and so on
and stuff like that
or so/or something/or somewhere

WORD LIST

Geographical features

bay *n C* **	/beɪ/
canal *n C* **	/kəˈnæl/
cape *n C*	/keɪp/
desert *n C* **	/ˈdezə(r)t/
falls *n pl*	/fɔːlz/
gulf *n C*	/gʌlf/
mount *n C*	/maʊnt/
ocean *n C* **	/ˈəʊʃ(ə)n/
peninsula *n C*	/pəˈnɪnsjʊlə/
strait *n C*	/streɪt/

Binomials

bits and pieces	/ˌbɪts ən ˈpiːsɪz/
black and white	/ˌblæk ən ˈwaɪt/
born and bred	/ˌbɔː(r)n ən ˈbred/
down and out	/ˌdaʊn ən ˈaʊt/
flesh and blood	/ˌfleʃ ən ˈblʌd/
forgive and forget	/fə(r)ˌgɪv ən fə(r)ˈget/
here and now	/ˌhɪə(r) ən ˈnaʊ/
long and hard	/ˌlɒŋ ən ˈhɑː(r)d/
pick and choose	/ˌpɪk ən ˈtʃuːz/
short and sweet	/ˌʃɔː(r)t ən ˈswiːt/
sick and tired	/ˌsɪk ən ˈtaɪə(r)d/
to and fro	/ˌtuː ən ˈfrəʊ/
tried and tested	/ˌtraɪd ən ˈtestɪd/

Describing landscape

a bare rocky ridge	/ə ˌbeə(r) ˌrɒki ˈrɪdʒ/
a deep narrow gorge	/ə ˌdiːp ˌnærəʊ ˈgɔː(r)dʒ/
a fertile wooded valley	/ə ˌfɜː(r)taɪl ˌwʊdɪd ˈvæli/
gentle rolling hills	/ˌdʒent(ə)l ˌrəʊlɪŋ ˈhɪlz/
a jagged snowy peak	/ə ˌdʒægɪd ˌsnəʊi ˈpiːk/
a sheltered sandy cove	/ə ˌʃeltə(r)d ˌsændi ˈkəʊv/
a tall steep cliff	/ə ˌtɔːl ˌstiːp ˈklɪf/

Other words & phrases

adamant *adj*	/ˈædəmənt/
affluent *adj*	/ˈæfluːənt/
artefact *n C* *	/ˈɑː(r)tɪˌfækt/
a tall order	/ə ˌtɔːl ˈɔː(r)də(r)/
Aussie *n C*	/ˈɒzi/
breed *v* **	/briːd/
buzz *n U/v*	/bʌz/
by and large	/ˌbaɪ ən ˈlɑː(r)dʒ/
circumnavigate *v*	/ˌsɜː(r)kəmˈnævɪˌgeɪt/
colony *n C* **	/ˈkɒləni/
controversial *adj*	/ˌkɒntrəˈvɜː(r)ʃ(ə)l/
correlation *n C* *	/ˌkɒrəˈleɪʃ(ə)n/
counterpart *n C* **	/ˈkaʊntə(r)ˌpɑː(r)t/
crawling *adj*	/ˈkrɔːlɪŋ/
crucial *adj* ***	/ˈkruːʃ(ə)l/
Dane *n C*	/deɪn/
deter *v*	/dɪˈtɜː(r)/
dispute *v* *	/dɪˈspjuːt/
down under *n U*	/ˌdaʊn ˈʌndə(r)/
dragon *n C*	/ˈdrægən/
epic *n C*	/ˈepɪk/
estuary *n C*	/ˈestjuəri/
euphoric *adj*	/juːˈfɒrɪk/
fjord *n C*	/ˈfjɔː(r)d/
fleet *n C* **	/fliːt/
flood *v* **	/flʌd/
footage *n U*	/ˈfʊtɪdʒ/
glossy *adj* *	/ˈglɒsi/
itinerary *n C*	/aɪˈtɪnərəri/
league table *n C*	/ˈliːg ˌteɪb(ə)l/
magnify *v*	/ˈmægnɪfaɪ/
mainland *adj*	/ˈmeɪnˌlænd/
maze *n C*	/meɪz/
navigate *v*	/ˈnævɪgeɪt/
ocean-going *adj*	/ˈəʊʃ(ə)nˌgəʊɪŋ/
out of the way	/ˌaʊt əv ðə ˈweɪ/
paramount *adj*	/ˈpærəmaʊnt/
pending *adj*	/ˈpendɪŋ/
perception *n C* **	/pə(r)ˈsepʃ(ə)n/
pipe dream *n C*	/ˈpaɪpˌdriːm/
plain *n C* **	/pleɪn/
plot *v* *	/plɒt/
Pom *n C*	/pɒm/
populate *v*	/ˈpɒpjʊleɪt/
repulse *v*	/rɪˈpʌls/
round *v* **	/raʊnd/
rural *adj* ***	/ˈrʊərəl/
satire *n U*	/ˈsætaɪə(r)/
set sail *v*	/ˌset ˈseɪl/
setting *n C* ***	/ˈsetɪŋ/
settlement *n C* **	/ˈset(ə)lmənt/
sizeable *adj*	/ˈsaɪzəb(ə)l/
skilled *adj* **	/skɪld/
spice *n C* *	/spaɪs/
step back *v*	/step bæk/
submarine *n C* *	/ˈsʌbməriːn/
supply *v* ***	/səˈplaɪ/
temporary *adj* ***	/ˈtemp(ə)rəri/
unspoilt *adj*	/ʌnˈspɔɪlt/
upside down *adv* *	/ˌʌpsaɪd ˈdaʊn/
vessel *n C* **	/ˈves(ə)l/
veteran *adj*	/ˈvet(ə)rən/
wash away *v*	/ˌwɒʃ əˈweɪ/
well-earned *adj*	/ˌwelˈɜː(r)nd/
workshop *n C* **	/ˈwɜː(r)kˌʃɒp/

12A | Loot

SPEAKING

1 Work in small groups. Look at the movie posters and discuss these questions.

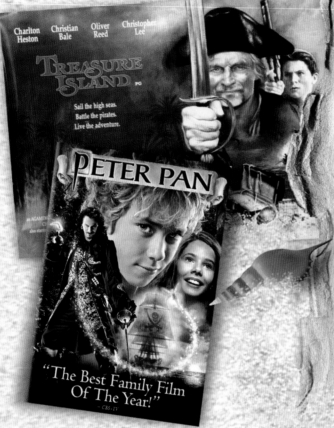

- What have these movies got in common?
- Do you know anything about the stories the films tell?
- Do you know of any other films or books that tell stories about pirates and treasure?

READING

1 Read the text about a real-life treasure island and answer the questions.

1 What kind of treasure is hidden there?
2 Has it all been found?
3 When was treasure last found there?

2 Read the text again and match the headings 1–5 to the sections A–E.

1 Success at last   4 Death by greed
2 A tale of trickery   5 Pirate base
3 A failed attempt

COCOS ISLAND

One small Pacific island became a treasure bank for a string of pirates and a magnet for treasure hunters. But even after 300 years, Cocos Island has not yet yielded up all its secrets. Cocos Island, 500km (300 miles) off Costa Rica, Central America, has been used by at least three pirates for hiding treasure. Treasure hunters are still drawn to the island, hoping that some of its riches can still be found.

A

In the 1680s, the English pirate Edward Davies used Cocos as a base for his ship, the *Bachelor's Delight*. He would attack passing ships and raid coastal towns before returning to the thickly-wooded island to store his treasure. No one knows if he collected it all before his mysterious disappearance in 1702.

In 1819, a Portuguese pirate named Benito Bonito carried out a raid on the Mexican port of Acapulco, making off with a cargo of gold and silver coins. He too headed for Cocos Island, hiding his treasure in an area known as Wafer Bay.

Two years later, Bonito was killed in a fight, leaving only a confusing map to indicate where the treasure might be.

B

The biggest haul of all was left by a Scottish sailor, William Thompson. During a revolution in 1821, the government of Peru hired him to carry their most valuable treasures to Panama to keep them safe. Thompson promptly stole them and buried them on Cocos Island.

The rulers of Peru forced him to take them back to the spot where he had buried the treasure, but he escaped and hid on the island until they had left. He was rescued by a passing ship, and planned to come back to collect the treasure. But he never made it. On his deathbed, he told a friend, John Keating, where the loot could be found.

3 Find the words 1–7 in the text and explain in your own words what they mean.

1 string   5 hoard
2 yielded up   6 scoured
3 haul   7 clasped
4 loot

4 Do you know of any stories of buried treasure in your country?

C

Many attempts have been made to track down the Cocos Island treasure – some more successful than others. In 1880, Benito Bonito's map fell into the hands of a German sailor, August Gissler, who realized that the island on the map must be Cocos. Gissler spent nearly 20 years searching the island. All he found was one single doubloon (a Spanish gold coin), and he died in poverty.

D

In 1846, John Keating, who had been given William Thompson's treasure map, set sail for Cocos with a companion named Boag. They found the cave Thompson had described, with a hoard of treasure which included a life-size solid gold statue.
But when they returned to their ship, the crew demanded a large share of the loot and threatened violence. Keating and Boag jumped overboard and swam to the island to escape. The sailors searched in vain for the treasure, then sailed away, leaving the two men behind. Boag died, but Keating escaped on a passing whaling ship.
No one knows what he took with him, but he lived the rest of his life a wealthy man, returning to Cocos several times before his death in 1882. He left his widow clues about how to find the treasure cave, but she was never able to decode them.

E

Other treasure hunters have scoured Cocos, but with little success. However, in 1966, a French team found fifteen gold bars and some gold coins. Nearby lay two skeletons, one with an axe clasped in one hand and a knife between its ribs, the other with a large hole in its skull. Two treasure hunters had obviously killed each other in their desperation to grab the loot for themselves.

GRAMMAR: passives review

1 Underline the passive verbs in the sentences.

1 Cocos Island, 500 km off Costa Rica, Central America, has been used by at least three pirates for hiding treasure.
2 Treasure hunters are hoping that some of its riches can still be found.
3 Two years later Bonito was killed in a fight.
4 Many attempts have been made to track down the Cocos Island treasure.
5 He was rescued by a passing ship.
6 On his deathbed, he told a friend, John Keating, where the loot could be found.

2 Work in pairs. Look at the text and find the sentences in exercise 1.

1 Look at the rules of use in the grammar box and discuss why the writer used the passive rather than the active.
2 Rewrite the sentences with an active verb.

3 Rewrite the phrases in italics in the passive. Do not include the agent (eg *by someone*) if it is unnecessary.

Saxon treasure found in garden

(1) *Someone found a priceless hoard of 3,000 Saxon coins* yesterday as a woman was digging in her back garden. (2) *Someone had packed the coins* into a wooden box which broke as (3) *she was digging it out* of the ground. The coins are in the care of a local museum where (4) *museum workers are cleaning them* in a special laboratory. (5) *Someone will then take them* to the museum in York for further examination. A legal expert said that even though Mrs Barrett found the coins on her property, (6) *the local authorities could still rule them* as the property of the state.

🔊 **2.28** Listen to check.

4 Work in pairs. Look at the headline and imagine a story to go with it. Use at least five passive verbs. Look at the verbs in the box for ideas.

> dig   call   give   clean
> leave   forget   take   lose

Hidden treasure found in children's park

Use a passive form when you want to bring the object of the verb to the front of the sentence
- in order to emphasize the object of the action or the action itself (rather than the subject of the active verb).
- because the subject of the verb is unknown, unimportant or obvious from the context.

Use *be* + past participle to form the passive.
*The treasure **is hidden** somewhere on the island.*
*He **may have been** killed in a fight.*

➤ SEE LANGUAGE REFERENCE PAGE 124

12B | Bounty hunter

SPEAKING & VOCABULARY: idioms (money)

1 Work in pairs. Can you think of any stories to illustrate the proverbs below?

Money is the root of all evil.
Money makes the world go round.
There's one law for the rich, another for the poor.

2 Put the idioms in the box into two groups: (a) being rich, (b) being poor.

> hard up   have money to burn   in the red
> in the lap of luxury   live hand to mouth
> on the breadline   worth a fortune
> be without a penny to your name

3 Replace the words in italics with the appropriate form of the expressions in exercise 2.

1 What would you do if you *had more money than you needed*?
2 Who would you turn to for help if you *had absolutely no money*?
3 Is it good for children to grow up living *in an extremely wealthy environment*?
4 Do you know anyone who is *short of money* at the moment?
5 What would you miss most if you were *really poor and only just had enough money to survive*?
6 Would it worry you if you were *in debt*?

4 Work in pairs. Ask and answer the questions in exercise 3.

5 Work in pairs. Can you think of three ideas to add to the list below?

TOP TEN WAYS TO MAKE MONEY

- **Go out with a metal detector**
- **Speculate on the stock exchange**
- **Inherit a fortune**
- **Marry into money**
- **Become a model, actor or pop star**
- **Write a bestseller**
- **Dig for gold**
- _____
- _____
- _____

Which way is ...

- the quickest?
- the hardest work?
- the most unlikely?
- the one you'd choose if you could?

LISTENING

1 **2.29** Listen to a story about Domino Harvey and answer the questions.

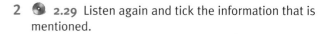

1 What is a bounty hunter?
2 Why is it surprising that Domino Harvey became a bounty hunter?
3 How did Domino Harvey become famous?

2 **2.29** Listen again and tick the information that is mentioned.

1 It is sometimes possible to borrow money to stay out of prison in the US.
2 Bounty hunters are illegal in most countries.
3 Domino was badly affected by the death of her father.
4 Her mother went to live with a restaurant owner.
5 She followed a training course to become a bounty hunter.
6 She worked for a time as the manager of a night club.
7 She was arrested for possessing drugs.
8 She was found dead in her bath.
9 In the film of her life, the role of Domino was played by Keira Knightley.

3 Complete the sentences with the missing words.

1 If the bounty hunter manages to catch _____ with the robber, he will collect the reward money.
2 Domino's time was running _____.
3 All the money and the glamour could not make _____ for the loss of her father.
4 Tony Scott tracked Domino _____ and persuaded her to sell her life story.
5 If you don't turn _____ for your court appearance, you lose the money.

Check your answers in tapescript 2.29 on pages 162–163.

4 Work in groups. Discuss these questions.

- Do you think that bounty hunting should be legal or not? Why?
- Have you seen the film of Domino's life? If so, what do you remember about it? If not, do you think it would make a good film?

PRONUNCIATION: sentence stress

1 🔊 2.30 Listen to an extract from a trailer for the film, *Domino Harvey*. Mark the stressed words. The first sentence has been done for you.

My <u>name</u> is <u>Domino Harvey</u>. I am a bounty hunter. You're probably wondering how a girl like me arrived here. What I say will determine whether or not I spend the rest of my life in prison. Let's start at the beginning.

2 🔊 2.30 Listen again and read the text at the same time as the recording.

GRAMMAR: passive reporting structures

We can use passive reporting structures to report opinions and facts without naming the source. Here are two common reporting structures.

It	is was	said thought believed reported known rumoured	that	+ clause.

It **is believed that** she took a course in acting.

He She etc	is was etc	said thought etc	to	+ infinitive be + verb + -ing have + past participle

Domino **was said to be** a very difficult child.
She **was reported to be feeling** unhappy.
She **was said to have worked** with the Ford agency.

⊙ SEE LANGUAGE REFERENCE PAGE 124

1 Rewrite the sentences using the words given.

1 Some papers have reported that she worked as a model.
   It has _____.
2 Certain members of her family have said that she was a difficult child.
   It has _____.
3 A number of people think that she was not comfortable in her mother's world.
   It is _____.
4 There are a lot of rumours that she was very unhappy with the film.
   It is widely _____.
5 People who knew her believe that the happiest years of her life were those spent on the streets of LA.
   It is _____.
6 Her bounty hunter colleagues knew that she carried a knife at all times.
   It was _____.

2 Rewrite the sentences 1–6 in the poster using the verbs in the box and the passive reporting structure *He is (said) to ...* .

believe	know	report	rumour	say	think

JAMES T GREENBERG

Wanted in connection with the murder of a police officer in Pennsylvania.

Do not approach.

Considered armed and extremely dangerous.

1 **he uses a number of different names**
2 **he is carrying a knife**
3 **he is extremely dangerous**
4 **he has a tattoo of a dragon on his left arm**
5 **he may be working as a barman**
6 **he may be travelling with a young woman and two small children**

A reward of up to $100,000 is being offered for information leading directly to the arrest of James T Greenberg.

3 Work in pairs. Imagine that you work for a magazine that reports gossip about celebrities in your country.

● Choose a celebrity that people are interested in reading about. Invent a news story about this person that will encourage people to buy your magazine.

● Use passive reporting structures to report your story.

● Work with other students and compare your stories. Whose story is (a) the most believable, (b) the least believable, (c) the best story to help sell the magazine?

12c | Scam

SPEAKING & VOCABULARY: phrasal verbs 2

1 Match the phrasal verbs in bold in questions 1–8 to the definitions a–h.

1 Have you ever been given something by mistake and then had to **hand it back**?
2 Have you ever been **ripped off** by a shop assistant or taxi driver?
3 Have you ever been **turned away** from somewhere because you were wearing the wrong clothes?
4 Have you ever **fallen for** a little lie?
5 Have you ever **got your own back on** someone who had done you a bad turn?
6 Have you ever **got away with** doing something bad?
7 Have you ever **made up** an excuse for being late?
8 Have you ever regretted **giving away** personal information?

a believed that a trick, a lie or a joke was true
b cheated (eg when someone charges you too much money for something)
c escaped without punishment
d invented
e punished someone for something they have done to you
f refused entry
g return something
h telling information or facts that you should keep secret

2 Work in pairs. Test each other's memories. Take it in turns to …

- cover the definitions and look at the questions. Can you remember the definitions?
- cover the questions and look at the definitions. Can you remember the phrasal verbs?

3 Work in pairs. Ask and answer the questions in exercise 1.

READING

1 Read the headlines and explain the connection between them.

1 **Police arrest internet scam gang**

2 **Tougher penalties for online crime**

3 **Scam victims fight back**

2 Read the article and choose the best headline 1–3 from exercise 1.

3 Read the article again and put the sections in the correct order.

4 Find the idioms 1–4 in the article and choose the correct definition, a or b.

1 take the bait
   a accept what is offered   b refuse what is offered
2 putting up a fight
   a not trying to achieve something   b trying hard to achieve something
3 play someone at their own game
   a do to someone what they have done to you   b make a lot of money
4 give them more teeth
   a make them less powerful   b make them more powerful

5 Work in pairs. Discuss these questions.

- Have you ever received emails asking you for money? What did you do?
- Do you know of any other scams, email or otherwise?
- What punishment do you think scammers should get?

1 It is estimated that scam victims in the US are ripped off to the tune of 200 million dollars every year. Many of them are fooled by an email that has got through their anti-spam system. It informs them that they have been singled out to receive a very large sum of money. All they have to do is send their postal addresses and bank details to a 'government official' in some distant country. Those who take the bait exchange emails for a few days before being told that the money is almost ready for transfer to their account. The only slight problem is that the small sum of US$80 is needed for bank charges. Hundreds of optimists around the world have the US$80 transferred to the

☐ ago that she would never see her money again, other victims have been more fortunate and have had their money handed back. In the US, internet service providers claim to be winning the war on scam after seeing a drop of 75% in the last two years. The war may not be over, but it has most certainly begun.

☐ a codeword on a piece of card and hold it in the photo. Amazingly, many of the conmen fall for the scam baiters' tricks. These photos are then posted on the websites in 'Halls of Shame'. The website galleries are full of photos of men and women holding pieces of card with ridiculous code words or, worse still, who have had their arms tattooed with something silly.

Other scam baiters have actually managed to get the would-be conmen to pay – for bank charges and the like. The emails from the conmen

☐ other side of the world. They will never see it again. The lucky ones stop there, but others will continue to pay advance fees, administrative costs, legal expenses and credit card charges in the desperate belief that they will soon be enormously rich.

Winnie Mitchell, a divorced mother of six from San Fernando, lost her life savings when she gave away her bank details after falling for one email scam. But Winnie's eldest daughter, Paloma, was not prepared to see her mother ripped off without putting up a fight. Paloma, a games programmer in nearby Mission Hills, joined a group of online scam baiters. The sport of scam baiting is to play the scammers at their own game. They deactivate the anti-spam controls on their own computers and wait, with pleasure, for the next email that offers them US$8 million and the

☐ are also forwarded to government agencies that are involved in the fight against internet crime. They have the emails traced so that the accounts can be shut down and the photographs are sent to local police forces who can make arrests. Anti-scam campaigners in many countries have got their governments to introduce tougher anti-scamming laws and these have given the police more teeth.

Although Winnie Mitchell accepted long

☐ chance to get their own back on the gangs that run the scams.

The scam baiters' achievements are posted on websites devoted to their hobby. Their stories are happy reminders that the bad guys don't always get away with it. One email exchange between a scam baiter and a would-be conman begins in typical fashion with a mail from a 'development commission' asking for help in transferring a large sum of money. The scam baiter replied that he was sure he could get his 'board of directors' to agree to help. He made up a story about how his directors wanted more information about the representative of the 'development commission'. Could he please have his photograph taken with a digital camera and attached to the next email? For 'security purposes', he asked the would-be conman to write

GRAMMAR: causative

1 Choose the correct form to complete the sentences. Check your answers in the article.

1 They have the money *to transfer / transferred* to the other side of the world.
2 He got the directors *to agree / agreed* to help.
3 He had his photograph *to take / taken*.
4 They had their arms *to tattoo / tattooed*.
5 They got the would-be conmen *to pay / paid*.
6 They had the emails *to trace / traced*.
7 They got the government *to introduce / introduced* tougher laws.

2 Complete the sentences with a phrase from the box.

> the Bahamas   his money   his portrait
> his personal fashion assistant   his yacht
> buy tickets for the World Cup Final   caviar
> his clothes   iron his newspaper

1 He has _____ served for breakfast every day.
2 He has _____ designed by _____.
3 He gets his secretary to _____ every morning.
4 He has had _____ painted five times.
5 He is going to get his PA to _____.
6 He's having _____ repaired.
7 He's had _____ sent to _____.

3 Work in pairs. How many more ways can you complete the sentences in exercise 2?

Compare your ideas with another pair of students.

Who has the funniest or most interesting ideas?

Use
- *have* something *done*
- *get* someone *to do* something
to talk about actions that you ask or persuade someone else to do for you.
  *I **had** my camera **repaired**.*
  *I'm **having** my shoulder **tattooed** next week.*
  *I **got** my company **to pay** the bill.*
  *I'll probably **get** a friend to help me.*

🔵 SEE LANGUAGE REFERENCE PAGE 124

12D | Dollar bill

SPEAKING

1 Work in pairs. Discuss these questions.

- How many different banknotes exist in your country?
- What colours are they?
- What denominations are there?
- What do the pictures show?

2 Work in groups. Look at a specific banknote or coin and share your ideas to answer the questions.

1 When and where was it made?
2 Has it travelled far?
3 Who had it before you?
4 What will you spend it on?
5 What will the next person do with it?

3 Work with a student from another group. Exchange your ideas from exercise 2.

LISTENING

1 Work in pairs. Look at the pictures on these pages for thirty seconds. Then close your books and describe the pictures in as much detail as possible.

2 🔘 **2.31** Listen to an extract from a radio programme and put the topics in the order in which they are mentioned.

- ☐ counterfeit dollar bills
- ☐ the meaning of the pyramid symbol
- ☐ burning dollar bills
- ☐ how to trace a dollar bill
- ☐ large denomination bills
- ☐ the manufacture of dollar bills
- ☐ the translation of the Latin inscriptions

3 🔘 **2.31** Listen again and explain the significance of the numbers in the box.

75	six months	$540	8,000
over 50	1776	five	70

4 Work in pairs. How much can you remember about the images in the US Great Seal?

FUNCTIONAL LANGUAGE: generalizing

1 Identify and underline the expressions in the sentences that show the speaker is making a generalization.

1 Generally speaking, people are thinking more about their coffee than the money in their hand.
2 They mostly last less than two years.
3 As a rule, it can be sold for more than four times its face value.
4 For the most part, the work was done by Jefferson.
5 By and large, the stories are more entertaining than probable.
6 Americans generally prefer dollar bills to dollar coins.
7 On the whole, most British people can understand most Americans.
8 Broadly speaking, the dollar has remained strong against other currencies.
9 I think that, in general, it's best to travel with dollars in your pocket.

2 Work in groups. How many generalizations can you make about the topics in the box?

banks criminal gangs the police spam
presidents the Secret Service tattoos

Do you agree with the generalizations of the other members of your group?

VOCABULARY: US & UK English

1 Work in pairs. Do you know the British English word that is being defined in the sentences below?

1 A game with eleven players and a round ball that is kicked. It is called *soccer* in the US.
2 An object for controlling how much water comes out of a pipe. It is called a *faucet* in the US.
3 An underground tunnel for people to cross a street. It is called an *underpass* in the US.
4 The piece of paper that tells you how much you must pay. It is called a *check* in the US.
5 A purple vegetable that is called an *eggplant* in the US.
6 The side of a street where people can walk. It is called the *sidewalk* in the US.
7 Fingers of potato that are fried and served hot. They are called *fries* in the US.

2 Work in two groups, A and B.

Group A: You are going to write definitions for four British English words. Turn to page 148 for help.
Group B: You are going to write definitions for four British English words: Turn to page 147 for help.

3 Work in pairs with one student from Group A and one student from Group B. Read your definitions to your partner. Does he/she know the words?

DID YOU KNOW?

1 Work in pairs. Read the information and discuss the questions.

The first credit card appeared in the US in 1950, but it was first thought of in a nineteenth-century novel by Edward Bellamy. The Diners Club card of 1950 was soon followed by American Express. Diners Club cards were originally accepted in fourteen New York restaurants, but can now be used to pay in 24 million locations worldwide. Shops and restaurants have to pay a fee of 2 or 3% of every transaction to the credit card company, and the customer pays about 13% interest.

American Express now has an annual profit of billions of dollars and is one of America's top 30 corporations. However, the average American owes over $8,000 to the credit card companies. On average, they also receive seven offers every year to extend their credit or apply for an extra card. One million American credit card holders declare themselves bankrupt every year. The situation in the UK is very similar where most people, including teenagers, have at least two cards.

- What are the most popular credit cards in your country?
- What sort of things do people buy, and not buy, with them?
- Is it easy to get a credit card?
- Should teenagers be allowed to have credit cards?
- Would you ever cut up a credit card? Why or why not?

GRAMMAR

Passives review

We use a passive form when we want to bring the object of the action to the front of the sentence. There are a number of possible reasons for doing this:

- in order to emphasize the thing or person affected by the action.
  The gold had been buried on a desert island.
- because the agent of the action is unknown, unimportant or obvious from the context.
  Its location was marked on an old map.

If we want to name the agent, we use *by*. We name the agent when it is important or unusual, or because we want to make this information more noticeable.
The map had been drawn **by Bluebeard himself.**

Use *be* + past participle to form the passive.

I	am/was/was being have been	
She He It	is/is being/was was being/has been/ had been	marked buried shown taught taken etc.
We You They	are/are being/were/ were being/have been	
	can be/must be/to be /being	

Passive reporting structures

We can use passive reporting structures to report opinions and facts without naming the source. Here are two common reporting structures.

It	is was	said/thought/believed /reported/known/ rumoured	that	+ clause

It is believed that his father was a fugitive.

He She etc	is was etc	said thought etc	to	infinitive be + verb + -ing have + past participle

His father **was thought to be** a fugitive.

Causative

We use the causative to talk about an action that you ask, persuade or arrange for someone else to do for you.
She's having her jewels valued.
We do not normally need to say who does the action, because this is usually understood from the context. We use *by* if we want to say who does the action.
She usually has it done **by** *experts from an auction house.*

subject	verb	object	past participle
He She They etc	has/have is/are having had is/are going to have	the house the TV it	painted tattooed repaired etc.

We can sometimes use *get* instead of *have* to form the causative. (eg *She's getting her nails painted.*)

We can indicate the person who we have asked or paid to do the action with *get* + someone + *to* + *do* (infinitive) something.
They **got** *the prisoner* **to walk** *the plank.*
I'll **get** *my family* **to help** *me.*

FUNCTIONAL LANGUAGE

Generalizing

Sentence starters
Broadly speaking
Generally speaking
As a rule
For the most part
By and large
On the whole
in general

Generally speaking, *they arrive quite late.*

Before the main verb
mostly
generally

They **generally** *arrive late.*

Word list

Idioms (money)

be hard up	/bi ˌhɑː(r)d ˈʌp/
be in the red	/biː ˌɪn ðə ˈred/
be on the breadline	/biː ˌɒn ðə ˈbredlaɪn/
be without a penny to your name	/bi wɪˌðaʊt ə ˌpeni tə jə(r) ˈneɪm/
be worth a fortune	/bi ˌwɜː(r)θ ə ˈfɔː(r)tʃən/
have money to burn	/hæv ˌmʌni tə ˈbɜː(r)n/
live hand to mouth	/lɪv ˌhænd tə ˈmaʊθ/
live in the lap of luxury	/lɪv ɪn ðə ˌlæp əv ˈlʌkʃəri/

Phrasal verbs 2

fall for	/ˈfɔːl ˌfɔː(r)/
get away with	/get əˈweɪ wɪð/
get your own back on (sb)	/get jə(r) ˈəʊn bæk ɒn/
give (sth) away	/ˌgɪv əˈweɪ/
hand (sth) back	/ˌhænd ˈbæk/
make (sth) up	/ˌmeɪk ˈʌp/
rip (sb) off	/ˌrɪp ˈɒf/
turn (sb) away	/ˌtɜː(r)n əˈweɪ/

US & UK English

bathroom **	/ˈbɑːθˌruːm/
toilet **	/ˈtɔɪlət/
check **	/tʃek/
bill ***	/bɪl/
eggplant	/ˈegˌplɑːnt/
aubergine	/ˈəʊbə(r)ˌʒiːn/
faucet	/ˈfɔːsɪt/
tap **	/tæp/
fries	/fraɪz/
chips **	/tʃɪps/
garbage can	/ˈgɑː(r)bɪdʒ ˌkæn/
dustbin *	/ˈdʌs(t)bɪn/
gas station	/ˈgæs ˌsteɪʃ(ə)n/
petrol station	/ˈpetrəl ˌsteɪʃ(ə)n/
pants *	/pænts/
trousers **	/ˈtraʊzə(r)z/
sidewalk	/ˈsaɪdˌwɔːk/
pavement **	/ˈpeɪvmənt/
soccer *	/ˈsɒkə(r)/
football ***	/ˈfʊtˌbɔːl/
stove *	/stəʊv/
cooker *	/ˈkʊkə(r)/
subway	/ˈsʌbˌweɪ/
underground *	/ˈʌndə(r)graʊnd/
underpass	/ˈʌndə(r)ˌpɑːs/
subway	/ˈsʌbˌweɪ/
undershirt	/ˈʌndə(r)ˌʃɜː(r)t/
vest	/vest/

Other words & phrases

alive and well	/əˈlaɪv ən ˈwel/
all-seeing adj	/ɔːˈlˈsiːɪŋ/
axe n C *	/æks/
and the like	/ənd ðə ˈlaɪk/
bail n C *	/beɪl/
bait n C	/beɪt/
bankrupt adj *	/ˈbæŋkrʌpt/
billfold n C	/ˈbɪlˌfəʊld/
bondsman n C	/ˈbɒndzmən/
bounty hunter n C	/ˈbaʊnti ˌhʌntə(r)/
cargo n C/U *	/ˈkɑː(r)gəʊ/
clasp v *	/klɑːsp/
codeword n C	/ˈkəʊdˌwɜː(r)d/
conman /conmen n C	/ˈkɒnmæn/ /ˈkɒnmen/
counterfeit adj	/ˈkaʊntə(r)fɪt/
deactivate v	/diːˈæktɪveɪt/
deathbed n C	/ˈdeθˌbed/
decode v	/diːˈkəʊd/
deface v	/dɪˈfeɪs/
denomination n C	/dɪˌnɒmɪˈneɪʃ(ə)n/
desperado n C	/ˌdespəˈrɑːdəʊ/
do (sb) a bad turn	/ˌduː ə ˌbæd ˈtɜː(r)n/
doubloon n C	/dʌˈbluːn/
embark on v	/ɪmˈbɑː(r)k ɒn/
enforce v **	/ɪnˈfɔː(r)s/
excess n U **	/ɪkˈses/
expel v	/ɪkˈspel/
face value n U	/ˈfeɪs ˈvæljuː/
fake adj/n C	/feɪk/
fall apart v	/ˌfɔːl əˈpɑː(r)t/
fall into the hands of (sb)	/ˌfɔːl ɪntə ðə ˈhændz əv/
fishpond n C	/ˈfɪʃˌpɒnd/
fool v *	/fuːl/
fugitive n C	/ˈfjuːdʒətɪv/
give (sb) more teeth	/ˌgɪv mɔː(r) ˈtiːθ/
grab v **	/græb/
haul n C	/hɔːl/
hoard n C	/hɔː(r)d/
inscription n C	/ɪnˈskrɪpʃ(ə)n/
life savings n U	/ˈlaɪf ˌseɪvɪŋz/
jet set n U	/ˈdʒet set/
loot n U	/luːt/
magnet n C	/ˈmægnɪt/
make off with v	/ˌmeɪk ˈɒf wɪð/
metal detector n C	/ˈmet(ə)l dɪˌtektə(r)/
on the trail of	/ˌɒn ðə ˈtreɪl əv/
overboard adj	/ˈəʊvə(r)ˌbɔː(r)d/
overdose n C	/ˈəʊvə(r)ˌdəʊs/
play (sb) at their own game	/ˌpleɪ ət ðeə(r) ˌəʊn ˈgeɪm/
provider n C *	/prəˈvaɪdə(r)/
put up a fight	/ˌpʊt ʌp ə ˈfaɪt/
raid n C **	/reɪd/
raid v	/reɪd/
ranch hand n C	/ˈrɑːntʃ ˌhænd/
recall v	/rɪˈkɔːl/
rumour n C/U **	/ˈruːmə(r)/
Saxon adj	/ˈsækʃ(ə)n/
scam n C	/skæm/
scam baiter n C	/ˈskæm ˌbeɪtə(r)/
scour v	/ˈskaʊə(r)/
seal n C **	/siːl/
serial number n C	/ˈsɪəriəl ˌnʌmbə(r)/
set in v	/ˌset ˈɪn/
single out v	/ˌsɪŋg(ə)l ˈaʊt/
skeleton n C *	/ˈskelɪt(ə)n/
spam n U	/spæm/
spammer n C	/ˈspæmə(r)/
speculate v *	/ˈspekjʊleɪt/
string n C ***	/strɪŋ/
the chances are	/ðə ˈtʃɑːnsəz ˌɑː(r)/
to the tune of	/tə ðə ˈtjuːn əv/
trickery n U	/ˈtrɪkəri/
ungirly adj	/ʌnˈgɜː(r)li/
want for nothing	/ˌwɒnt fə(r) ˈnʌθɪŋ/
whaling adj	/ˈweɪlɪŋ/
wooded adj	/ˈwʊdəd/
would-be *	/ˈwʊdbiː/
yield up v	/ˌjiːld ˈʌp/

Abbreviations for word lists

n	noun
v	verb
adj	adjective
adv	adverb
prep	preposition
sb	somebody
sth	something
C	countable
U	uncountable
pl	plural
s	singular

*** the most common and basic words

** very common words

* fairly common words

1 | Writing A job application

SPEAKING

1 Work in pairs. Read the two quotes and answer the questions.

A: *I've travelled widely in a number of countries outside the UK.*

B: *I've been abroad a few times.*

Which person, A or B, is probably exaggerating the truth?
Which answer would it be best to give when applying for a job? Why?

2 Think of an exaggerated truth for each of these sections in a CV.

1 Languages spoken
2 Computer skills
3 Job responsibilities
4 Personal qualities
5 Work experience

READING

1 Look at the job adverts and the CV. Which job do you think Antonia is interested in? Why?

Professional footballer seeks personal assistant.

Duties will include accompanying him on trips abroad. Knowledge of at least three major world languages essential. Previous experience of a similar post preferred. Apply with CV and covering letter to applications@dreamjobs.com

---

Small, dynamic TV production company seeks youthful, enthusiastic office assistant. The successful candidate will have a degree in media or film studies, and a keen interest in sport. Apply with CV and covering letter to jobs@TV3.com

---

CURRICULUM VITAE

Antonia Piper
0156 233784
toniap@newmail.ac.uk

Personal Profile
An enthusiastic, energetic undergraduate, I am experienced in coordinating and supporting the work of others as well as motivating myself to work alone. I am currently looking for a short-term placement within the sports and leisure industry.

Education
2007–present   BSc Sports Science Newham University
2000–2006   International Baccalaureat: Newham Girls Grammar School

Work Experience
Part-time editor, Newham University, 2007–present
As part of my degree in Sports Science I am currently working ten hours a week as sub-editor of the sports page for *The Word*, the Newham University weekly newspaper. My duties include writing articles, editing the work of fellow students, and liaising with local and national press agencies.

Secretary, Newham University Film Society 2007
As secretary of the film society I initiated a student discount system with a local DVD rental firm and organized local sponsors for a student film production which was subsequently shown at the local film festival.

Retail assistant,   The Corner Shop 2005–2007
Initially I worked as a part-time cashier and following a brief training period I was promoted to shop assistant. My duties included opening the shop, arranging the window display and informing customers about promotional campaigns.

Skills
Fluent Spanish, conversational French, intermediate Italian
Webpage design
Full driving licence

Interests
Independent film: I try where possible to attend both local and national film festivals.
Amateur dramatics: I was an active member of my school drama club prior to entering university
Football: captain of the university women's football team.

References
Ms Gill Stallcott
Senior Lecturer
Faculty of Sports Science,
Newham University,
Newham
g.stallcott@newmail.ac.uk
0156 257889

2 Look at the CV again. Which of the following pieces of information 1–6 has Antonia included in her CV? In which section?

1 her university studies
2 voluntary work
3 the kind of job she's looking for
4 the languages she speaks
5 date of birth
6 the sports she's interested in

3 Read the information sheet about writing a good CV. Has Antonia followed all the advice given? Answer Y (yes), N (no) or D (don't know).

How to write a good CV

- Use headings and bold to make your CV easier to read.
- Use bullet points to make lists more attractive.
- Write your education and work experience with the most recent events first.
- Include a brief description of any work experience, highlighting your responsibilities and achievements.
- Include the names of at least two referees. One should be your present employer or tutor where possible.
- Never tell lies or exaggerate on your CV. You will get caught out.
- Remember to check your spelling and punctuation.

LANGUAGE FOCUS

1 Find examples in the CV for each of the rules for using capital letters.

Use capital letters

- to begin a sentence.
- for names of people and their job titles.
- for names of places (street names, towns).
- for names of organizations.
- for languages, nationalities and countries.
- for titles of books, films, etc.
- for headings and subheadings.

2 Add capital letters to the CV extract where necessary.

skills
fluent german and working knowledge of hungarian
full driving licence
interests
journalism and writing
i work as a voluntary reporter for the newsdesk at newham fm radio station one or two nights a week, filing reports on local news and events.
i have contributed articles to the arts and culture section of the newham gazette, a local weekly newspaper.
references

dr j.k. smithers,	professor james tann,
the old vicarage	newham business school
12, orchard lane,	newham university
newham	newham

3 Find ten spelling mistakes in the CV extract below.

Extra Information

I worked as a voluntary secretery for a local children's charity for a breif period, suporting the work of field workers and child carers alike.
I have attended various web design courses and have my own web page and blog which I update whenever posible.
I was asistant to a local independant candidate during the recent local goevernment election campaing.
I hold a full driving lisense.

4 Find words or expressions in the CV that mean:

1 I have experience of …
2 helping other people with their work
3 My job involved …
4 My aim is to find ….
5 I took an active part in …
6 at the moment
7 at first
8 after that

5 Look at the CV again and underline any other useful phrases or expressions.

WRITING

1 Write a CV for yourself. Look back at the information sheet about writing a good CV. You can invent information if you like.

REMEMBER TO …

- use capital letters where appropriate.
- check your spelling.
- use bullet points, underlining and bold to make your CV attractive and easy to read.
- use formal language (eg no contractions).
- include short, concise descriptions of work experience and interest where necessary.

2 | Writing A composition

SPEAKING

1 Work in pairs. Which of the things in the box do you associate with India?

> computer technology   elephants
> movies   nuclear weapons
> palaces and temples   poverty
> space rockets   the Taj Mahal
> traditional religious ceremonies

2 In what ways do you think that the following are different in India from your country?

- an average family home
- a popular festival
- a typical market
- a typical meal
- people's clothes

READING

1 Read the composition and choose the best title 1–3.

1 Indian information technology
2 Poverty in contemporary India
3 The face of modern India

2 Read the composition again. Match the paragraphs 1–3 to one of the summaries a–f below. Three of the summaries are not needed.

a an example of an appropriate image of contemporary India
b examples of modern tourism in India
c examples of traditional images of India
d information about population growth in India
e reasons why India is still an agricultural society
f reasons why traditional images are unsatisfactory

1

When most people think of India, they probably imagine a brightly-coloured land of exotic animals, temples and markets, and of people washing their clothes in the river. India would seem, from these images, to be a very traditional society that
5 has little or nothing to do with the industrialized twenty-first century.

2
These images, however, do not do justice to the incredible variety of the country – geographically the seventh largest in the world with a population of over one billion people. Although it is undeniable that the lives of many Indians, especially in the countryside, have hardly changed
10 for hundreds of years, India, as a whole, has been transformed in the last twenty-five years. It is a world leader in computer technology, has its own space programme and is a nuclear power. In Bollywood, India has the world's largest film industry.

3
For all these reasons, it could be argued that the usual images of India
15 give a very false impression. Perhaps a better symbol of contemporary India would be HITEC City in Hyderabad, a state-of-the-art business park and convention centre in the south of the country, and home to such multinational giants as Microsoft, General Electric and HSBC. The ultra-modern architecture and facilities of HITEC City may come as a surprise
20 to many, but as a reflection of the second fastest-growing economy in the world, it is fair to say that it represents contemporary India better than photos of tigers, elephants or the Taj Mahal.

LANGUAGE FOCUS

1 Divide the composition into three paragraphs.

Traditional tourist images of Wales usually show dragons, mining valleys and male voice choirs. The dragon is a national symbol and features on the Welsh flag. Coal mining was, for many years, the country's main industry and the Welsh are understandably proud of their singing traditions. Most people would agree, however, that these images do not reflect contemporary Wales. The dragon, of course, is a mythical beast; the coal mines have nearly all closed down and male choirs are not the most popular form of music among the majority of Welsh people. It seems to me that a more accurate image of modern Wales would include large wind farms or computer factories, but these might not be very appealing to potential tourists. Wales has spectacular mountains where visitors can take part in a wide range of outdoor sports, so a more attractive alternative would be photographs of paragliding, hill-walking or whitewater rafting.

2 Read the information in the box and underline the topic sentences in the compositions about India and Wales.

Useful language

It is common to begin paragraphs with a topic sentence which introduces the main topic of the paragraph. The rest of the paragraph develops the idea of the topic sentence.

3 Match the topic sentences 1–4 to the beginnings of the paragraphs a–d.

1 Images of traditional costumes such as these could easily be replaced with something more modern.
2 Many of the most well-known images of the country show members of the royal family.
3 Picturesque villages may appeal to visitors to the country, but they are misleading.
4 These images, however, belong more to the past than to the present.

a Most of the monuments were built in the nineteenth century. Few people now wear traditional costumes.
b The king is probably the most popular. Royal palaces are also very common.
c First of all, very few people these days actually live in houses like these. In fact, most of the population live in flats very similar to any other large city.
d An up-to-date photo of the city centre would be one possibility. This would, at least, show how people dress.

4 Mark the expressions for giving opinions 1–9 I for the ones in the India composition, W for the Wales composition and N for neither.

1 It could be argued that …
2 It is fair to say that …
3 It is generally recognized that …
4 It is reasonable to say that …
5 It is undeniable that …
6 It seems to me that …
7 Many people feel that …
8 Most people would agree that …
9 There is no doubt that …

5 Work in pairs. Complete the phrases in exercise 4 with nine different pieces of information about your country.

WRITING

1 Work in small groups.

● Think of at least six different images that are often used to advertise your country.
● Decide which of these images are old-fashioned.
● Think of two or three images that show a more contemporary aspect of your country.
● Choose the best of these images and explain your reasons.

2 Use your ideas from exercise 1 to write your composition.

REMEMBER TO …

● organize your composition into three logical paragraphs.
● begin each paragraph with a topic sentence.
● use a variety of phrases from Language focus exercise 4 to introduce your ideas.
● use formal language.

3 | Writing A review

SPEAKING

1 Work in pairs. Which sentences 1–5 are true for you?

1 I prefer to watch stuff at home on DVD, but I go to the cinema from time to time.
2 I like to know about the latest films and I probably watch three or four movies a week.
3 The films they make these days aren't as good as they used to be.
4 I like watching movies but I forget about them as soon as I've seen them.
5 I prefer to go to the cinema with a friend.

2 Which of the following ingredients influence your opinion of a film (1 = very important, 2 = quite important, 3 = unimportant)?

- the action
- the cast and the acting
- the direction
- the plot or the script
- the setting

READING

1 Which of the reviewers 1–6 liked the film?

1 An extraordinary story of two people who struggle to communicate.
2 Scarlett Johansson is absolutely stunning, but the film is about as exciting as watching paint dry.
3 Beautifully-shot and lovingly-directed, this won't appeal to everybody, but it's a pleasant way to spend the evening.
4 Scarlett Johansson doesn't have to say much, but she's one of the finest actresses of her generation.
5 With 17th-century Delft as a stunning backdrop, we see the details of the life of a beautiful young servant.
6 Johansson is very pretty, the camerawork is very pretty and the film is pretty boring. Another costume drama for cinema-goers who don't mind if nothing much happens.

MOVIES TODAY

Nominated for three Oscars when it was released in 2003, *Girl with a Pearl Earring* tells the story of the Dutch painter, Vermeer, and the creation of one of his most famous paintings. It is an adaptation of a novel by Tracy Chevalier of the same name. The
5 subject of the portrait, *Girl with a Pearl Earring*, is Vermeer's servant, Griet, who gets to know the artist while sitting for the picture.

The role of Griet is played to perfection by Scarlett Johansson, who also starred in the memorable *Lost in Translation* of the same
10 year. Colin Firth *(Bridget Jones' Diary, Love Actually* and *Nanny McPhee)*, is excellent in the role of Vermeer, and Tom Wilkinson is convincingly revolting as Vermeer's patron, Van Ruijven, who wants to buy Griet.

What is most memorable about *Girl with a Pearl Earring* is its
15 hypnotic beauty. The scenes are shot in lovingly recreated Delft of 1665 and the light and the detail come straight out of one of Vermeer's paintings. The cast are dressed in lavish costumes by the Dutch designer, Dien van Straalen, and the camerawork of Eduardo Serra is exquisite. *Girl with a Pearl Earring* received
20 mixed reviews, but it has stood the test of time well. The film appeals to more adult tastes and carries a PG-13 certificate.

Nominated for 10 BAFTAS and 3 ACADEMY AWARDS including Best Actor and Best British Film

COLIN FIRTH SCARLETT JOHANSSON TOM WILKINSON
GIRL WITH A PEARL EARRING
BASED ON THE BEST-SELLING NOVEL

2 Match the quotations in exercise 1 to the categories in Speaking exercise 2.

3 Read the review and answer the questions.

1 Is it generally positive or negative?
2 What aspects of the film did the reviewer like?

4 Read the review again and put the questions in the order in which they were answered.

☐ What are best features of the film (acting, direction, script, soundtrack, etc)?
☐ What do you remember most about the film?
☐ [1] What is the plot about?
☐ What kind of people does the film appeal to?
☐ When was it released?
☐ Where is it set?
☐ Who are the main characters?
☐ Who stars in it?

LANGUAGE FOCUS

1 Complete the sentences with a preposition.

1 Tom Hanks is perfect in the role _____ the professor.
2 Audrey Tautou is extremely convincing _____ a code-breaker.
3 She gives a performance that is worthy _____ an Oscar.
4 The film is set _____ Paris.
5 The film tells the story _____ an attempt to solve a mysterious murder.
6 It's an adaptation _____ a book by Dan Brown.

2 Think of a film or TV programme that you liked. Replace the words in italics with information about that film or programme.

1 *Lost in Translation* was directed by *Sofia Coppola*. It was made in *2003*.
2 The film stars *Scarlett Johansson and Bill Murray*.
3 It is set in *Tokyo* and tells the story of *an aging film star and a young woman who find themselves together*.
4 *Scarlett Johansson* is excellent in the role of *the young wife who is looking for her role in life*.
5 Most of the action takes place *in the hotel bar*.
6 What is most memorable about *Lost in Translation* is *the performance of Bill Murray*.
7 The film appeals to *people who want more than Hollywood entertainment*.

3 Which tense is used in reviews to give details of the plot?

Griet gets to know the artist while sitting for the picture.
Vermeer's patron, Van Ruijven wants to buy Griet.

4 Expand the notes. Use present simple and any other words that you need.

> ***Lost in Translation:* plot summary**
> Charlotte / meet / Bob / Tokyo hotel. They / both bored. They / spend / few days together / he / talk / about / his wife / children. She / talk / her husband / photographer. They / become / good friends / important experience / their lives.

WRITING

1 Work in pairs. Think of a film or TV programme that you have both seen. Look at the questions in Reading exercise 4 and prepare your answers together.

2 Decide the best order in which to organize the information and your opinions about the film/TV programme.

3 Work with another pair of students. Tell them about the film/TV programme.

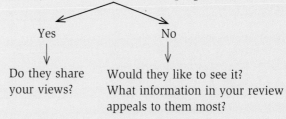

Have they seen the same film/TV programme?

Yes   No

Do they share your views?

Would they like to see it? What information in your review appeals to them most?

4 Write your review.

> ### REMEMBER TO ...
>
> • organize your review into appropriate paragraphs.
> • use a selection of phrases from Language focus, exercise 4.
> • use appropriate verb forms to talk about the film.
> • look twice at the prepositions you have used.

4 | Writing An email to a friend

SPEAKING

1 Work in pairs. Think of three reasons why you would email a friend rather than phone or text them. Then answer the questions below.

- When do you prefer to text and when do you prefer to phone?
- When was the last time you received an email from a friend?
- Why did he/she write to you? What did he/she have to say?

READING

1 Read the email and answer the questions.

1 What's the relationship between Polly and Kay?
2 Why is Kay writing to Polly?

2 Read the email again and decide if the sentences are true or false.

1 Kay has never done a fell running race before.
2 Her sister persuaded her to do it.
3 She's always been keen on keeping fit.
4 Polly lives near the Lake District.
5 Polly's about to start a new job.
6 Polly's going to run in the race too.

3 Work in pairs. Imagine that Kay phoned Polly instead of writing an email. Roleplay the telephone conversation between the two friends.

         keeping in touch

From: Kay Green
To: Polly
Subject: keeping in touch

Hi Polly, how are you doing? I can't believe it's been three months since we last spoke! It sounds like things are going really well for you. The new job sounds superb. And your new man ... I can't wait to meet him!

Me and Bruce are going to be in your neck of the woods in about a month's time. The weekend of the 23rd. Are you going to be around? You're not going to believe this, but we've signed up for a fell running race in the Lake District. 18 miles mostly uphill – and Britain being Britain, probably in the pouring rain. I know. We're mad!
It was all my sister's fault. We were at a party at her house a couple of months back and we got talking to this guy who actually runs the whole thing. He was dead enthusiastic about it all and well, the next thing we knew we'd signed up to do it too!
So, anyway, we've become complete fitness freaks. We're down in the gym practically every night. We're going on a trial run in Wales next weekend and there's a group of us going up to the lakes on the 23rd. We're going to rent a house for the weekend. Do you fancy coming to stay? It's got an open fire and a great little pub right next door! Check out the photos.
We'd love to see you … and Nick, of course! What do you reckon? We've booked the house already so there's no need to make a decision right away. I really hope you'll be around and if you decide to come and join us for the weekend that'd be great!
Right, got to go now. It's my turn to make supper!
A huge hug and speak soon
K

LANGUAGE FOCUS

1 Rearrange the words to make sentences.

1 phoned   was   sorry   out   I'm   when   I   you.
2 today   you   phone   I'll   on   later.
3 ringing   got   now,   the   go   phone's   I've   to.
4 moment   from   all   that's   me   the   for.
5 know   soon   me   let   write   and   again.
6 long   been   sorry   haven't   touch   for   so   in   I.
7 doing   hi,   are   you   how?
8 great   thanks   they're   photos,   for   the!

2 Look back at the sentences in exercise 1 and decide which you would use to open an email (O) and which to close it (C).

3 Choose the correct word to complete the invitations below.

1 What about *meet / meeting* up sometime over the weekend? We could go out for a drink or something.
2 Would you like *to do / doing* something at the weekend?
3 I was *wonder / wondering* whether you might like to meet up sometime.
4 Do you fancy *come / coming* along with us? It'll be great fun.
5 What do you reckon to *go / going* out for a meal tonight? We could try that new Greek restaurant.
6 Mr and Mrs Smythe Hamilton *request / requesting* the pleasure of your company at their daughter's wedding.

4 Decide which invitations in exercise 3 are:

a very informal (VI).
b neutral (N).
c formal (F).

5 Work in pairs. Invite your partner to do something this evening. Make any necessary arrangements.

WRITING

1 Work in pairs. A friend you haven't seen or spoken to for almost a year has just emailed you with his/her news. You're going to write a reply. Decide which of the following you will include in your email and in what order.

☐ comment on your friend's news
☐ invite your friend to come and stay with you
☐ suggest going out together one evening
☐ suggest a visit to your friend's home
☐ promise to phone your friend very soon
☐ send your regards to your friend's family
☐ encourage your friend to write back soon
☐ attach a photo
☐ explain your news and plans
☐ ask your friend for more details about his/her news

2 Make notes on …

● any changes in your life over the last twelve months.
● what you're doing at the moment.
● any plans you've got for the near future.

Useful language

Have you heard the latest?
You know I was thinking of … well …
Did I tell you about … ?
We've been thinking of …
I don't know if you know, but …
We've got some great news!

3 Write your email. Remember to thank your friend for his/her email and to suggest meeting up very soon.

REMEMBER TO …

● open and close the email appropriately.
● thank your friend for his/her email.
● use informal language (eg contractions) and a friendly tone.
● use appropriate verb forms to tell your news and describe your plans.

5 | Writing A story

SPEAKING

1 Work in pairs. Use the words in the box to make up a story about a rescue.

> canyon   paramedics   walking
> water   coyotes   collapse   hero

2 Work with a different partner. Compare your stories. How similar are they?

3 Choose one of your two stories and write a dramatic headline for it.

READING

1 Read the story. Then work in pairs and make up a suitable headline.

2 Work in pairs. Answer the questions without re-reading the story.

1 Where was Renée Zellweger?
2 Who was she with?
3 What were they doing?
4 What did they see?
5 What did Renée do?
6 What did her friend do?
7 What did the paramedics say?
8 What did the witness say?
9 How did the story end?

Read the story again to check your answers.

3 Match the words in bold to the three women in the story, R (Renée Zellweger), P (her personal trainer), W (the walker).

1 ... **they** saw **her** when **she** fell into the canyon
2 ... talking to **her** and offering **her** water, while **her** friend called for help.

4 Work in pairs. Roleplay an interview between a journalist and Renée Zellweger about the experience.

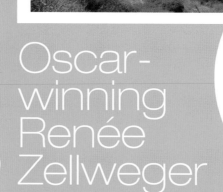

Oscar-winning Renée Zellweger

became a true life heroine when she saved a walker in LA's remote Runyan Canyon.

Renée and her personal trainer were taking a walk when they saw a fellow hiker collapse and slide off the path into the canyon below.
5 Renée immediately ran to the walker's rescue. She scrambled down the steep side of the canyon, risking her own safety to help the woman.

'Renée and her friend were about 50 yards behind the lone woman hiker. Luckily, they saw her when she fainted and fell into the canyon,'
10 said a witness.

The actress stayed with the injured walker, talking to her and offering her water to drink, while her friend called for help.

The paramedics praised the Hollywood star's quick thinking, saying that anything could have happened. The canyon is known to be full of
15 coyotes, and without water the woman could have fallen into a coma or even died.

The Hollywood heroine made light of the situation and, once she had made sure the woman was in good hands, she continued with her workout as if nothing had happened.

LANGUAGE FOCUS

1 Look at the story in the reading section and find three expressions used …

- to refer to Renée Zellweger.
- to refer to the person she rescued.

2 Work in pairs. Replace the words in italics in the story below with phrases from the box.

- Mr Ford
- the lost teenager
- the stupid boy
- the 13-year-old
- the heroic superstar
- the Hollywood actor
- handsome Harrison
- the Utah schoolboy
- Indiana Jones himself
- the unlucky lad

Harrison Ford flies to the rescue

Harrison Ford volunteered to fly his own helicopter to rescue a boy scout who had got lost on a camping expedition in Yellowstone National Park. After a search with dogs failed to find the *boy scout*, two air rescue teams were called in.

Harrison Ford, better known for his heroics as the archaeologist, Indiana Jones, was piloting one of the helicopters which searched the Wyoming forest throughout the night. *Harrison Ford* and his team eventually found the *boy scout* early the next morning. He was cold and tired but very excited when he found out that not only was he going to ride in a helicopter, but that he had been rescued by *Harrison Ford*.

3 Read the explanation in the box and punctuate sentences 1–5.

1 he's a real live hero said one fan
2 it was like something from the movies one onlooker said
3 was that really who I think it was asked the young woman
4 she's just as beautiful in real life as she is on screen commented one of the people who witnessed the rescue
5 I just couldn't stop thanking him the boy's mother said

Use speech marks (' ') to indicate speech. All punctuation (commas, full stops, exclamation marks etc) goes inside.
> *'Thank you,'* he said.
> *'I can't believe it!'* she screamed.

The reporting verb and subject are often inverted.
> *'She saved her life,'* said one paramedic.
> *'Is that Renee Zellweger?'* asked a passer-by.

But not when the subject is a pronoun.
> *'She's a real life heroine,'* ~~said she~~.

WRITING

1 Work in pairs. Look at the pictures and discuss what is happening. Use the questions below to help you.

1 What are the men in the first picture doing? Where are they?
2 What is the connection with the second picture?
3 What's happening in the second picture?
4 What do you think happened between the second and third picture?

2 You are going to write a short news story about what happened in the pictures. Which of the following will you do and in what order?

- [ ] describe how the story ended
- [ ] report an eyewitness account
- [ ] set the scene
- [ ] comment on the heroic action
- [ ] summarize the story
- [ ] describe how the story developed
- [ ] describe the main event

3 Write the story. Remember to include a headline and a quote from one of the people concerned or a witness.

REMEMBER TO …

- use a variety of expressions to talk about your heroes and victims.
- use adjectives to make the description more lively.
- use correct punctuation with quotations.
- divide your story into clear paragraphs.

6 | Writing A report

SPEAKING

1 Think of a film or TV documentary you've seen recently which showed some spectacular scenery. Use the questions to prepare to tell a partner about it.

1 What was it about?
2 What was the scenery like?
3 Was the scenery central to the film or was it just a backdrop?
4 Do you know where it was filmed?
5 Is this information important in order to understand the film?

2 Work in pairs. Tell your partner about your film, then answer these questions.

* Have you seen the film or documentary your partner described?
* If yes, did you enjoy it too?
* If not, would you like to see it? Why or why not?

READING

1 Complete the film location report with the headings a–e.

a Accommodation   d Location
b Description   e Other important information
c Facilities

2 The producer of the film made some notes as she was reading the report. Put the questions in the order in which she wrote them.

☐ Could we get permission to build a small road?
☐ Do the local people have experience of this kind of work?
☐ How cold is it up there in the winter?
☐ How much would it cost per night for the entire team?
☐ What sort of training are they thinking of?

3 Work in pairs. If you were film producers, which of the questions in exercise 2 would be most important to you?

Preliminary location report: ROCCA CALASCIO

Introduction
The purpose of this report is to provide basic information about the suitability of Rocca Calascio as a location.

1 _____
The ruined castle of Rocca Calascio is dramatically situated in the Gran Sasso mountains of central Italy. It stands at the top of a mountain 1,400 metres above sea level and is surrounded by other snow-covered peaks. The castle overlooks the picturesque village of Calascio and has spectacular views of the valleys below.

2 _____
Although Rocca Calascio lies above the snowline in the winter, it can easily be reached by car at any time of year. Road connections are good and Rome, with its two international airports, is only a short drive away.

3 _____
The village of Calascio offers only very limited accommodation with no email or internet facilities. However, the neighbouring town of L'Aquila, with a good range of four and five-star hotels, could easily accommodate all the staff and cast.

4 _____
The village and castle have both power and water supplies provided by the local council. There are no roads leading through the village or up to the castle so all equipment will need to be carried by hand.

5 _____
One of the conditions for obtaining permission to film is that we work closely with the local employment office in recruiting extras and catering staff. We will also be expected to cooperate with the local film school in L'Aquila offering training sessions for both students and teaching staff.

Conclusion
Despite some practical difficulties, I would recommend that we include Rocca Calascio on our short list of possible locations and commission a fuller report.

LANGUAGE FOCUS

1 Put the phrases below into two groups: (a) beginning a report, (b) ending a report.

1 My own view is that Rocca Calascio would (not) be an appropriate location.
2 This report outlines the advantages and disadvantages of …
3 The information below provides essential information about …
4 The purpose of this report is to examine the suitability of …
5 Taking everything into consideration, Rocca Calascio would (not) seem to be suitable for our purposes.
6 To sum up, it may be concluded that …

2 Complete the text with words from the box.

> drive   neighbouring   offer   overlooks
> situated   stands   surrounded   views

The village of Beynac (1) _____ on the River Dordogne in the south-west of France. The castle is (2) _____ on a rock which (3) _____ the village and has breathtaking (4) _____ of the river valley.
Beynac is (5) _____ by beautifully unspoilt countryside, but the major cities of Bordeaux and Toulouse are only a short (6) _____ away. The village of Beynac and the (7) _____ town of Sarlat (8) _____ a wide choice of accommodation and restaurants.

3 Work in pairs. Think of a village that you know. Describe its location using the language in exercise 2.

4 Choose the correct word to complete the sentences.

1 *Although / Despite / However* Rocca Calascio lies above the snowline, it can easily be reached by car.
2 The village of Calascio offers only limited accommodation. *Although / Despite / However*, L'Aquila could easily accommodate all the staff.
3 *Although / Despite / However* some practical difficulties, I would recommend that we include Rocca Calascio on our short list of possible locations.

5 Work in pairs. Insert the name of a village or small town in your country in the yellow box. Then complete each sentence in three different ways.

1 _____ is extremely picturesque, although …
2 It is popular with tourists in the summer. However, …
3 Despite the fact that … , it …

WRITING

1 Work in groups. A film company is looking for a range of interesting locations in your area. They have asked you to write a report on one of them. Follow the steps below to help you prepare your report.

1 Decide on a location and the kind of film it would be suitable for
2 Choose five adjectives that describe the location
3 Write a sentence describing the location to someone who's never seen it before
4 Make notes on its precise location and distance from major towns and airports
5 The type of accommodation in the area
6 Facilities that will be useful to the film crew (electricity, running water, etc)
7 Any other information that might be important

2 Use your ideas from exercise 1 to write the report.

REMEMBER TO …

- use clear headings and subheadings.
- explain the purpose of the report.
- recommend the location.
- suggest any follow-up action.
- use any useful expressions from the Language focus section.
- check your spelling and punctuation.

Communication activities

10B Speaking exercise 1 page 98

#9 You go and help the woman. She is badly hurt and needs to go to hospital. She explains that she is terrified of ambulances and asks you to call a taxi instead. Turn to card #26 on page 140 if you agree to call a taxi. Turn to card #19 on page 141 if you decide to call an ambulance anyway.

1C Speaking exercise 1 page 10

An easy guide to analyzing signatures

Size
Large: people who have a lot of confidence in themselves – they are probably quite outgoing and sociable.
Small: quieter, more introverted people
Slant
To the right: good communicators, friendly and warm
Vertical: independent people who are happy to do things on their own
To the left: emotional, sometimes passionate, often shy
Legibility
Hard to read: active and energetic, but sometimes selfish
Easy to read: organized, careful, possibly lacking in self-confidence
Pressure
Heavy: hard-working and serious, possibly defensive with a tendency to overreact
Light: kind and gentle, interested in other people
Other features
Looped letters: imaginative and creative, possibly a little romantic
Underlining: ambitious and sometimes impatient

10B Speaking exercise 1 page 98

#3 You don't lend her your phone, but she says that she understands. However, she asks you to accompany her to the train station, which is about one kilometre away. She explains that she is frightened of meeting the men who robbed her. Turn to card #8 on page 148 if you agree to accompany her. Turn to card #7 on page 143 if you refuse to accompany her.

2D Speaking exercise 1 page 23
Student A

9D Functional language exercise 2 page 93
Student C

Take it in turns to read out your sentence openers. One of your partners will have the matching sentence ending.
Openers:
3 Fewer and fewer young people are joining the armed forces
6 In spite of the fact that they are often teenage idols,
Endings:
e even though they have to work pretty hard and put up with a lot of attention from the press.
f although tax inspectors are hardly the world's most popular people either!

10B Speaking exercise 1 page 98

#24 It's quite cold, so you keep your coat on. You finally arrive at the station. The woman buys her ticket and you accompany her to the platform. She gets on the train without saying *thank you* or *goodbye*. How do you feel?

10B Speaking exercise 1   page 98

#4 You hand her your phone. She dials a number, but she gets no reply. She then asks you to accompany her to the train station which is about one kilometre away. She explains that she is frightened of meeting the men who robbed her. Turn to card #8 on page 148 if you agree to accompany her. Turn to card #7 on page 143 if you refuse to accompany her.

4A Functional language exercise 3   page 37
Group A

- Fear of crossing bridges
- Fear of speaking in public
- Fear of electricity
- Fear of vegetables

Choose a phobia from the list.
Complete the sentences below for your phobia in as many ways as you can think of.

1 Sufferers of this phobia have to _____, otherwise _____.
2 They need to _____ so that _____.
3 They always _____ in case _____.

4D Speaking exercise 1   page 43
Student C

C

5A Speaking exercise 1   page 47
Group A

- commited suicide
- doctors cut off her leg
- got married to the painter, Diego Rivera
- had a bus accident
- had affairs with other people
- the Mexican Revolution took place
- was questioned by the police

5B Speaking exercise 2   page 49
Student A

Underline the answers to the questions.

What is your role?

Which work of art do you think the company should buy? Why?

Your position in the company: _____

DIRECTOR OF FINANCE

The managing director of the company has decided that it would be a good idea to put some art in the reception area of your office. You have been given a budget of $25,000.

The short list	Your point of view
The glass sculpture	☹
The bricks	☹☹☹
The horse	☹☹☹☹☹

Extra information:
- *It would not be safe to put the glass sculpture in the reception area.*
- *The managing director told you that he didn't like the bricks.*
- *The horse looks like something you buy from a cheap souvenir shop.*

10B   Speaking exercise 1   page 98

#26 You call a taxi which arrives very quickly. In the taxi, the woman suddenly smiles. She is clearly very well! She explains that she is making a reality TV programme called *How Kind Are You?* and she shows you the camera that is on the front seat and pointing at you. She asks you if you would like to take part in the programme next week in the studio.
What do you say?

6A   Speaking exercise 1   page 56

Student A

Charlie Chaplin blacklisted
Film star and director, Charlie Chaplin, has been refused entry to the US following an investigation into his political activities. The House of Un-American Activities Committee asked Chaplin to …

Stars pull out of Oscars ceremony
A small group of Hollywood celebrities have refused to take part in this year's Oscars ceremony in protest at the American government's foreign policy. The group, which includes Will Smith, Angelina Jolie and Tom …

Spice girl stars in election programme
Former Spice Girl, Geri Hallywell, has agreed to star in a new promotional broadcast for Britain's ruling Labour Party. In the film, Hallywell serves tea to a …

10B   Speaking exercise 1   page 98

#25 You agree to deliver the envelope. When you arrive at the address, you see that it is a TV production company. The receptionist explains that they are making a reality TV programme called *How Kind Are You?* and that a hidden film crew has been filming you for the last few hours. She asks you for permission to use the film and says that the company will pay you £100.
What do you say?

6B   Grammar exercise 3 page 59

Actress Winona Ryder in the Beverley Hills Municipal Court for shoplifting

Charles and Diana on tour in Canada

6B   Pronunciation exercise 3   page 59

Student A

Ask your partner these questions.
1 There are two major political parties in the USA, the Republicans and the … ?
2 What do we call a person who has studied economics?
3 What adjective do you use to describe the political party that is in government?

2D   Speaking exercise 1 page 23

Student B

10B Speaking exercise 1   page 98

#19 You call an ambulance anyway. The woman becomes very upset and explains that, last year, her husband died in a car accident with an ambulance. She begs you to call a taxi. Turn to card #26 on page 140 if you agree to call a taxi. Turn to card #27 on page 147 if you decide to wait for the ambulance.

5A Speaking exercise 1   page 47
Group B

- suffered from depression
- got married
- had over 30 operations on her leg
- got pregnant
- fell in love with the Russian Communist leader, Leon Trotsky
- drank and took drugs
- got divorced

7B Speaking exercise 1   page 69
Student B

Solar cooker
The Solar Sizzler is a solar-powered cooker that concentrates the sun's rays to create heat. You can fold it away and put it in your backpack when you go camping. Or use it in the garden for a barbecue. It is easily available online and prices are very low.

4D Speaking exercise 1   page 43
Student A

A

5B Speaking exercise 2   page 49
Student B

Underline the answers to the questions.

What is your role?

Which work of art do you think the company should buy? Why?

Your position in the company:

DIRECTOR OF MARKETING
The managing director of the company has decided that it would be a good idea to put some art in the reception area of your office. You have been given a budget of $25,000.

The short list   **Your point of view**
The glass sculpture   😊☹️
The bricks   😊😊
The horse   😐😊☹️

Extra information:
- *The managing director is going to retire next year (this is a secret that nobody else knows). You will almost certainly get his job.*
- *Charles Andrews has offered to share the $25,000 with you if his work is bought.*
- *The glass sculpture is not safe for the reception area and the horse is too small – nobody would see it.*

7B Speaking exercise 1 page 69

Student A

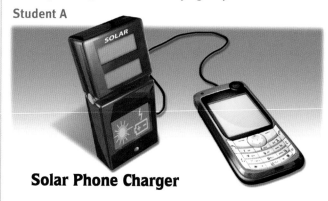

Solar Phone Charger

Made by the Dutch firm, Soldius, this solar charger can power up a mobile phone in a couple of hours. It is compatible with all the major phone manufacturers and the company is developing a version that will work with MP3 players, laptops and cameras.

10B Speaking exercise 1 page 98

#11 You tell the caller to wait and run after the woman. You hand her the phone. After a short conversation in a language you don't understand, Empanda explains that someone is coming to get her. She asks you to wait until they arrive. Turn to card #15 on page 144 if you agree to wait. Turn to card #20 on page 145 if you decide not to wait.

7C Speaking exercise 1 page 71

Group A

Here is a step-by-step model for how to run a coaching session

Stage 1: find out what your client is worried about, or what change they would like to make in their lives
Stage 2: encourage your client to explain exactly what his/her short term goals are
Stage 3: explore the problems and barriers blocking the client's way
Stage 4: explore practical options and set realistic time limits
Stage 5: encourage your client to commit to their goals – help them visualize how their lives will be happier if they succeed.

Think of at least one useful question to ask at each stage. Think of three things you can say to encourage your client to stick to his or her goals.

8A Speaking & vocabulary exercise 4 page 76

Student A

Roleplay 1: calling in sick
You are calling in sick from home. You've got a sore throat, a bad cough and a temperature. You feel guilty about phoning in sick because it means you'll miss an important meeting. You spent most of last night preparing documents for the meeting. Offer to send your work by email.

Roleplay 2: at the chemist
You are the customer. You've been bitten by an insect of some sort. The bite is red, swollen and painful. Show it to the chemist and ask for their advice.

Roleplay 3: at the doctor's
You are the doctor. You think that there is probably nothing seriously wrong with your patient. You do not want to prescribe any medicine if possible. Suggest simple home remedies instead.

10B Speaking exercise 1 page 98

#23 You go to find out what has happened. The woman is unconscious and you think she has had a heart attack. You call an ambulance but you think it is too late.
How do you feel?

4D Speaking exercise 1 page 43

Student B

B

8B Speaking & vocabulary exercise 3 page 78

How much of a hypochondriac are you?

1 You're feeling a bit under the weather. Do you (a) decide to wait for a day or two to see if you feel better? (b) take some of your favourite medicine? (c) go to see a doctor?

2 You hear on the news that there is a new flu bug going round. Do you (a) quickly forget what you have heard? (b) find out more about it on the internet? (c) immediately think you will catch it?

3 You've been feeling unwell, but the doctor gives you a clean bill of health. Do you (a) believe the doctor? b) ask the doctor to give you some medicine anyway? (c) go to another doctor for a second opinion?

4 You discover a large black spot under your arm. Do you (a) try to clean it with soap and water? (b) make an appointment to see the doctor? (c) know you are at death's door?

5 You are watching a TV drama series that is set in a hospital. Do you (a) have no idea what the doctors are doing most of the time? (b) watch with interest and learn some new medical facts? (c) know exactly what the doctors are doing all the time?

6 You go to the doctor's because you have a stomach bug. It's very important for you to know (a) how quickly you will feel better. (b) which medicine you should take. (c) the scientific, technical name for the infection.

10B Speaking exercise 1 page 98

#22 You leave. You've done enough for one day! Later that evening on the TV news, you hear a report about a foreign ambassador's wife who was robbed in the street. After the robbery, she suffered a heart attack and died. You recognize from the photo that it is the woman you helped earlier in the day.
How do you feel?

8D Functional language exercise 3 page 82

Student A

You need to use the following four words or phrases in a conversation with your partners. Use suitable language to help you change the subject.

- aromatherapy
- sore throat
- train station
- cinema tickets

Start the conversation with this phrase 'Have you seen the new Brad Pitt movie yet?'

10B Speaking exercise 1 page 98

#7 You don't want to accompany her, so you say goodbye. A few moments later, your phone rings. The caller asks to speak to 'Empanda' and describes her. Empanda is obviously the woman you just left. Very strange! She is only 100 metres away. Turn to card #11 on page 142 if you decide to run after the woman and hand her the phone. Turn to card #12 on page 145 if you decide to hang up.

6A Speaking exercise 1 page 56

Student B

Star raises $6 million for Democrat cause
Hollywood star, Barbra Streisand, has helped to raise $6 million to help the Democrats fight the next election. Streisand said that she would do anything …

Rock fans walk out of protest concert
Dozens of Pearl Jam fans walked out of one of the group's concerts in Denver Colorado after the lead singer took the opportunity to protest against US president …

Live 8's message to world leaders
Concerts in ten cities round the world have brought together the world's top musicians as part of a campaign to encourage world leaders to fight world …

10B Speaking exercise 1 page 98

#17 You hang up. In the distance, you can see that the woman has fallen over. Turn to card #23 on page 142 if you decide to go and see what has happened to her. Turn to card #22 on page 143 if you decide to ignore the woman.

6B Pronunciation exercise 3 page 59

Student B

Ask your partner these questions.
1 What do you call the study of thought and ideas?
2 What name do we give to a person who works in politics?
3 Who is responsible for making laws in the UK?

10B Speaking exercise 1 page 98

#15 You wait with her. After 30 minutes, nobody has arrived. Turn to card #16 on page 147 if you decide to carry on waiting. Turn to card #20 on page 145 if you have had enough and decide to leave her.

5B Speaking exercise 2 page 49

Student C

Underline the answers to the questions.

What is your role?

Which work of art do you think the company should buy?

Why?

Your position in the company:

DIRECTOR OF HUMAN RESOURCES

The managing director of the company has decided that it would be a good idea to put some art in the reception area of your office. You have been given a budget of $25,000.

The short list	Your point of view
The glass sculpture	☺☺☺☺
The bricks	☹
The horse	☺☺☺☺☺

Extra information:
- *Most of the staff that you have spoken to say that they prefer the glass sculpture.*
- *The bricks are depressing. Nobody likes them.*
- *The managing director would be very happy with the horse. He's very keen on horses.*

7B Speaking exercise 1 page 69

Student C

Solar bricks

Strong enough to support the weight of a heavy truck, these polycarbonate plastic bricks contain solar panels and a light source. Just one hour of sunlight will power the bricks for three nights, and they can be used for walls, roads and pathways. They could even do away with the need for street lighting.

9D Functional language exercise 2 page 93

Student A

Take it in turns to read out your sentence openers. One of your partners will have the matching sentence ending:

Openers:
1 Traffic wardens are at the top of most people's hate lists
4 More and more young people want to become accountants and bankers

Endings:
a despite large increases in salaries.
b they do come pretty high up on the list of the most respected professions.

10B Speaking exercise 1 page 98

#1 You decide to give her the money. While you are getting out your money, she explains that she urgently needs to make a phone call. She asks if you will lend her your phone. Turn to card #4 on page 139 if you agree to lend her your phone. Turn to card #3 on page 138 if you don't want to lend her your phone.

10B Speaking exercise 1 page 98

#28 You carry on walking. After a few minutes, you are stopped by a man with a microphone and a film crew. They explain that you have been taking part in a reality TV show and that you are on live TV.
How do you feel?

10B Speaking exercise 1   page 98

#12 You hang up, but the phone rings again almost immediately. It is the same caller, begging you to speak to the woman. The woman is now 300 metres away. Turn to card #11 on page 142 if you decide to run after the woman. Turn to card #17 on page 144 if you decide to hang up again.

8D Functional language exercise 3   page 82
Student B

You need to use the following four words or phrases in a conversation with your partners. Use suitable language to help you change the subject.
- new coat of paint
- babysitter
- runny nose
- postcard

Student A will start the conversation.

10B Speaking exercise 1   page 98

#20 You feel a little guilty because you could have been more helpful, but enough is enough. That evening on the TV news, you see a report about the woman. She is interviewed and she explains how she was robbed. But she adds that the worst thing about the experience was that absolutely nobody would help her. That would never happen in my country, she says.
How do you feel after watching the news report and interview?

3C Speaking exercise 1
page 31

10D Speaking exercise 1   page 103
Group A

Look at the job description below and prepare five questions to ask the candidates. Remember for reasons of fairness you must all ask the same questions. Look at the areas below to help you.

- present job
- relevant past experience
- qualifications
- plans for the future
- personal qualities important for the post
- strengths and weaknesses
- specific responsibilities
- knowledge of the geographical area

Post: Regional Training Officer
NewStart is a non-profit organization that provides basic skills training (literacy, numeracy and computer skills) for people who cannot access formal or private training.

Main responsibilities:
- Actively seek out new sponsors amongst local businesses
- Establish contacts with local press and media
- Prepare and distribute promotional materials
- Represent the organization at conferences and promotional events
- Liaise with the central offices of the organization
- Coordinate and publicize courses
- Recruit and train new volunteers
- Manage the day-to-day running of the training centre. Some teaching may also be required

10B Speaking exercise 1   page 98

#10 You carry on walking, but every now and then you turn around to have a look. Nobody else in the street has helped the woman and now a little dog has got the woman's dress between its teeth. It is pulling and tearing. Turn to card #9 on page 138 if you decide to go and help the woman. Turn to card #28 on page 144 if you decide to carry on walking.

10B Speaking exercise 1   page 98

#5 You refuse her offer and begin to walk away. You suddenly realize that she looks like someone you have seen in a film. Is she a famous actress? Turn to card #1 on page 144 if you decide to call the woman back and offer her the money. Turn to card #6 on page 148 if you still want to walk away.

4A Functional language exercise 3 page 37
Group B

- Fear of phones
- Fear of flying
- Fear of the number 13
- Fear of stairs

Choose a phobia from the list.
Complete the sentences below for your phobia in as many ways as you can think of.

1 Sufferers of this phobia have to _____,
   otherwise _____,
2 They need to _____ so that _____,
3 They always_____, in case _____,

10B Speaking exercise 1 page 98

#21 You continue to wait. After a long, long time, a large black limousine arrives. The driver gets out and gives the woman a beautiful fur coat. She thanks you, gets into the car and says goodbye. The car leaves before you realize that she still has your money. How do you feel?

8A Speaking & vocabulary exercise 4 page 76
Student B

Roleplay 1: calling in sick
You are the boss. There is a very important meeting this morning. It's essential that all members of staff attend. You suspect that some of your staff are taking time off sick when they don't really need to.

Roleplay 2: at the chemist
You are the chemist. There has been a plague of tiger mosquitoes in your area. The local health authorities have asked chemists to report any unusual insect bites. You need to take the name, age and nationality of the patient and details about where and when they were bitten as well as a contact address or phone number.

Roleplay 3: at the doctor's
You are the patient. You haven't been sleeping well recently. It's beginning to affect your work and your boss has started to comment on your lack of energy. You've tried all kinds of home remedies but they don't work. Ask the doctor to prescribe you some sleeping pills.

7B Grammar exercise 3 page 68
Student B

Choose one of the questions below and spend two minutes preparing what you are going to say.

Speak for 30 seconds without pausing or repeating. Do not tell your partner which question you are answering.

How much free time do you have next week?
What are you looking forward to in the next few days?
How much money do you expect to spend tomorrow?
When and where is your next holiday?
What will be the worst thing that happens to you tomorrow?
How will tomorrow be different from today?
Repeat the activity with a different question.

10B Speaking exercise 1 page 98

#18 You agree to wait. Before getting on the train, she thanks you for waiting with her and asks if you can do one more thing for her. She takes an envelope out of her pocket and asks you to deliver it to an address which is a fifteen-minute walk away. Turn to card #25 on page 140 if you agree to deliver the envelope. Turn to card #20 on page 145 if you decide that you do not want to deliver the envelope.

7C Speaking exercise 1 page 71
Group B

You must each choose a different problem from the list below.

- You aren't enjoying your university course and want to leave university. You know your parents won't approve.
- You want to get fit to take part in a local sports event.
- You need to save money, but you can't stop shopping.
- You hate your job and you want to find a new one.
- You don't get on very well with your mother-in-law and this is making your partner unhappy.

Decide …
1 exactly how much of a problem it is and why it is a problem.
2 what you want to do about it.
3 what is stopping you from doing anything about it at the moment.

3c Speaking exercise 2 page 31

12d Vocabulary exercise 2 page 123

Group B

Here are the four words you need to write a definition for. Remember, don't use the British English term.

1 vest (UK)
undershirt (Am)

2 underground (UK)
subway (Am)

3 trousers (UK)
pants (Am)

4 dustbin (UK)
garbage can (Am)

10b Speaking exercise 1 page 98

#16 You wait for one hour, and still nobody has arrived. Turn to card #21 on page 146 if you decide to carry on waiting. Turn to card #20 on page 145 if you have had enough and decide to leave her.

8d Functional language exercise 3 page 82

Student C

You need to use the following four words or phrases in a conversation with your partners. Use suitable language to help you change the subject.

- foot massage
- new neighbours
- flu
- lottery ticket

Student A will start the conversation.

10b Speaking exercise 1 page 98

#27 You wait for an ambulance, which arrives very quickly. But when the ambulance comes, the woman stands up with a smile on her face. A film crew gets out of the ambulance, and the woman explains that you have been taking part in a reality TV show. How do you feel?

2c Vocabulary exercise 1 page 21

mad /mæd/ adj * *
1 very silly or stupid: CRAZY. * **stark raving mad** = extremely crazy **barking mad** = extremely crazy * **sb must be mad to do sthg** *mainly spoken* used for saying that someone is doing something very stupid.
2 [never before a noun] *informal* angry. * **hopping mad** = extremely angry
drive sb mad *informal* to make someone feel extremely angry, upset or bored
go mad *informal* **1** to become mentally ill **2** to start behaving in an uncontrolled way **3** to become extremely excited and happy **4** to become crazy because you are so bored, upset etc. **5** to do something that is not very sensible or wise **6** to become extremely angry
like mad **1** very quickly and with great effort **2** a lot **3** in a way that you cannot control or stop.
mad about sb *informal* very much in love with someone
mad about/on sth *informal* very enthusiastic about something
mad keen (on) *Br E* extremely enthusiastic about something

10b Speaking exercise 1 page 98

#2 You make an excuse and say that you cannot lend her the money. She then offers to give you her gold ring in exchange for £5. Turn to card #1 on page 144 if you agree to the exchange. Turn to card #5 on page 145 if you refuse her offer.

10B   Speaking exercise 1   page 98

#6 You walk away, but after a few seconds you hear a scream. You turn around and see the woman on the pavement. She has been knocked over by someone on roller-blades, who has not stopped. Turn to card #9 on page 138 if you decide to go and help the woman. Turn to card #10 on page 145 if you decide to carry on walking.

9D   Functional language exercise 2   page 93

Student B

Take it in turns to read out your sentence openers. One of your partners will have the matching sentence ending:

Openers:
2 I think that everyone would agree that footballers have a pretty good job
5 Although police officers are not always seen as the friendliest of people,

Endings:
c most pop stars are hardly respected at all.
d even though these are not considered to be glamorous or interesting jobs.

10B   Speaking exercise 1   page 98

#14 You offer her your coat. Eventually, you arrive at the station and the woman buys her ticket. The next train is in one hour and she asks you to wait with her. Turn to #18 on page 146 if you agree to wait. Turn to #20 on page 145 if you decide not to wait.

10B   Speaking exercise 1   page 98

#8 You agree to accompany her. As you are walking, you notice that the woman seems unwell. She is cold and shivering. Turn to card #14 on this page if you decide to offer her your coat. Turn to card #13 on page 149 if you decide not to offer her your coat.

7B   Grammar exercise 3   page 68

Student A

Choose one of the questions below and spend two minutes preparing what you are going to say.

Speak for 30 seconds without pausing or repeating. Do not tell your partner which question you are answering.

What plans do you have for the weekend?
What will the rest of today be like for you?
What do you imagine your retirement will be like?
How many different people will you speak to in the next twenty-four hours?
How will your appearance change in the next ten years?
What are you sure that you will do tomorrow?

Repeat the activity with a different question.

12D   Vocabulary exercise 2   page 123

Group A

Here are the four words you need to write a definition for. Remember, don't use the British English term.

1 petrol station (UK) gas station (Am)

2 waistcoat (UK) vest (Am)

3 toilet (UK) bathroom (Am)

4 cooker (UK) stove (Am)

3D   Pronunciation exercise 4   page 33

1   Student A must think of a word that starts with the consonant cluster in the first block and say the word in the block.

2   Student B then chooses one of the blocks below and says a word starting with those letters.

3   Student A then chooses a block either next to or below the previous block and says a word.

4   Continue until you have reached the last block. The student who says the word in the last block is the winner.

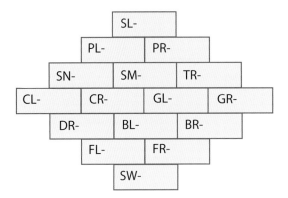

```
            SL-
      PL-         PR-
   SN-      SM-       TR-
CL-     CR-     GL-      GR-
   DR-      BL-       BR-
      FL-         FR-
            SW-
```

7A   Speaking exercise 1   page 66

1   Eat one less meat meal each week.
2   Only buy fruit that is in season.
3   Switch your TV, DVD and hifi off standby mode at night.
4   Wash up in a bowl or bucket and save the water to flush the toilet.
5   Give your newspaper to someone else when you've finished reading it.
6   When you're waiting for your bath or shower to run warm, use a bucket to catch the cold water and use it to water your plants.
7   When it's hot, use a hand-held fan rather than an electric one.
8   Buy a second-hand bike and a bike trailer so you can cycle to the shops.

10B   Speaking exercise 1   page 98

#13 You continue walking without offering your coat. After a while, she tells you that she is feeling cold and asks if she can borrow your coat. Turn to #14 on page 148 if you decide to lend her your coat. Turn to #24 on page 138 if you decide not to lend her your coat.

10D   Speaking exercise 1   page 103
Group B

Look at the job description below and the handwritten notes. Look back at the advice on page 102 and prepare for the job interview.

Post: Regional Training Officer

NewStart is a non-profit organization that provides basic skills training (literacy, numeracy and computer skills) for people who cannot access formal training.

Main responsibilities:
* Actively seek out new sponsors amongst local businesses
* Establish contacts with local press and media

1 last 6 months volunteer at local radio station - know lots of people in the local media

* Prepare and distribute promotional materials
* Represent the organization at conferences and promotional events

2 present job - basic skills trainer at the local further education institute - attended the national basic skills training conference in Glasgow last year

* Liaise with the central offices of the organization
* Coordinate and publicize courses

3 part of present job

* Recruit and train new volunteers
* Manage the day-to-day running of the training centre

4 volunteer literacy trainer with the organization for six months three years ago - know how the courses and the centre works

Some teaching may also be required

4D   Speaking exercise 1   page 43
Student D

D

Tapescripts

1B Listening exercise 2 🌐 1.1

J = Jayne   H = Harry   D = Dave

H: So, are you ready for the big day, then? When are you going? Tomorrow, isn't it?

D: Yeah, that's right …

J: What's happening tomorrow then?

H: Dave's got his paintball championship finals.

J: Paintball championship? I didn't know such a thing existed …

H: Yeah, Dave's three time national champion …

J: National champion? You, Dave? You dark horse! How long have you been doing that then?

D: Er, well, I haven't been doing it for that long really, I started a couple of summers ago.

J: So, paintballing eh? I didn't know you were into war games …

D: It isn't a war game.

J: Uh-oh – have I touched a raw nerve there? Are you a bit sensitive about it?

D: No, I don't think so, not especially, it's just that it's always the same – you mention paintballing and people think you're Rambo or something …

J: And it isn't true? I mean, isn't the whole point of it to dress up and play soldiers? You know, shooting each other with paint, re-enacting famous battle scenes and all that? Sounds like a war game to me.

D: No, it doesn't have to be. It's no more a war game than chess – or draughts.

J: Sorry, you've lost me there. What are you saying?

D: It's a game of strategy. You have to think ahead and plan how best to eliminate the other side.

H: Yeah, and don't loads of companies use it now for team building and stuff like that?

D: Yeah, that's how I got into it actually. We went on a team building weekend, you know, getting to know each other better … it was great fun.

J: What – shooting at each other? I can think of better ways of getting to know your workmates! I mean come on – those are real guns you're using out there. They may be gas-powered and they may be shooting paint pellets, but they're real and the whole purpose of the game is to shoot and kill, or sorry, should I say 'eliminate' other players. I mean, who started it off? Wasn't it designed for training soldiers?

D: No, it wasn't actually. The paint markers were designed for branding cattle, if you must know.

H: Really? Oh, I didn't know that.

D: Yeah, they used them in the States to shoot paint at the cattle.

H: Not what you'd call a military action, eh Jayne?

J: Possibly not, but it doesn't really matter what their original use was – they're being used now to shoot at people. I mean, you must have heard that story about the madman driving around shooting people out of his car!

H: Oh yeah, in um Barry or somewhere wasn't it? What happened? Did anyone get hurt?

J: No, luckily enough, he was only shooting paint at them … but that's pretty frightening – I mean they thought they were being shot at by a real gun … and it can be dangerous. Those paintballs can hurt.

D: So what are you saying? Are you suggesting the sport should be banned because there are a few nutters out there who take things too far?

J: Yes, I am, I do think it should be banned. I think it's dangerous, paintguns are dangerous weapons. They are not toys. What happens if someone gets killed one day?

D: So, would you call for a ban on baseball in the same way because some people use baseball bats in fights?

J: Yeah, but baseball bats are supposed to be used for hitting balls – not people – unlike paintguns. Paintballing is not a sport, it's violent, it's dangerous and it glorifies …

H: Hey, Jayne, don't you think you're going a bit too far? Dave doesn't strike me as being a blood-crazed maniac. He's just a normal sort of bloke who likes to let off steam at the weekend. He's not about to go out and shoot somebody, is he?

J: OK, OK, sorry Dave, I got a bit carried away. I didn't mean to get personal.

H: Maybe you should give it a go sometime. I heard Bill's arranging a trip for his 30th birthday. You should sign up. You might change your mind!

J: No way! You must be joking! I think I'll just get him a card instead!

1D Listening exercises 1 & 2 🌐 1.3–1.7

1: I've always had a thing about football, not that I'm any good at it, mind, and at school we used to hang around in the playground every day, and everyone would have their pile and we'd go through them, 'got, got, got, need, got, got, need' and so on, and then we'd do swaps and try to collect the whole set. And then when I left school, I just sort of carried on because I still had some missing, and what I couldn't bear was, just, you know, giving up without getting the whole set. I don't know why really, it's just one of those things. I've got all the World Cups since 1990 in Italy – those are the ones I'm most proud of. If I ever have a kid myself, I know he'll enjoy looking at my collection in years to come.

2: My friends like to joke that my husband is the star attraction in my collection because he's got these bulging eyes. I don't mean that in a nasty way, but it's true that he does look a bit like one. What he doesn't know is that they call him Kermit, you know, from *The Muppet Show*. But, um, let me see, I've got about a thousand altogether, we always buy a few when we go on holiday. Slovenia's good, we've been there twice, because they're very popular there, little clay models painted green, but there are some beautiful ones in the Far East, made of precious stones. It's a good thing we've got quite a big house because I wouldn't know where to put them all otherwise.

3: We all used to wear them at university, but it's a thing of the past now. I mean, you do get some kids wearing them, but it's not like it used to be. In those days, you used to get market stalls, shops even, that sold nothing else. Anyway, I kept all mine and one day I got them out and I found them, I don't know, I just found them really interesting. And then, I started buying a few more and discovered that there are loads of people out there who are into it. Most of them collect the old enamel or metal ones from before the war, but not me. I prefer stuff from the 1970s. What I like best are the political ones with anti-nuclear slogans, 'No more war' and stuff like that.

4: It started off as a bit of a joke, really. I just wanted something to liven up the garden and I bought my first one at a car boot sale. And then I really got attached to it, I gave him a name, actually I give them all names now, and then I thought he was looking a bit lonely out there on the lawn all on his own, and that's when a gentleman friend of mine gave me another, and then, well, one thing led to another, and before I knew it I had about thirty of them, all different. What I didn't realize at first was how many different kinds there are, but now I only really get special ones, because they can be quite expensive, so I don't buy as many these days.

5: I read the other day that Bratz are the in-thing these days. They've been voted 'People's Choice Toy of the Year' three years running in America, but what people see in them is beyond me. They're just plain ugly for one thing. I guess we didn't have much choice, although some girls had Sindys. I was lucky because I had two sisters so when we played together, we had an incredible wardrobe and hundreds of accessories. Our parents used to disapprove, I never quite knew why, but it was all those hours dressing and undressing them that probably made me decide to be a fashion designer. And now, well obviously I don't play with them any more, but you can learn a lot from looking at them. Did you know that there are versions designed by Versace and Armani? Some of them are worth a fortune. I'd love to be invited to design an outfit for her myself one day.

2B Listening exercises 3 & 4

🌐 **1.11**

P = Presenter J = Jean T = Tom

P: Following the arrest yesterday of four urban fox lovers on the steps of the town hall, in today's *Face to face* we will be finding out more about the urban fox problem. In the studio with us this morning, we have Jean Baker, chairperson of the Residents' Association which is calling for action against the growing numbers of foxes plaguing our town, and Tom MacFaerne, spokesperson and founder member of Urban Fox Lovers, the organization responsible for the protest outside the town hall. Jean, if I could turn to you first. Following a series of attacks on household pets your association is calling for a cull on urban foxes in your area. Could you tell us more about why you think this is necessary?

T: Sorry, could I just clear up one thing before we start? I don't know who the four people who were arrested were, but I'm absolutely certain they were not members of Urban Fox Lovers. They had nothing to do with us. I just wanted to make that clear from the start.

P: Jean?

J: Yes, thank you. The fight outside the town hall was certainly very unfortunate, but if you ask me, what we need to do now is put it behind us, sit down calmly and discuss what can be done to tackle the growing problem of urban foxes. And, let's face it, they are a serious nuisance. Quite simply, there are too many of them, 35,000 at the last count. To be perfectly honest, we think it's about time we did something to control their numbers.

T: Kill them, you mean.

P: Tom, please, we'll turn to you in a moment. Jean, you were saying?

J: Yes, well, although we respect the views of the Urban Fox Lovers, we are absolutely convinced that measures need to be taken to control all fox numbers. There are a number of reasons for what we're saying. In our area alone, we have had a large number of attacks on domestic animals. We know that a hungry fox will break into hutches and eat pet rabbits and guinea pigs. We also have reason to believe that foxes are also attacking cats and small dogs. Personally, this is what upsets me – and many other people I know – the most. On top of that, there are minor irritations, like the problems with rubbish bins, for example. Foxes are forever turning over the bins to look for food, which is both messy and extremely unhygienic, and they keep digging holes in gardens round here to bury their half-eaten food.

T: I'm sorry, but I really must butt in here. Frankly, this is absolutely ridiculous. Cats will rip open rubbish bags more often than foxes and dogs are always digging holes everywhere. Do you want to control their numbers, too?

J: True, but the difference is that people choose to have dogs and cats and they don't choose to have foxes. Foxes are pests, like rats or mice, and all we are asking is for the local council to take steps to control them like other pests.

P: OK, I see your point. Tom?

T: Sorry, but foxes are not pests. They actually help keep down pests – they kill and eat rats, and mice, too. Our cities would actually be much dirtier if it wasn't for the foxes. And, on top of that, there are a lot of people who like seeing foxes in their gardens. People who will actually put food out for the foxes, you know, to encourage them to come into the garden.

P: Yes, but I really don't think everyone agrees with you there, Tom. I may be wrong, but not everyone actually wants foxes in their gardens ...

T: Well, it they don't want them to come in, they can always keep them out! There's no need to kill them to keep them out! There's all sorts of things you can do instead, put special chemicals down on the grass, put up foxproof fences, that sort of thing, I mean, it's not difficult.

J: And what about the attacks on other animals? Or children?

T: Oh, come on! You don't really believe that, do you? I don't believe for a minute that foxes will attack children. It's totally absurd! Foxes do everything they can to keep out of people's way. But in any case, you miss the point completely. The whole idea of a cull is a waste of time. Foxes control their own numbers and if you start killing them, other foxes will just move in to take the places of the ones you kill, and you'll end up having to kill them too. So, it's not only cruel, it's pointless. So, I'm sorry, but Jean's marvellous plan to kill all the foxes just doesn't add up.

J: We are not suggesting that we get rid of foxes altogether – and you know that. All we are saying is that their numbers have got out of hand, and that because there are so many of them, it's because there are so many of them that they are becoming more aggressive and we need to do something about it. We've got to draw a line somewhere.

T: But what you're suggesting just won't work!

J: I'm sorry Tom, but basically we think it's time to do something about this problem, and it is a problem, even you must see that ...

T: No, I don't see it. As far as I'm concerned there is no problem.

J: We can't just allow their numbers to keep on growing. We're animal lovers, too, but when we are constantly seeing our pets attacked, it's simply time that something was done about it.

P: Jean, sorry, but I think it's time now to hand things over to our listeners. We have our first caller on the line from ...

2B Pronunciation exercises 1 & 2

🌐 **1.12**

<u>Frankly</u>, it's about time <u>Tom</u> faced <u>facts</u>. // Urban foxes are not only a <u>nuisance</u> // they're a real <u>menace</u>! // The authorities need to do something <u>now</u>, // before <u>homeowners</u> start taking the <u>law</u> // into their own <u>hands</u>!

2D Listening exercise 2

🌐 **1.14**

P = Presenter   B = Beth

P: In today's *On the job* we're looking at working with animals. Later on in the programme we'll be paying a visit to London Zoo to talk to some of the keepers there, but first of all we're going to be talking to a dog trainer from the Guide Dogs for the Blind Association to find out what it takes to become a guide dog trainer. Good morning Beth, thanks for joining us this morning.

B: It's a pleasure to be here.

P: So, Beth, how did you first get involved in training guide dogs?

B: Well, first of all, I got interested in the puppy walking side of things, 'cos there was someone I knew who did it.

P: Puppy walking?

B: Yes, a neighbour of mine used to take in pups for the Guide Dog Association. She had the job of doing basic training with the pups, getting them used to walking on a lead, to noisy and crowded places, that kind of thing. It's important that when they start their guide dog training they're already used to busy roads and traffic and don't get scared by loud noises. So, anyway, we got talking and I volunteered to take on a pup and it all just grew from there. About a year later I was training as a guide dog trainer.

P: So, er, what did you do before?

B: I used to be a postwoman – ironically – as some dogs really hate postmen!

P: So, is life very different as a dog trainer?

B: Yes, it definitely is! I don't think it could be more different really.

P: What's the most rewarding part of the job?

B: I think training the people rather than the dogs. Sometimes it's hard work. But when it works out it's great. I once trained a man with quite severe mental problems who didn't actually speak to me for about two weeks!

P: That must have been difficult!

B: Yes, but then the bubble burst and from then on we got on fine ... he really benefited from getting a guide dog.

P: What's the most difficult part of the job?

B: Well, sometimes partnerships just don't work out, for whatever reason. Maybe the dog and the owner just don't get along and a change has to be made. We train about 750–800 people a year and it's inevitable that things don't always work out, but I still hate to see a partnership falling apart.

P: So, what advice would you give someone who wants to become a trainer?

B: Well, find out what it's all about first – and remember it's not just about dogs, it's about people too. It took me some time to get used to that side of things.

P: Do the owners need to have had previous experience of owning a dog?

B: It isn't essential, but it helps. No, it's actually far more important that the owners are already mobile to some degree, that they're used to getting around with a white stick, for example, and that they have a realistic idea of what a dog can do for them. A dog can't replace their eyes, but they can be an enormous help in making day-to-day life much easier and happier.

P: How long does it take for the dogs to get used to their owners and their new homes?

B: It depends, but it's usually very quick … two or three days. Some partnerships hit it off straight away, others take longer to get to know each other. All the dogs need a breaking-in period, when they get used to their owners' daily routines, the routes they usually take, the walks they usually go on. Dogs pick things up very quickly, but I always feel that a dog and owner REALLY gel together after two years … when the dog is about four years old.

P: What's the hardest thing for the dogs to learn?

B: To deal with traffic, especially bicycles – they can be pretty unpredictable.

P: I've seen people out and about with their guide dogs and I'm always amazed at how quickly and smoothly they get around …

B: Um, yes, one of the basic things the dogs need to be able to do is judge their owner's size and to match that with possible obstacles. They need to be able to decide if, for example, an overhanging branch is too low for their owner's head, or a gap in the crowd is too narrow. It's amazing to see how they get so good at it, and how quickly the two of them get used to picking their way through a crowd, whether it's on the street or in a crowded shop. Going back to one of your earlier questions, maybe that's the most rewarding thing – seeing a dog and its owner working as a team and feeling that they really don't need me anymore. That my job's over and the two of them can just get on with it. That's a great feeling – a feeling of a job well done.

P: Well, thank you for joining us today and good luck to you and your guide dogs. And if you want to know more about becoming a guide dog trainer, get in touch with the Guide Dogs for the Blind Association on www.guidedogs.org.uk

3B Listening exercises 1 & 2
🔊 1.15–1.16

W = Woman M = Man

1

W: Are you going to get changed for this evening?

M: Yeah. In a minute.

W: You could try to look your best for once. It is their anniversary after all.

M: I really don't think your parents are terribly bothered what I look like. You're the only one who gets upset about it.

W: I don't get upset. I just don't like the looks we get when we're in a posh restaurant and you're wearing that dirty old fleece.

M: What? The one you gave me for my birthday?

W: Yes, that horrible old grey thing. The one I gave you about five years ago. Although by the look of it, it could have been about ten years ago. In fact, the next time I see it, I'm going to chuck it in the bin.

M: I like it. I'm very attached to it. And don't you dare throw it in the bin.

W: Oh, come on, Philip, be reasonable. Here, I got this catalogue from *Next*. There are some really nice jackets in here. It'll only take a minute to look through. There's bound to be something that you like.

M: If I really must.

W: Here, what about this, for example? That would suit you.

M: Yeah, OK.

W: You like it?

M: 'S all right, I suppose.

W: Or something a bit more modern-looking, perhaps. What about this one?

M: Both jackets look exactly the same to me, except that one's brown, which is probably my least favourite colour. I prefer the black one.

W: Do you want to order it?

M: If you want.

W: Right. Decided. Now, what are you going to wear this evening?

M: This evening? Well, after what you just said, I think I'd better wear my fleece tonight. Which is probably the last chance I'll get to wear it.

W: You know, I had a funny feeling you'd say that.

2

M: Bren?

W: Yeah?

M: You got any plans for tomorrow?

W: No, nothing special. Why?

M: Oh, I just thought you might like to go and do a bit of shopping. You know, see what they've got in the sales.

W: What? With you, you mean?

M: Yeah, why not?

W: Well, it's just the first time you've ever wanted to go shopping with me.

M: Just a thought. Thought we might get you something to wear for that dinner tomorrow night.

W: Oh well, if you're offering. Come to think of it, I was having a look in the window of *Next* the other day. There was a pair of black linen trousers that would go well with my white jacket. Nice. Quite cheap, too.

M: Oh right. Trousers. Um, I was thinking maybe, I mean, you've got loads of trousers, haven't you?

W: Yes. And?

M: No, well, it was just that maybe, you know, you could wear something a bit more feminine-looking, maybe.

W: You mean a little black skirt like all the other wives that are going to be there? You want me to go for the *Desperate Housewives* look?

M: No, I don't mean that. But, I mean, you know, you've got great legs. What's wrong with a skirt?

W: Nothing wrong with skirts. Just I feel more comfortable in trousers, that's all.

M: Well, it was just a thought. Look, forget I said it.

W: But you can still buy me the trousers I liked, if you want.

M: Only if you promise to see what they've got in the way of skirts and stuff. Maybe try one or two on?

W: You know what? I think perhaps I might just go to the shops tomorrow with Petra. But it was sweet of you to offer.

3D Listening exercises 2 & 3
🔊 1.17

1: Because I met a photographer, who was a friend, and he was always taking pictures, and I was eighteen and I had just arrived in New York, I'd left high school and I'd come to New York to go through college, and he took pictures of everyone, of me, and one day he said 'Oh, you're really photogenic and could be a model', and I'd never thought of, about it before, and then he sent some of my photos to an agency, and they said they'd like to meet me, so I had an appointment to meet the people at the agency, and they took some more photos, because you have to put a book together, you know, a book of photos, with photos, and they send the book to the clients, and, you know, it just sort of started from there.

2: I started with some photo shoots, and then I did a few catwalk jobs, really, really not my kind of thing, I'm too shy, I just don't have the right kind of mentality, you have to be psyched up for that work, and besides I'm not tall enough, you have to be a lot taller than me, and you have to be not only relaxed, but also kind of like an actress, but I did a few and realized it wasn't my kind of thing, so I was offered a few jobs, the first one was for a hair spray, and then, yeah, the hair spray and, oh, I nearly forgot, I did an advertisement for brandy, and then quite quickly, I got more work, and they sent me to Milan, in Italy, and Greece, other trips to Europe, as well as work in New York and the west coast, but in Greece, there was an agency that was interested in me, so I was in Greece for a month, and they worked me really hard, work every day, mostly magazines.

3: Erm, most of all, the travel, I had a lot of work with foreign agencies, a month in Italy, a month in London, and I liked that, and they give you an apartment and money to live on, and, in addition, you live well and I had an independence I didn't have at home, you know, living as a student. What else? The money, the money was good, I could make two or three grand in one week, you work hard but the money's good, but I used to blow all the money, so I lived well for a week or two, do the things I wanna do.

4: The biggest drag is you have to be so passive, you can't show any initiative, you have to do exactly what the photographer and the client want you to, the less you exist as a person, as a human being, the better it is, you can't have any personality, you have to be able to obey, it's really passive. And, on top of that, some of the photographers, you know, they really want you to know who's the boss, and you can have a rough time if you don't do exactly what they want. One time, this guy wanted me to, this was in New York, and this photographer, a real big mouth, he wanted me to bite a necklace, a pearl necklace, and I thought it was so dumb and I just said 'Hey, I'm not gonna do that' and he went nuts, so you have to keep your cool. In fact, yeah, the biggest, the worst were the photographers, frustrated artists who'd prefer, who don't want to be doing advertisements, they can be a real drag.

5: Not in my private life, no, yeah, there was a curiosity, a lot of people thought that it was a weird world, everyone took drugs, yeah a lot of people had a lot of fantasies about what it was like to be a model, so there was a curiosity and people asked a lot of questions, but maybe it was mostly, it was people from back home, from Indiana where I grew up. They kinda looked at me like I was from another planet, sometimes, I guess. And then, some people treated me like an airhead 'cos I was a model, like, you know, as if, so you're a model, so you have to be real dumb.

6: I felt bad, half the time I'd arrive at a job and I thought they'd send me home, 'she's not what we're looking for,' I never had much confidence, I thought they wouldn't want me. I remember one time I was feeling very low, and I hadn't had time to wash my hair, and, what's more, I had this spot on my chin, and I was feeling beat because we'd been working non-stop for weeks, no, I've never really liked the way I look.

4B Listening exercises 1 & 2
🌐 1.26

K = Kay J = Jay

K: Hi Jan, how are you doing?
J: Fine thanks. Kay. And you?
K: Not too bad, can I get you a coffee?
J: Yeah, thanks.
K: How's Suzi getting on? Have you heard from her recently? Has she picked up an Italian boyfriend yet?
J: Not that she's mentioned! But yeah, she seems to be getting on fine. She phoned last night and said she's really enjoying it.
K: How long has she been out there now?

J: Almost three months. She's got another three months to go on her contract, but she's talking about extending.
K: Have you been out to see her yet? Here you go Jan, here's your coffee.
J: Ooh, Thanks, Kay. No, I haven't been out there yet, but I'm planning to go next month for a week or so, I haven't been before, I'm really looking forward to it.
K: Oh, you'll love it.
J: Have you been then?
K: Yeah, a couple of times. Rome's beautiful, it really is.
J: Yeah, so I've heard, Suzi raves about it.
K: Bet she's got a long list of places to take you to when you go over …
J: Yeah, and you're not going to believe it, but she's got me fixed up to do a gladiator course.
K: A gladiator course? Did I hear that right?
J: Yes you did: female gladiators, it's the latest thing, apparently.
K: That's so Suzi, but I can't believe she's roped you in too, sounds a bit scary to me.
J: Yeah, me too! But I think that's the whole point, you know, confront your fears and all that.
K: Yeah, I suppose once you've faced a real live gladiator in the ring there's not much that can frighten you … I still think it's a bit extreme though.
J: Yeah, well it's supposed to be the latest thing in stress-busting and confidence boosting …
K: So what is it then, a whole week's course?
J: No, no, not that bad … just a weekend – a two day intensive course, you learn about sword fighting and dress up in Roman costumes, eat Roman food and stuff and apparently you get to fight in a proper ancient Roman arena at the end of it – a kind of mini coliseum.
K: Where you 'face your fears and come out stronger' I suppose?
J: Yeah, that kind of thing …
K: But why? I mean, surely there are better things to do in Rome? You know, see the sights, enjoy the food, do some shopping …
J: Yeah, but I can do all of that during the week … and well, Suzi fancies it and it's something different.
K: You can say that again!
J: Suzi's really into it. She's doing a course at the moment, two nights a week. She loves it. She said the first time she actually fought in front of an audience was fantastic. A real adrenaline buzz. And she reckons it's done loads of good to her confidence.
K: Does she need it? She's never struck me as being particularly shy. In fact I've always thought she was Miss Confident.
J: Not in Italy, it seems! They've got a totally different concept of shy over there! in fact it was her boss over there that suggested she go. Said she was a bit too quiet, a bit too timid and needed to be a bit more assertive, stand up for herself a bit more. So she signed up two months ago, and she's been really happy with it from the word go.
K: And has it worked?

J: I don't know. I'll have to see when I go out there. But it sounds fun. And Suzi says she's made loads of friends through it.
K: Suzi always makes loads of friends!
J: Yeah, well, I think the main reason she's invited me to go is that she's got to take her final test when I go out. She's got to fight the resident Amazon – she's already fought her a couple of times and she lost on both occasions, apparently this woman walked all over her. She's got to win this time or she won't pass the course. I think she wants some moral support.
K: Yeah, I can understand that, but can't you go as a spectator? I mean, do you really want to do the whole gladiator bit? Sounds a bit violent to me.
J: Yeah, I do actually. It's something different and anyway, I need a bit of confidence building too! Especially after today …
K: Hum, why's that?
J: Haven't I told you? I've just heard that I've got to give a big presentation at work – you know, in front of everyone? I've never done anything like that before and the thought absolutely terrifies me!
K: It would me too!
J: Thanks, that's a lot of help.
K: No, I mean, I'm sure you'll be fine, but it is pretty daunting! So gladiator school, hey? Well, remember to take plenty of photos – I'd love to see the two of you dressed up in your togas …
J: You never know, once you've seen all the photos and heard all the stories, you might be the next one signing up for the course.
K: No way! I'd rather not have my confidence boosted thank you very much. I'm happy enough as I am!

4D Listening exercises 3 & 4
🌐 1.27

P = Presenter   C = Chick
K = Kathryn

P: In recent weeks we've been exploring the weird and wonderful world of America's Deep South, and our journey has taken us through Florida, Georgia and Alabama. Today we travel to the very heart of Texas, and discover the terrifying world of rattlesnake round-ups and rattlesnake sacking. Later in the programme, I'll be meeting a real-life rattlesnake mama from the town of Sweetwater, home of the 'World's Largest Rattlesnake Round-up', and we'll visit the Rattlesnake Sacking Championships in the town of Taylor. But first, I spoke to herpetologist, Chick Ferragamo, who introduced me to my first rattler.
C: This one that you're looking at right now is the Western Diamondback Rattlesnake, 'Crotelus atrox', and this is the one that you'll see at the rattlesnake shows. He's about two foot in length, so he's still young … The rattle on the end of the tail is a warning signal, but he's not gonna bite.

Don't move and he'll stay still, too. In principle anyway! You're too big to go in his mouth. They generally swallow their prey whole.

He sure doesn't like you! You see that little drop of yellow on the fang? That's the venom, and if that gets into your blood, you have about thirty, say forty, minutes to get medical help. And that's our work here in this lab, we keep the rattlers here to collect their venom, and the venom is then, er, we use the venom to manufacture the antivenin. But there are many small, small differences between the venoms of different snakes and we need to ensure that we give people the right antidote. We've been studying rattlers here for nearly fifteen years, and we still haven't identified all the variations.

P: Feeling better informed, but not particularly reassured, it was time to move on to Sweetwater, American City, a small town of about 12,000 people. This is agricultural land, cotton and cattle, rodeos and cookouts, but we're here because, as the publicity proudly announces, 'This city has been organizing the 'World's Largest Rattlesnake Round-Up since 1959.' My guide for the day is Kathryn Rogers – or *Rattlesnake Mama* as she calls herself. Kathryn took me to the Nolan County Coliseum, the main venue for the event.

K: This is the Nolan County Coliseum and this is where all the main action is happening. Folks can watch the snake handling shows throughout the day, or you can join a guided rattlesnake hunt at the registration desk over there. Then we have food stalls serving deep-fried rattlesnake meat. Come on, I'll treat you.

P: Mmm, it's, er, it's quite – nice. A bit like chicken. Mmm. Thanks.

K: You're welcome. Now, if you're ready, let's go to the weigh-in.

P: Hunters have been bringing in snakes since the show opened yesterday morning, and although we're only half-way through the three-day event, the guys here have already weighed over seven hundred kilos of rattlesnake.

K: The round-up started way back when a group of farmers and ranchers from the County wanted to do something about the number of rattlers. But the show has grown and tens of thousands of people from all over the world come every year. It's organized by the Jaycees, the Junior Chamber of Commerce, and the proceeds all go to good causes – the boy and girl scouts, the Red Cross, the homeless.

P: My day at the Sweetwater Rattlesnake Roundup ended with a visit to the Gun, Knife and Coin Show. Guns and knives I could understand, but coins? I'm on my way to Taylor, in Williamson County and the moment I've been waiting for. We've been driving round Texas for over a month and we've done hundreds and hundreds of miles, but finally here we are: the National Rattlesnake Sacking Championship in Taylor, Texas, and I have to say - it's something of a disappointment. In many ways, this is no

different from what we saw in Sweetwater: snake handlers bring in their rattlers for the round-up, an arts and crafts fair – no guns, knives and coins this time, but plenty of stalls selling fried rattlesnake, rattlesnake kebabs, barbecued rattler, or just plain baked rattlesnake. You could have a three-course meal and eat nothing but snake. I don't know what I'd been expecting, but I've been surprised by the simplicity of the sacking. Two people stand inside a sort of glass box with ten rattlesnakes. One of them holds a sack, and the other has a kind of stick. The idea is to pick up the snake in your bare hands and throw it in the sack. You have to do it as quickly as possible, and the fastest time wins. That's it. The world record of seventeen seconds is held by Jackie Bibby, who also holds records for sitting in a bathtub with 81 rattlesnakes and holding nine rattlesnakes in his mouth. It takes all sorts, I guess. But for me, I have to say that I'm getting tired of the whole thing, tired of the show and thinking that, just maybe, there was something about the burger I had for lunch that didn't agree with me.

5B Listening exercises 2 & 3
🌐 1.30

P = Presenter L = Lucy

P: The world of art hit the front pages this week with the news that a London hospital has appointed an arts curator on a salary of £42,000 a year. The curator's job will be to arrange art exhibitions and other events at University College Hospital to 'improve patients' experience in hospital'. The new appointment follows the installation last month of a £70,000 stone sculpture outside the hospital's main entrance. The unveiling of the sculpture was greeted with disbelief by the popular press and some patients' groups, who described it as 'a load of rubbish' and 'a complete waste of money', and the appointment of the new curator has fuelled the debate. According to a statement from the management of the hospital, an artistic environment is a positive factor in attracting and keeping staff, as well as helping in quicker recovery rates for the patients. Critics of the hospital's policy, however, were unimpressed. I spoke to Lucy Haddon-Peters, an independent art consultant and a curator herself, for an expert opinion on this controversy.

P: Lucy, thank you very much for coming along today …

L: You're welcome.

P: We're standing outside University College Hospital on the busy Euston Road with the controversial stone sculpture by artist John Aiken just in front of us. Lucy, could I ask you first of all your opinion of the sculpture? Is it a masterpiece or is it, as some have said, a load of rubbish?

L: Well, erm, it has a, it has a certain organic charm, um, and it, er, it fits, I think it looks quite nice, but, erm, but …

P: You're not convinced?

L: No, no. I think that, I think, whatever you think of it, I don't think that anybody would say it's a masterpiece.

P: Worth £70,000?

L: Well, it certainly sounds a lot of money, but I don't think it's overly expensive for a work of this kind. But I'd just like to say, if I may, that, erm, I read in one of the papers this morning, one of the papers that was very anti, very critical, that the hospital should have, that they should have spent the money on more staff, more doctors and nurses and so on. That they shouldn't be wasting money on paying for an arts curator and so on, but the money actually comes from charitable donations, from money that er, that people have given.

P: Why is that more and more public institutions, hospitals for example, and, er, private companies, local governments, etcetera are spending money on art projects?

L: Yes, I agree that this seems rather new, but in some ways, this country is simply catching up with other countries, like France, for example, in fact, erm, wherever you go in France, you see large public arts projects all around you, everywhere, and many of these are very popular, so it's not really new as such, although the idea is still new to some people here, here in England.

P: And the reasons?

L: Well, there's no doubt that many environments could be improved, made more attractive, more interesting with well-chosen works of art as a, as a focal point, a point of interest, and people often feel more positive, they feel proud of where they live or where they work, and I think that art can also help to bring people together, to, er, encourage people to talk about, to react to the art and share their views, whether they like it or not, and so on. In fact, in all the companies I've worked for, yes, all of them, in fact, whenever we unveil a work of art, people always get together and talk about it, so, yes, I think there are many reasons, why public art projects can be very exciting for everyone.

P: But only if they like what they see, I suppose?

L: Well, yes, obviously, and I think it also depends on why a company invests in an art project. There was one company, a paint factory it was which wanted art for their office buildings, where I acted as a consultant to help them in selecting and buying the work, and then we worked together to decide the best way to exhibit the work in the offices, but the place was absolutely awful, coffee stains on the carpets, broken-down vending machines everywhere, no redeeming features at all. And the smell of paint, the smell was so strong, so overpowering. I got the commission because they wanted to smarten the place up, make it look nice, you know, but the smell of paint was really, that a couple of prints on the walls or a nice sculpture or whatever simply wasn't going to make the slightest difference. I mean, really, who was going to think, for a second, that because they had an extremely valuable painting on the walls, that they were a decent, respectable company. Which they clearly weren't. It turned out that they were breaking every regulation in the book. They should really have spent the money on smartening the whole place up.

5B Speaking exercise 4
1.32

There is no record of an artist with the name of Charles Andrews, although a man of that name was recently arrested by police in the south of Spain. It is possible that the dealer who is selling this pile of bricks is dishonest. There is a well-known artist called Carl André, who makes sculptures from bricks, but he has no connection to the bricks in the photograph. The sculpture of a horse is made of imitation brass and has been painted green so that it looks old. It was bought in a souvenir shop in Volterra and is absolutely wortless. Diocletus the Etruscan is an invented name. The most valuable work of art in this collection – in fact, the only object here that is worth anything at all – is undoubtedly the glass sculpture, 'Hanging Spirit' by Stephen Knapp. Stephen Knapp has been commissioned to create sculptures and other work for many public buildings in the US, and his work is exhibited in many galleries.

5D Listening exercises 1 & 2
1.34

P = Presenter   J = Juliet

P:
In this week's *Book Corner*, we turn our attention to the winner of the National Book Foundation's 50th anniversary gold medal. Voted one of the most influential people of the twentieth century by *Time Magazine* and named by *Forbes Magazine* as the world's most powerful celebrity, she became the first-ever African-American woman billionaire and was honoured in the Hall of Fame of the National Association for the Advancement of Colored People. A tireless campaigner against child abuse, she fought for the National Child Protection Act which became law in 1993, and was named after her. Nominated for an Oscar for her role in Steven Spielberg's *The Color Purple*, she is also the co-founder of a successful cable TV network. Her own TV talk show is the most successful in television history and is watched by over thirty million viewers in more than one hundred countries around the world. The show won so many Emmy awards that she asked for it not to be considered any more. In case you hadn't guessed, we're talking about Oprah Winfrey. Juliet Evans looks into the background.

J:
Oprah was a talented child but no one thought her life would turn out such a success. Born in Mississippi, Oprah Winfrey was brought up by her grandmother on a farm, before she joined her mother in Milwaukee. The victim of abuse, Oprah ran away from her home and, at the age of thirteen, was sent to a juvenile detention centre. The centre, however, was full and Oprah was turned away. With nowhere else to go, Oprah went to live with her father in Nashville. Her father, Vernon, was strict, but, according to Oprah, he saved her life. As part of the regime, Oprah had to learn five new words every day, and each week she had to read a book and write a report on it.

After studying at Tennessee State University, Oprah worked as a TV reporter and newsreader, before taking over a Chicago talk show. The public took to her immediately and Oprah's career took off. Within two years, her show was broadcast nationally and Oprah received the first of her many Emmy awards. In the mid 1990s, Oprah came up with the idea of a book club, of introducing a regular book slot on her show. Her idea was to encourage Americans to read more, but even she must have been surprised at its success. As part of the show, Oprah put forward a book which she had read and enjoyed and discussed it on the programme. She chose only contemporary writers and the media coverage that these novels received turned them into best-sellers overnight. For the publishing world, it was a godsend, but the writers were less impressed when Oprah suspended her book club in 2002, because, she said, not enough contemporary novels lived up to her expectations. A year later, Oprah's book club returned, but this time with the classics. After describing Tolstoy's *Anna Karenina* as 'one of the greatest love stories of our time', Oprah told viewers that the book's 837 pages shouldn't put them off. Such is the trust that she inspired in her viewers, Anna Karenina shot to number one in the *New York Times* bestsellers list. The Oprah Winfrey Book Club logo on the front cover of a novel is now enough to ensure huge sales for even the most unlikely of titles, such as a boxed set of three of William Faulkner's novels.

Oprah Winfrey's influence on the world of books would be colossal if it stopped there, but the book club phenomenon just grew and grew. Other chat show hosts, such as Britain's Richard and Judy, have taken up where Oprah left off. Inspired by Oprah's example, hundreds of thousands of people, mostly women it has to be said, have joined or set up their own reading groups, and meet up on a regular basis to discuss their book of the month. The craze has even inspired writers to use the idea of a book club for the plot of their novels. *The Jane Austen Book Club* and *Angry Housewives Eating Bon Bons*, to name but two works of contemporary fiction, follow the lives of groups of women who belong to reading groups.

Not everyone has been impressed by the Oprah Winfrey book club phenomenon. One novelist, Jonathan Franzen, turned down the chance to have his book, *The Corrections*, featured on the *Oprah Winfrey Show*. Franzen was afraid that it might affect his reputation in literary circles, but he quickly regretted the comments he made. Franzen's comments came across as pretentious and elitist, and his reputation nosedived anyway.

P:
In the studio with me here, my guest is the author, Matthew Jones, whose latest novel will be published next week. I asked Matthew to evaluate the books on Oprah Winfrey's list. A superstar she may be, but is Oprah any judge of books? Matthew?

6B Listening exercises 1 & 2
1.35

P = Presenter

P:
The world has come a long way since Grover Cleveland, the twenty-second president of the United States, said, in 1905, that 'sensible and responsible women do not want to vote' and added that the positions of men and women in society had been determined by God. Cleveland would be horrified to know that, only one hundred years later, women not only had the right to vote but had been elected to the highest positions of power around the world. With the recent election of the first woman president in Africa, there are now few parts of the world where women have not been heads of state.

However, despite the progress, women remain extremely unrepresented in politics. Ninety-one per cent of the members of national parliaments worldwide are men. Even in countries like Sweden, with a very high proportion of women in politics, men still hold over fifty percent of the parliamentary seats.

In order to tackle the problem, many political parties and some national governments have introduced or are considering the introduction of quota systems. These systems vary, but the basic idea is simple. When political parties prepare their lists of candidates for elections, they include a balance of the sexes. Some parties, such as the Greens in Germany, have lists that are fifty per cent men and fifty per cent women, although a lower figure of between twenty and forty per cent is more common. In Argentina and Belgium, for example, every third person on candidate lists for elections must be a woman.

But the quota system, sometimes referred to as 'positive discrimination', is not popular with everyone, and it's not only men who are arguing against it. Later in the programme we'll be asking you for your opinions, but first we'll be hearing the views of two women, both members of the ...

6B Listening exercises 1, 2 & 3
🌐 1.35–1.36

W = woman

W1:

Can I say first of all that what I want to see, what I think we all agree we need, is to see, to have more women in politics. I don't think there's really much disagreement about this, I think that probably all the major political parties wish they had more women standing, representing them. The more women we have, the more political parties can represent the electorate, and let's not forget that there are more women out there than men, and some of the things that matter to me, some of the big issues like equal pay and childcare and health, for example, will get more attention if we have more women Members of Parliament. So we're not really arguing about the end, the outcome, it's about how we get there, and er, positive discrimination, the quota system, is clearly not the way to go about it. First of all, I'd like to say that, as a woman, I find the idea of quotas, as a woman, condescending and offensive. I think it was Oprah Winfrey who said that excellence is the best way to fight discrimination, and I think she was absolutely right. How would you feel if you were appointed to your job simply because you were a woman, or because you were black or whatever? That you got the job, not because you were the right person for the job, but simply because you were a woman. And, how would you feel, as a man, let's say a man who had been doing a job for a long time, and doing it very well, if you had to step aside, if you were to lose your position just because your party or the government or whoever decides that it ought to be a woman in the job? Or as a voter and there's someone you'd really like to vote for, and you find yourself saying if only he wasn't a man! It simply doesn't make any sense and quotas will simply alienate an awful lot of people. What we need, and when I say 'we', I mean both men and women, is to have people in positions of responsibility who are good at what they do. Excellence. And let's face it, many politicians are bad enough as it is, without replacing them with people who are even less competent. We all want to see the end of discrimination but the quota system is just another kind of discrimination, and even if we call it 'positive discrimination'; it's still discrimination. Two wrongs do not make a right and this is not the way to make progress.

W2:

People say that the quota system, a quota system that makes it possible for women to be elected to national or regional parliaments, people object to this system because they say that it is another form of discrimination, that we are replacing one kind of discrimination with another. You know, they say that we'll be replacing a good man in a job with a stupid woman, but, I mean, really, there are so many stupid men in politics that if we have one or two stupid women, I really don't think it's any big deal. Is it? But seriously, I think this is missing the point and, in any case, I don't

think we should be using the term 'positive discrimination' anyway. 'Positive action' is a much better way of describing the quota system. It doesn't discriminate against men – it simply gives women a fairer chance. And that is what this is all about. Quotas may not be perfect, they may not be ideal, and I can understand it when people say if only there were some other way of achieving equality. But the fact is that there isn't. Nobody has suggested anything else that will work, and we know from experience, from quite a lot of experience now, that quotas for women bring results. If you look at countries where there are large numbers of women in parliament, places like Denmark or Sweden, it is because the political parties there introduced a quota system. I mean, if you ask yourself why the Germans elected a woman Chancellor, it's because the political parties there also have a quota system. This is the only way we know to get more women into politics. We can't go back now. The world of politics is changing because there are more women in it, and there are more women in politics because quotas have made this possible. I only wish that we'd introduced the system a hundred years ago when women got the vote.

6D Listening exercises 2
🌐 1.40

A = Anne   D = Di

A: Hi Di, heard the news?

D: What news?

A: Frank's been given the sack

D: The sack? Really? Are you sure? But he's been with us forever.

A: Yes, well, and he's been a pain forever too. I'm surprised they didn't get rid of him sooner.

D: What do you mean?

A: Well, he's hardly Mr Popular is he? Especially with the new boss.

D: Yes, you've got a point, what with all his sexist jokes and all that laddish banter all the time.

A: Yeah, do you remember the time he asked her to get him a cup of coffee at that first department meeting?

D: Do I remember? She was so angry! She was practically breathing fire! I think we all felt sorry for him then! But what are you saying? That she's got rid of him because of his sexist comments? Has he made one joke too many?

A: He may well have done, and it probably hasn't helped his case, but no, that's not what I'm saying. Apparently it's come from higher up. He's really messed it up big time.

D: So what's he done then?

A: Well, apparently he was asked to write the ad for the new receptionist ... you know, after Fiona left ... so anyway, they asked him to write this advert ...

D: But that isn't really his job, is it?

A: No, I don't know how he came to be writing it, actually ... so anyway, he scribbles something down, he doesn't think to ask anyone to check it ...

D: Well, he wouldn't, would he?

A: It gets sent to the local paper and before anyone's seen it, it's in print and the damage is done. Someone complained to the government organization and they're taking the whole thing very seriously. Sex discrimination ... amongst other things ...

D: What exactly did he put in it? 'Attractive blonde receptionist required, 5 inch heels essential ...'?

A: Almost!

D: So go on, what did it say?

A: Yeah, well, first of all he used the adjective 'young'. 'Suit young graduate' I think it was ...

D: Uh oh – ageist, too. He obviously hadn't read the memos about age discrimination ...

A: ... and then he goes and slips in a completely unnecessary 'she'.

D: What do you mean? I don't follow.

A: Look, here's a copy ... see, here 'she should also be ...'

D: Oh no, the idiot! I bet he didn't even notice. Poor Frank. I mean, it's not as if he did it on purpose ... I feel quite sorry for him actually ...

A: Sorry for him? The man's a liability!

D: Yeah, I know that, but it really is a lot of fuss about nothing.

A: What, the government organization is taking us to court and you call it a lot of fuss about nothing. The company could face massive fines. What are you saying?

D: I know, I know, but what I meant to say was that we all know what he's like, I mean, he's not the most articulate person we know, is he? Whoever asked him to write the ad should really have written it themselves or at the very least they should have asked to see it before it got sent off.

A: So, basically you're saying that he's incompetent? That he can't actually do his job without someone overseeing everything he does. I mean, he's supposed to be a senior manager, he's supposed to be supervising other people's work, not having his work supervised!

D: Now, that's unfair. That's not what I said. He's very good at his job. He's an excellent engineer. He just isn't very good with words, that's all. I mean, yes, it was a big mistake ... and a stupid one too. But it was a mistake and I really don't think he deserves to lose his job over it.

A: I can't believe it! And from you of all people! You're forever complaining about his bad jokes and macho behaviour.

D: Yes, OK, OK, I know, I know. He's sexist. There's no denying it. And something should be done about it, I'm not disputing that. But my point is that I don't think someone should lose their job for making an honest mistake.

A: And what about for being a sexist pig? Or for being totally un-pc?

D: Yeah, well I'm not sure what the unions would say about that. Is it fair grounds for dismissal?

A: Sure as hell should be!

7B Listening exercises 2 & 3

🔘 2.1

N = Nell B = Becky
W = Winston

N: Becky, hi!
B: Nell, darling! Have I come at a bad time?
N: No, come in, come in. I'll just move this out of the way. Mind all the dust and rubble and stuff. How're you doing?
B: Fine, fine. I was just passing and I thought I'd pop in and see how the work's going.
N: Yes, come in, come in. Do you fancy a drink? Or would you like to have the guided tour first?
B: The guided tour, I think.
N: Winston! It's Becky!
W: What?
N: I said it's Becky. I don't think he heard.
B: Wow! It looks like you're taking the whole house to pieces!
N: Yes, well not exactly. We're putting in solar panels. Winston's just knocking a hole in the wall to get the wiring through.
B: And you're doing that all by yourselves? Can't you get a man to come in and do it for you?
N: Winston! Can you shut up for a minute? Ah, that's better. Winston! Where were we? Ah, yes, the panels. You get a grant from the local council. You pay for the panels, they pay for the installation, so if we do the installation ourselves we keep the cash.
B: Oh right, makes sense. And what else are you doing to this 'green home' of yours? Didn't you say you were putting it in for a competition or something?
N: Yes. It's called 'Ecohome of the Year'. Winston's got a few weeks' holiday and we're making the most of it to get as much work done as we can.
B: Well, you're not going to win any ecological competitions with all those old car tyres outside the front door.
N: Er, actually, we're going to use them to insulate the back wall. It's north-facing and really damp and it'll make a difference to our heating bills. With a bit of luck, we won't need any central heating at all.
B: And you're living here while all this is going on? You must be completely mad.
N: Um, it might sound mad to you but if we win they'll pay for all the work we've done, so it's worth giving it a go! The judging doesn't start till next spring and they take plans and work in progress into account as well so I reckon we'll be in with a chance.
B: So what does it all involve then, apart from the solar panels?
N: Well, first of all we're stripping the house down to its bare bones: brick walls and bare floorboards. It makes it easier to see what else we want to do. We've done most of it already, but there's still the bathroom left. We're doing that next week. Winston will have some fun smashing up all the tiles with his sledge hammer.
B: What, you mean you aren't going to recycle them?

N: Course we are. I'm going to build a mosaic wall in the kitchen!
B: You are kidding now, aren't you?
N: No, straight up.
B: And you and Winston are doing all this on your own?
N: Most of it, yes. Winston's hired one of those sanding machines, you know, for sanding the floorboards. He enjoys that. But he's going to need help with the wiring and the plumbing.
B: How long's it going to take, do you think? You know, to do the whole lot.
N: We're reckoning on at least seven to eight months. But it could be longer. We don't really know when all the materials and fittings are going to be delivered. We don't know when the greywater tank is coming, for example.
B: Greywater? What's that?
N: That is the pièce de résistance. We're going to have a special system installed that recycles all the water from the bath, the shower and the washing machine … that's the greywater. Dirty, but not too dirty … to flush the toilet.
B: Charming. So what other delightful features is your 'ecohome' going to have?
N: Well, we're going to change all the windows. The previous owners put in PVC windows with double glazing, we're going to replace them with wooden windows with triple glazing. And after that …
W: Do you know where the first-aid kit is, Nell? I've cut my arm.
B: You're bleeding!
N: Oh no, not again.
W: It's not my fault. There's something wrong with that drill.
N: Come on, let's all have a cup of tea.

7D Listening exercises 2 & 3

🔘 2.3–2.5

1
If the turn of the century was marked by the drive for super sizes, then the next twenty years will be marked by a demand for ever-decreasing sizes. Mini-portions will be more and more fashionable. Even the big fast-food chains will be bringing out their own mini food, things such as mini-burgers and mini-pizzas … and all at mini-prices! And not only will the portions be smaller, but the food itself will also be fresher. Advances in packaging technology will mean that we will be able to keep food fresh and tasty out of the fridge for much longer. For example, new ultra-light materials will mean that thermos bags and bottles will be lighter, smaller and easier to carry, and we'll be able to take our pocket-sized sushi to work without worrying about it going off. As well as encouraging a taste for smaller portions, the interest in healthier food will also mean that we will be eating more and more organic food – approximately 60% of the food we eat will be organic – and less and less meat. And watch out for a huge increase in the consumption of all kinds of seafood. Seaweed, in particular, will be taking off as the number one health food product and we'll be eating seaweed supplements along with most of our meals.

2
As always there'll be a whole host of new fashion ideas. Teenagers will be buying interactive T-shirts which can screen their favourite movie, and their dads'll be investing in kilts and sarongs as skirts for men become a definite fashion possibility. A whole range of clothes will be developed that can integrate electronics with fabrics. For instance, we'll be able to play our favourite music videos on our T-shirts or read the football results on the palm of our gloves. What's more, we'll be able to make phone calls without needing a phone, it'll be built into our jacket. Heat-sensitive fabrics will also be coming into their own with a hundred and one different uses, beachwear for children which will warn parents to get the kids out of the sun when it's too hot or sweatshirts that will show it's time to put on another layer when it's too cold, to name but a few. Besides being used for clothes, these heat-sensitive fabrics will also find their uses in the house. Soft furnishings, like blankets and cushions, will be particularly useful for the elderly, flashing warning signals to grandma when she needs to turn the heating up in winter, or take a couple of layers off in summer.

3
Virtual reality will have revolutionized spectator sports, combining the joys of TV sports and actually going to the game. VR options will include, among other things, the possibility to change your seat at any time. For example, you want to see the action from behind the goal, just press a button and you're there, or maybe you want to see the players coming out of the tunnel, pay a supplement and you'll be standing there, rubbing shoulders with your sporting heroes. And besides that, and more excitingly, we'll also have the virtual ability to be on the field during the action, to watch the kicks from any angle, and much, much more. And if you're bored of watching the TV, then thanks to your virtual gym you'll have no shortage of fitness options in your own living room. You could take part in a virtual Tour de France on your exercise bike for instance, or run the London marathon. Virtual workouts will be all the rage. We'll still be running to keep fit, but in virtual scenery that our present day dreams are made of. Fancy a run along your favourite beach for example, or a cycle ride over the Pyrenees? It'll all be possible from the comfort of your own gym, thanks to VR helmets and special VR suits. And it won't only be workouts that are given the VR makeover. Virtual reality could also mean the end of traditional telephone calls with conversations being replaced by virtual walks. Imagine you are away from home on business, and your partner is home alone on a wet, winter's day. Thanks to the new virtual phones you could both meet up for a romantic walk on a virtual beach, enjoying the Pacific breeze and a spectacular sunset.

8B Listening exercises 2 & 3
🌐 2.6

N = Newsreader   S = Sonia

N:
Figures released in America today show that one in seven doctors are now refusing to deliver babies because they cannot afford the insurance policies they need to protect themselves if anything goes wrong. Insurance costs for doctors in the US have risen by up to 75% in the last five years and could rise further. Here in the UK, where doctors work for the National Health Service and do not require private insurance, the government has announced that it is putting aside nearly eight billion pounds to cover compensation claims in the next ten years. Our health correspondent, Sonia Razzaq, reports.

S:
A 30-year-old rugby player, Adrian Bowe, went to his doctor, complaining of headaches and a loss of vision in one eye.
After examining the patient, the doctor decided that he must be suffering from a migraine attack. However, not long after, Mr Bowe collapsed, the victim of a stroke that has left him permanently disabled and requiring a wheelchair to leave his house. Earlier this year, a judge ruled that the doctor was guilty of 'clinical negligence'. With a correct diagnosis of Mr Bowe's condition, the stroke might have been avoided. Mr Bowe is now entitled to compensation and this could run into millions of pounds.

The tragic story of Adrian Bowe is not an isolated case. Each year, Britain's National Health Service considers up to 7,000 claims for compensation where operations have gone wrong or doctors have made errors of judgement. Critics of Britain's under-fire health service fear that the country may soon find itself in a similar situation to the United States where many doctors are refusing to perform certain operations. They point to the increasing pressures that doctors are now working under. Shortages of staff and increased workloads have led to shorter consultation times and, say the critics, more and more errors are inevitable.
It is a suggestion that is rejected by others in the profession. A spokesman for one London hospital said that the increase in compensation claims cannot be the result of more medical errors, because the number of claims is not increasing. Courts are awarding higher compensation payments, but there is no evidence that doctors are making more mistakes. What is happening, he added, is that people seem to be forgetting that medical diagnosis is not an exact science.

He points out that Adrian Bowe's symptoms could have been caused by a migraine and it is impossible for doctors to make the correct diagnosis. Similarly, a patient who is feeling under the weather, stiff and generally run-down, may be going down with the flu, but they might also be showing the first signs of something much more serious. Computerized databases of symptoms and illnesses are now widely available, and these may result in better diagnoses, but doctors will always need to use their personal judgement and experience. Online databases are also being used by patients who think that their doctor may have made a mistake, but medical experts warn that such websites can lead to people who are in perfectly good shape worrying over nothing. One of these sites, wrong diagnosis dot com, lists 145 illnesses, some of them very serious, which have no symptoms at all. Hypochondriacs may enjoy identifying a hundred possible explanations for why they feel at death's door, but the only sensible course of action remains a visit to your GP.
The government's decision to set aside nearly eight billion pounds for compensation claims may sound extremely high, but this represents less than 1% of the NHS budget. Britain is still a long way from the situation in the United States, and although we can expect to hear about more cases like Mr Bowe, there seems, for the moment at any rate, to be no reason to be alarmed.

8C Grammar exercise 3
🌐 2.8

I was bored with my job. Sometimes I had to answer as many as 300 calls a day. I wasn't allowed to leave my desk, not even to stretch my legs. Then the headaches started. One day I was talking to a customer on the phone and she mentioned that she was an acupuncturist. We arranged to meet. That meeting changed my life! She cured my headaches and I didn't have to pay her a penny. But she also saved me from my dead-end job. Now I'm a fully trained acupuncturist. I still have to work long, hard days, but I don't have to ask someone else what I can and can't do. I'm my own boss and it's great! I feel like a new person.

8D Listening exercises 2 & 3
🌐 2.9–2.13

1   B = Bob   J = Jen

B: By the end of the week? Ooh!
J: You still haven't been to see a doctor, have you?
B: Why? What's the point? He won't be able to do anything to help …
J: At least he'll be able to prescribe some painkillers …
B: Listen, I appreciate the concern, but I'd rather just put up with it, OK?
J: How about getting a massage then? I know a really good physiotherapist – he does these special lower back massages – they're great – they really help – a couple of hours a week and you'll be like new. Tom went to him – he says he works miracles.
B: Oh, that reminds me – I need to call Tom. I'd promised I'd get back to him today …
J: OK, ignore me! But it's for your own good.
B: Look, thanks for the suggestions but I've had this problem for years now – it comes and goes – I just live with it.

J: OK, have it your own way. Anyway, as I was saying, I reckon we can get the report done by the end of the week, or the beginning of next week at the very latest …

2   M = Mike   B = Bob

M: Hi Bob, how's your back?
B: Don't ask!
M: So, no football again this week then?
B: No, sorry mate. You'll have to do your best without me!
M: You really should see someone about it you know. How long have you had it now? It's been weeks since you last played.
B: I know, I know. It'll sort itself out. It always does.
M: Look, I know I've said this before, but I know a really good osteopath. My mother swears by her. She does this spinal manipulation thing …
B: Sounds painful!
M: It probably is, but it works, I tell you, you really should try …
B: By the way, how is your mum?
M: Don't change the subject! Look I've got her number here.
B: Who, your mum's?
M: No! Look, phone her. Get yourself an appointment. It'll be worth it, you'll see.
B: Yeah, well, maybe … but I really don't think it'll work.
M: You are just so stubborn! I don't know how Linda puts up with you!

3   L = Linda   B = Bob

L: How long are you going to keep putting it off? It's not fair, you know, you're not the only one who has to put up with it. It makes you irritable and moody – you get tired and snap at the kids … I'm sick and tired of telling you to see a doctor … and I'm sick and tired of your bad moods and your moaning and grumbling. I know, I know, it's no fun having a bad back, you've told me that a million times – but it's no fun for us either. There are a hundred things you could do – take some painkillers for a start – buy a new chair for your desk – make an appointment with the osteopath – I know Mike's given you her number.
B: Her number? So it was your idea was it? You put him up to it …
L: Yes, I did. And what's wrong with that? I thought you might listen to Mike – seeing as you don't listen to me!
B: Ah, yes, come to think of it, Mike did mention you when he gave me the number, I should have known.
L: Bob! I just don't get you. I'm being serious here – and you're not even listening! I have had enough. Do something about your back or …
B: Or … ?
L: Or … I don't know. I'll have to put painkillers in your food or something!
B: Listen, I'm sorry, I really am. You're right, I need to do something about it and I promise I will.
L: Hmm … I'll believe that when I see it!

B: Come here – you know you look beautiful when you're angry … so, what's for dinner?

L: Ah, talking of dinner, it's your turn!

B: My turn? Again? Oh, aw, I don't think I can … I've got a bad back …

L: Bob Davis, I swear , I'll …..

**4 B = Bob A = Ann K = Kate
G = Greg**

B: Yeah, and well, she just flew off the handle, I mean she was really, seriously angry with me …

A: I'm not surprised. You can be really stubborn sometimes you know …

G: Yeah, and you get pretty tetchy too.

B: I know, I know, I should try and control my temper.

A: And as for what she was saying, well, she's right you know. You do need to do something about it. There's no medal for suffering in silence.

K: Not that you do suffer in silence … I wish you would!

B: Thank you Kate! But yeah, I know what you're saying – even little Jo was telling me off the other day. 'Dad, can't you be happy sometimes?' he said …

G: Bright for a three-year-old, your Jo!

B: Yeah, I know, but it's a bit much getting told off by your own son!

A: Well, there you go, as I was saying, you'll have to do something about it, won't you?

5 B = Bob L = Linda

B: Anytime this week, well, really in the evening if possible. I finish work at about 6.30. Thursday, 7.15? Yes, that sounds fine. Thanks great, thanks a lot. Goodbye. I've done it!

L: What have you done?

B: I've made an appointment to see the osteopath.

L: You have! At last!

B: Oh yes, and by the way, have I told you I love you?

9B Listening exercises 2 & 3
🔘 2.15

1

And finally, one of the strangest stories to have come our way for a long time. Over the last few days, reports have been coming in of strange things happening in Tunbridge Wells. For those of you not familiar with Tunbridge Wells in the county of Kent, the town is not known for its serious crime, although, like any town of its size, it is not entirely free from minor problems. But Tunbridge now has its very own superhero – a masked man in an orange suit, brown underpants and cape – who patrols the town, sorting out life's little inconveniences. Monkey Man, as he is known, was sighted earlier this week when local resident, Gladis Webb, suddenly became aware of a strange masked man behind her.

In a letter to the *Kent and East Sussex Courier*, she explained that the man had tapped her on the shoulder and returned the purse that she had lost earlier. In other reported sightings,

Monkey Man has helped motorists change their tyres, helped old ladies across the street and put rubbish in the rubbish bins. Until yesterday, Monkey Man's acts of goodness had been restricted to the kind of thing that any good citizen is expected to do. But the Tunbridge superhero came to the rescue of a young woman in the town centre. Monkey Man arrived in time to save her from a group of aggressive young men. A spokesman for the local police said they were always sympathetic to acts of good citizenship, but they hoped that Monkey Man would understand that some situations were better left to professional police officers. Their views were repeated by the town's mayor, Stanley Ward, who supported Monkey Man's acts so long as they remained 'community-minded'.

Meanwhile, national newspapers like *The Sun* and *The Daily Express* have picked up on the story and are asking their readers if they know the identity of the mysterious masked Monkey Man. A Polish tourist, Wozyck Wozyck, who was visiting the town, was lucky enough to take a photo of the Tunbridge superhero with his mobile phone and sent it to the *Kent and East Sussex Courier*. *The Daily Telegraph* suggested that the masked man might be Darren Hasell, a 35-year-old sports coach with a black belt in karate. But local people do not think he is connected to the man in the orange suit.

9B Listening exercises 5 & 6
🔘 2.16

2

And finally, we turn to an update on the story of the Tunbridge Wells superhero. The orange-suited Monkey Man has been involved in a number of incidents that have been reported as far away as Australia and New York. Helping old ladies cross the road, picking up litter and dutifully putting it in the rubbish bins, saving a young lady in danger from a group of aggressive youths, Monkey Man's time has been devoted to improving the day-to-day life of the good citizens of Tunbridge Wells. But it seems that the press has got a lot of egg on its face. We can now reveal that the identity of the caped crusader of Tunbridge Wells is none other than Matt Lees, a 31-year-old hairdresser, who, along with two friends, Chris Shaw and Rachel Bishop, was responsible for the strange series of events. The three friends made everything up from the start. Beginning with a handful of letters to the local newspaper, they were pleased and more than a little surprised when the paper believed the letters. Mr Lees pretended to be Gladis Webb and also dressed up as Monkey Man. Rachel Bishop took photos of him in the street and pretended to be the Polish tourist with the unlikely name when she sent the photo to the *Kent and East Sussex Courier*. National newspapers were so intent on publishing the story that they never checked out the sources. If they had, they would have quickly discovered that none of the witnesses actually existed. Prankster Chris Shaw insisted that it was all a joke but said that it was interesting to see how the press

could be so gullible. 'You wonder what else they print,' observed Mr Shaw.
And now over to Brian Moloney with all the latest sports news …

9D Listening exercises 1 & 2
🔘 2.17

S = Steve A = Amanda

S: Right, so it's back to the studios to take a closer look at today's news stories. So, Amanda, what have you got for us today?

A: Well, Steve, there's a great survey that's just come out to find the UK's top ten most hated professions.

S: Most hated professions?

A: Yes, that's right. Care to guess what comes in at number one?

S: I reckon number one has got to be tax inspectors.

A: Well, no, actually, you're wrong. In fact, surprising as it may seem, they're not actually in the top ten at all, although you're not going to be at all surprised to find out who the number one most hated profession is.

S: Well if it's not tax inspectors, then I guess it must be traffic wardens?

A: Yes, that's the one. It seems that despite admitting that traffic wardens are a necessary evil, there was still no doubt in people's minds that they are the number one high street villains.

S: I can believe it. I can remember the last time I got a ticket. I was furious. I'd only gone in to the shop for five minutes, and there she was, writing out the ticket, and even though I said I was going to move the car straight away, she still booked me. I couldn't believe it!

A: You and a thousand others like you, Steve! But it seems that the traffic wardens themselves aren't too happy with the results. They claim that they're only trying to keep our town centres free of unwanted traffic, and that, despite all the stories to the contrary, they are not vindictive and often give drivers a second chance if they say they're moving on.

S: I can't say I've ever seen that happen! So, who else is in the list? Lawyers? Journalists? Paparazzi?

A: No, actually, none of those made it to the top ten.

S: None of them? I find that hard to believe! So, who are the people we love to hate?

A: Well, there are quite a few I agree with, and I think you will too: telesales reps, for example. And although I know it's not their fault, and they're only doing their job and all that, I absolutely hate being disturbed at home by cold callers.

S: Yeah, and the phone companies themselves are the worst. I don't answer the phone anymore. Anyone who wants to get hold of me can text me or leave me a message!

A: Yes, and I don't suppose anyone's going to stand up and defend nightclub bouncers or estate agents either.

S: Are they there, then?

A: Yes, at numbers 2 and 3 respectively. Followed by motorcycle couriers and bus drivers.

S: There must have been a lot of stressed-out city drivers answering that survey!

A: Yes, and although I tend to agree with most of what's on the list, there are some surprises too. Footballers, for example? I thought they were everybody's heroes, not one of the top ten villains.

S: Yeah, well, they're supposed to be heroes aren't they, but in spite of their special hero status and all the perks and privileges of their job, they can be real arrogant, obnoxious thugs at times. I think that's the thing. Despite the fact that they're paid like gods, they often behave like pigs: swearing, spitting, starting fights. Hardly the stuff that heroes are made of.

A: Yeah, well then you'll agree with the next one too Steve: reality TV show contestants.

S: Yes! Definitely. Famous for being famous. What kind of a job is that? Not really a job at all. In fact I think I'd put them at number one.

A: Well they're actually at number ten, after PR people and politicians.

S: Ah, the professional liars! I'm sorry, is that very cynical of me? So what about the flip side? Do they say anything about the most respected jobs? Radio show host maybe? Disc jockeys?

A: No, I'm afraid not, despite your own dazzling performance Steve, I think you're going to have to content yourself with not being one of the baddies … no, the most respected professionals are members of the armed forces, followed by rescue workers, nurses, vets, teachers, ambulance drivers and firefighters.

S: Hum, just as it should be. Right, all interesting stuff, thanks Amanda. If you've got any comments please drop us a line on somethingtosay@radiotn.com
And now for a quick look at the weather. Chris, what have you got in store for us today?

10B Listening exercises 1 & 2
🌐 2.20

W = Woman   M = Man

W: An extraordinary thing happened at work today.

M: What? Moira turned up on time for once?

W: No – she was the usual fifteen minutes late!

M: So what happened then?

W: Well, a few weeks ago, I was giving Moira a hand going through the clothes from the recycling bin as usual, and there was this black leather coat, a man's one, and it was quite nice, much nicer than most of the stuff we get, and Moira said she thought we could probably get three or four hundred pounds for it, so we put it in the window, and, you'll never guess what.

M: What?

W: Well, we sold it the same day, after only a couple of hours as a matter of fact, this woman came in, and she said she'd seen it in the window and without asking how

much it was or anything, she said she'd give us five hundred pounds for it.

M: Five hundred quid. That's all right, innit?

W: Yes, not bad at all – but that's not the funny bit about it.

M: Oh? So?

W: Well, the thing is, the next day, this man walked in – smart, good-looking, expensive suit …

M: Just Moira's type!

W: A City type, merchant banker or something, but he seemed all embarrassed, he sort of gave the impression that he'd rather be anywhere in the world than there, you know, in a second-hand clothes shop. He could probably have bought the whole shop if he'd wanted to. Anyway, after a minute or two, he came up to us and asked if we had any black leather coats. So Moira told him that we'd sold a really nice one just the day before, but we didn't have any others. So then he asked us if we could describe the coat, which we did, and his face sort of lit up. 'That's my coat!' he said.

M: So why had he given it away?

W: Well, Moira asked him the same question. She, she fancied him a bit actually, well, actually, more than a bit, you know Moira, and the man explained that his girlfriend – his ex-girlfriend – had put the coat, which was his favourite coat, in the recycling bin after they'd had an argument. And now he wanted to know if there was any way to get it back. So Moira took his phone number and said she'd give him a call if she saw the woman who bought it again.

M: You're not going to tell me that Moira and this man are, um, …

W: Hang on, I'm getting to it. Give me a second. Anyway, so, this was, what, I don't know a week or two ago, and we never saw the woman again, and then this morning, me and Moira were going through a new pile of stuff from the recycling bin and Moira was saying how she'd been thinking about the man, the one who wanted his coat back, and how, maybe, she might give him a call, anyway, you know, just to say that we hadn't seen the woman, but then, there, at the bottom of the pile of stuff, there it was.

M: What? The black coat?

W: Yes.

M: The same one?

W: Yes, there it was. The very same black coat. Moira was on the phone in a flash and she told him that we'd found his coat, and that, if he wanted, she'd take it round to him.

M: And did she?

W: Well, yes, I think so, I mean, that's what she said she was going to do … but I haven't heard from her since lunchtime, because, erm, so we gave the coat a quick clean, got rid of the fluff and stuff, and then I felt that there was something in one of the pockets. There was this envelope and when we opened it – inside there was two thousand pounds in twenty pound notes. Two thousand. Can you imagine? That's more than we make in a week. So then Moira said we, she said it was a bit

risky having that much money in the shop and that she'd take it to the bank on the way to meeting the coat man. I haven't seen her since.

M: What do you mean you haven't seen her since? Wasn't she supposed to come back to the shop?

W: Yes, but well, it wasn't that busy and you … they might have got talking or whatever, you know … but anyway, that's not the end of the story, because later on this afternoon, another man came into the shop, and he came straight up to the counter and asked me if we had a black leather coat. I just shook my head and said sorry, no, and he started to give me this long explanation about how his wife had given him this coat, but he really didn't like it and the smell of the leather gave him a headache, bla, bla, bla, so he told her, his wife that it had been stolen from his office, but, in fact, he'd put it in the recycling bin. But then he realized that he'd left some money in the pocket and that's why he wanted to get the coat back.

M: So did you tell him?

W: No, no I didn't … I took his number and said I'd call him if his coat turned up.

M: But what about the money? I mean, it's his, isn't it? He must be worried sick …

W: I know, I know, but I was waiting to see what Moira thought. Oh, that must be her now. Hello? Moira?

10D Listening exercises 1, 2 & 3
🌐 2.21

I = Interviewer   A = Annette

I: Hello, come in, please sit down.

A: Thank you.

I: So, erm … Annette? Can you tell us something about your work experience to date?

A: Erm, yes, well, I've been working in the communications sector since I left university. To start with, I worked as a volunteer at a local radio station, covering local news and human interest stories. More recently I've been working as a press officer for a local homeless charity. Um, the job involves attending conferences, giving talks and, most importantly, taking part in the grassroots work of the charity, on the street, coordinating the work of the volunteers and setting up self help groups for the homeless people we work with.

I: I see, and why are you interested in the post of Communications Coordinator?

A: Um, well, for several reasons. First of all because it would be the logical next step in my career. In my current job I write press releases for the local press and liaise with local volunteers to develop stories and case studies and I think this post would give me the chance to develop my skills in this area. Um, secondly because I want to keep working in the non-profit sector and I'm particularly interested in the grassroots development work, you know facilitating the local projects, and coordinating the work of the local volunteers. That's an area that I would really like to learn more about. When I was studying at university I took three months out to travel around Latin America and I was lucky enough to get involved in some voluntary conservation work in Costa Rica. I actually came across some volunteers who were working for the RPA …

I: Ah, so you know something about our work out there already?

A: Yes, I do and I was very impressed by what I saw.

I: I'm sorry, I interrupted you, you were saying?

A: Erm, yes, and thirdly because I would love to live and work in Central America. I fell in love with that part of the world when I was out there and I've always wanted to go back.

I: I see. Thank you. And what do you think you personally can bring to this job?

A: Well, as my CV shows, I've got quite a lot of experience of writing promotional materials, I've been running the press office single-handed in my current position since our senior communications officer retired last year. I've worked on various projects where I had to coordinate the work of small groups of volunteer workers. I'm aware of – and interested in – the issues surrounding your work in Central America. And maybe most importantly I'm hardworking, keen and enthusiastic.

I: Fine, erm, what do you see as your strengths, Annette?

A: Well, I enjoy a challenge. When I started my present job I'd never written a press release before, but I soon learnt. I think I'm a quick learner and I take pride in my ability to meet tight schedules and deadlines. I think I work well under pressure and I'm usually good at setting priorities and keeping to them. I think this is probably important in this post as there are so many different responsibilities that need juggling.

I: Um, and what about your weaknesses?

A: Well, I know I have a tendency to get carried away sometimes and that I can sometimes spend far too long on one project to the detriment of others, so, as I said before, I always make sure I set my priorities and don't waste time on tasks that can be dealt with later.

I: Are there any aspects of the job that worry you? Any aspect you think you may need extra help or support with?

A: No, not really. Um, although the context is new and the job is probably a lot bigger than anything I've tackled before, I don't think I'll have any particular problems. In fact I'm really looking forward to being able to improve my Spanish.

I: Ah, and your level of Spanish is pretty good then?

A: Yes, I think so. I'm certainly capable of getting by in most day-to-day situations.

I: Right, thank you Annette and now, let's turn to some more practical issues, if we may …

11B Listening exercises 2 & 3

🌐 2.24

G = Gavin   M = Mark

M: What's this, then?

G: A map of the world.

M: Not as I know it!

G: Yeah, well it wouldn't be, would it? You'd have London at the centre, with England about five times the size of the United States!

M: Yeah, yeah, but what is it? I mean, where did you get it?

G: On the internet. There's this great website, 'mapping the world', it's got loads of really interesting stuff, just about every map that was ever drawn, from the Romans to the Aussies!

M: Is that what this is, then, the Aussie map of the world?

G: Sort of. It's based on an Australian map …

M: Yeah, I can see … it's upside down!

G: You're bound to say that, aren't you? And why is it 'upside down' then?

M: Well, because all maps have North at the top …

G: All maps, eh? All the maps you've seen, maybe. So North is up, is it? Is that some kind of absolute truth?

M: I don't know, I suppose not, but it is weird though, isn't it?

G: Yeah, that's what everybody says … and every time someone sees it for the first time, they do exactly what you're doing now too!

M: What's that? What am I doing?

G: Trying to turn it around!

M: What do you mean?

G: Well, look at you, with your head on one side like that, trying to put North back on top!

M: Oh yeah, sorry! It just takes some getting used to!

G: Yeah, you Pom! That's why it was designed, to get people like you to rethink your prejudices! There's a good story to it actually. Want to hear it?

M: Have I got any choice?

G: No!

M: Go on then, if you must.

G: Well, back in the sixties there was this schoolboy, Stuart McArthur his name was, and he drew a South-is-up map for his geography homework. Thought it was pretty cool, but his teacher told him he'd have to draw it the 'right' way up if he was going to pass his assignment and it got him thinking. Then a couple of years later he was on a school exchange in Japan with a load of other exchange students, mainly from the States, and he got sick and tired of them going on an on about how he came from 'down under' and 'the bottom of the world' and all that stuff, so he decided to put things right and designed the first South-is-up map, took him a couple of years, but in 1979, when he was just 21 years old he published his map with Australia right there in the middle and on top of the world.

M: Um, and this is it?

G: Yeah, this is it. With a couple of bits and pieces that I've added.

M: What? You've added?

G: Yeah right. On this website I was telling you about you design your own map. You select the basic map you want to use as your background and then you pick and choose the places that are most important to you. And you magnify them.

M: Oh, right. Nice idea!

G: And each of the places you choose can be magnified as much as you like. Like here, on the Melbourne map, see the smaller circle inside?

M: Yeah …

G: That's where my mum lives!

M: And what about the others?

G: Well, this is a beach on Koh Tao, turtle island, the best holiday of my life, just after finishing school, me and some mates, travelled around Thailand for a couple of months looking for the perfect beach … and this is it! Probably crawling with tourists by now. But at the time it was practically deserted, each of us had our own personal palm tree!

M: Not bad. Ever been back?

G: No, I think about it more or less every day, but it was a once in a lifetime holiday, couldn't be repeated.

M: What's this one then? You've actually highlighted something in Europe? Oh, I see, it's your wife's, Bel's, parents' place, isn't it? Somewhere in the South of Portugal? The Alentejo or something isn't it?

G: Yeah, that's right. Zambujeira. Not a bad place for a holiday, either! You ever been?

M: No.

G: You should go.

M: More beautiful beaches?

G: Yeah, of course! And the surf's not bad … well for Europe.

M: How's Bel doing, by the way?

G: She's loving it. Things are going really well for her. All the people in Washington are really great, and she's doing a lot of travelling. To and fro between Washington and New York every couple of days. Sounds fun. For her. But she's coming back home on Sunday for a week or so. Short and sweet, but better than nothing.

M: Yeah, I guess. OK, one more, what's this then? I mean, I can see it's New Zealand, but why's it highlighted?

G: Ah, that's a pipe dream.

M: What do you mean?

G: Well, I've always, always wanted to go there on holiday. I think maybe every Aussie I know wants to go! It's beautiful, the whole island is just one big natural paradise. It's got to be seen.

M: Planning on going there soon?

G: No, not unless I win the lottery!

11D Listening exercises 1 & 2
🌐 2.27

P = Presenter   S = Sophie

P: Hello and welcome to *Talking Pictures*. Today we've got Sophie Matthews in the studio with us. Sophie's a veteran location scout and she's going to let us in on some of the secrets of location hunting. Sophie, what exactly is a location scout?

S: Well, a location scout is someone who, as the name suggests, finds locations – for films, TV programmes or adverts. And it could be any kind of location: a street, a building, a historic setting, or a particular kind of landscape.

P: What kind of work do you usually do?

S: All sorts, I mean it very much depends on the kind of project you're working on. When I was starting out I used to do all sorts – and I used to work as a location manager as well – but that side of the job is just so stressful.

P: What's the difference?

S: Well, a scout finds the locations, and a manager makes sure the filming can happen.

P: Ah ha.

S: Yeah, you know, finds out who owns the location, gets permission to film there, finds accommodation for everyone, even makes the tea and sandwiches if necessary! It was fine to start with, I mean, I really enjoyed the buzz of it all, you know, meeting the stars and all that, but there's always so much to do and so little time to do it – it's such hard work and everything has to be done so quickly! It gets really exhausting. Now I just do the scouting – the fun bit!

P: And what kind of locations do you scout for?

S: I still do all kinds, but I particularly enjoy hunting out natural landscapes.

P: And what exactly does that involve? A lot of travelling I imagine?

S: Yes, it does and I really love the travelling. But I also do a lot of the research work from home – surfing the internet, watching travel documentaries, reading photography journals and travel magazines and then once I've got some clear ideas, I start travelling.

P: Do you work on your own?

S: Yeah, usually, just me and my camera. I get as much footage as I can of the locations I'm interested in and then take them back to see if they match the image in the director's head. That is definitely the most difficult thing to do. I mean, the script might just say 'rolling green hills' so off you go looking for rolling green hills. You reckon you've found exactly what the director wants, a wide green valley surrounded by wooded hills, and when you take the photos back to the studio, they say, 'where are the corn fields?' or 'I wanted some mountain peaks in the background' and then it's back to the drawing board.

P: So what are you working on at the moment?

S: I'm looking at locations for a new big budget adaptation of *Gulliver's Travels*.

P: Ah, *Gulliver's Travels*?

S: Yeah, it's going to be an epic – it's going to cover all four voyages – which means a lot of locations to find – and just to add a bit of spice, the studios have asked for them all to be within easy reach of each other!

P: That sounds like a tall order.

S: Yes, it is and there are so many factors to take into account: accessibility – film needs to be sent back to the studios for processing every day, so we need to be within easy reach of an airport, accommodation – there are so many people involved in the making of the film – it can be up to 100, 150 people all told and there has to be somewhere for them all to stay. So it's best if the location is within easy reach of a sizeable town. But for a big budget movie like this, it's not too important. The main challenge for us with Gulliver is translating the imaginary world into a real one on the screen. It needs to be spectacular enough to make a really strong first impression but spectacular scenery tends to be well known.

P: Though sometimes it's the film that puts the scenery on the map.

S: Very true, take Cappadocia in Turkey for example.

P: Yeah ...

S: It's an incredible place – a maze of narrow valleys and gorges, full of incredible rock formations and caves. When the *Star Wars* producers first found it it was a quiet little place – now it's a buzzing tourist resort. It was a perfect location, so out of the way, so untouched by the modern world – and that's so important. There were no roads, or power lines or modern buildings in the way. And it's such an incredible place, there's nowhere else like it in the world. That's the scout's challenge: to find somewhere that looks like it only exists in the film.

P: Like Middle Earth in the *Lord of the Rings* trilogy?

S: That's right. That's another excellent example – all the filming there was done on location in New Zealand – the director's home – and the scenery really is amazing – and so varied too.

P: And the films have done a lot to boost the tourist industry over there too, haven't they?

S: Yes, there are so many tour operators offering tours of Middle Earth, it's incredible.

P: So going back to *Gulliver's Travels* then. Have you come up with anything?

S: Yeah, we think we have, it's not totally decided yet and things could change but it's looking like it could be the Azores.

P: The Azores? Why the Azores?

S: For a number of reasons. First of all, the islands are so remote, so far from everywhere, it feels like a world apart already. Then they've got such a huge variety of scenery and landscapes. They've got golden beaches and gentle rolling hills, but they've also got dramatic cliff faces and dark, dense rain forest. It's just such a magical place. And more importantly, so few people know it, I mean, so few people visit the islands that they're practically unknown. We had looked at the Canary Islands as another possibility, I mean, the Canary Islands have got the same variety of landscapes – if not more – but they're too well-known – so many people go there on holiday, and there's so much footage of the islands on holiday programmes and friends' photos that they're not such a good choice – when you're creating an imaginary world, it needs to be a world apart, the landscape needs to be out of the ordinary – something you're seeing for the first time – and we think the Azores will give us all that.

P: So, what's the next step?

S: Well, if the director goes for it, then I need to go back again, do some more detailed scouting and match places to scenes in the film, and then it'll be time for me to step back and let the location manager take over from there ... and good luck to her!

P: And what about you? Back to your armchair?

S: No, not at the moment. I haven't got any other projects pending so I'm going to do a bit of non work-related travelling.

P: Anywhere interesting?

S: Yes, the fjords of Norway.

P: Plenty of scope there for more locations ...

S: Yes, one day, you never know.

P: Well, thanks a lot for being with us today Sophie.

S: Thank you.

12A Grammar exercise 3
🌐 2.28

A priceless hoard of 3,000 Saxon coins was found yesterday as a woman was digging in her back garden. The coins had been packed into a wooden box which broke as it was being dug out of the ground. The coins are in the care of a local museum where they are being cleaned in a special laboratory. They will then be taken to the museum in York for further examination. A legal expert said that even though the coins were found on Mrs Barrett's property they could still be ruled as the property of the state.

12B Listening exercises 1 & 2
🌐 2.29

Ask most people what they know about bounty hunters and they'll probably think of a Clint Eastwood-like hero from a Hollywood cowboy movie. In the wild Wild West of Hollywood fantasy, the bounty hunter is the ultimate macho man, on the trail of a bank robber who is wanted dead or alive. If he manages to catch up with him, the bounty hunter will collect the reward money before identifying another desperado and riding off, once more, into the sunset.

In twenty-first century America, the 'dead or alive' posters have long gone, but it may come as a surprise to learn that bounty hunters are still alive and well.

If you are arrested for many crimes in the US, you can remain free, until the time of your trial, if you pay bail or a sum of money to the court. If you're too hard up to pay the money yourself, you can often borrow it from a 'bail bondsman'. When you appear in court, the money is returned, but if you don't turn up for your court appearance, you lose the money. This is where the bounty hunter comes in. If someone has borrowed money from a bail bondsman and then doesn't appear in court, the bondsman will employ a bounty hunter to find the person and get the money back.

It's an unpleasant job and one that is illegal in most countries. Bounty hunters are tough and cynical and many are ex-criminals themselves. When times are good they have money to burn, but most of their lives are spent on the breadline. It is perhaps the last job in the world where you would expect to find someone like Domino Harvey. Domino was born in Britain. Her father, Laurence, was a well-known actor and her mother, Pauline Stone, was a model for *Vogue*. From birth, Domino wanted for nothing, living in the lap of luxury, but all the money and the glamour and the privileges could not make up for the loss of her father who died of stomach cancer when she was only four years old. Domino was suddenly worth a fortune and never needed to worry about money again. But, she was said to be a very difficult child. She was described as aggressive and ungirly, preferring to fight with the boys, rather than play with dolls. By the time she was old enough to leave school, she had already been expelled from four of them.

Domino moved into an apartment in west London and worked briefly as a DJ and she designed and sold T-shirts in a market. Friends say that she was relaxed and happy and seemed to be enjoying her life but again boredom set in and she was soon looking for new sources of excitement. It has been reported that she started a career in modelling. She certainly had the looks for it, and her mother had all the necessary contacts. She was said to have worked with the Ford modelling agency, but when questioned, none of the staff there could recall ever having come across anyone with the name of Domino Harvey. It's also believed that she took a course in acting – possibly with the intention of following in her father's footsteps. But, once again, if this is true, there is no firm evidence for it.

In 1989, she moved to the States to join her mother, but instead of joining the Hollywood jet set, she embarked on a series of adventures. She is rumoured to have worked first as a ranch hand in San Diego and then as a volunteer fire fighter on the border of Mexico. It was during this period that she took a two-week course to become a bounty hunter. The instructor on the course, Ed

Martinez, later became her partner. In their time together as bounty hunters, Domino and Ed are known to have caught more than 50 fugitives.

While she was working with Ed Martinez, chasing criminals across California and beyond, news got to journalists in the UK of a beautiful teenage model who had decided to become a bounty hunter. An interview in a Sunday newspaper came to the notice of Tony Scott, a Hollywood producer. He tracked Domino down and persuaded her to sell him her life story. He is said to have paid more than $300,000 for it.

The film was finally released in 2005 but this was one Hollywood story that was not to have a happy ending. Domino was reported to be feeling unhappy with the way her life had been portrayed in the film. She was thinking of making a documentary to tell the real story, but her time was running out. After a lifetime of excess, she was arrested for possession of drugs. Domino had no problems organizing bail, but she never made it to court. At the age of 35, while she was under house arrest in her luxury home in the Hollywood Hills, Domino Harvey was found dead of a drug overdose.

12D Listening exercises 2 & 3
🔊 2.31

Next time you take a dollar bill out of your billfold, the chances are you won't give it a second's thought. Generally speaking, people are thinking more about the coffee they're about to buy than the dirty piece of paper money they're holding in their hand. They see dollar bills every day of their lives but never look at them. They probably don't realize that the paper in their hand isn't actually paper at all. Dollar bills are a mixture of 75% cotton and 25% linen, and if you burn a bill, you'll see that it burns in a different way from paper. That's not to say that I would recommend you begin burning the money in your hand. Burning, damaging or in any way defacing a dollar bill is a federal crime. The maximum penalty is six months in prison and the law is enforced by the American Secret Service. So look out.

Every day, the Federal Reserve prints more than 540 million dollars worth of bills. Most of them are single dollar bills and, they mostly last less than two years before they are replaced. In those two years, they can change hands hundreds of times and they can be folded eight thousand times before they begin to fall apart. If you want to know who had your dollar bill before you, you can check out a website called 'Where's George?'. Users of the site post the serial numbers of dollar bills in their possession. These serial numbers are then used to track a dollar bill from owner to owner across the country.

Regular visitors to the 'Where's George?' website sometimes specialize in particular denominations. Some folks are attracted to the rare two-dollar bill, but the best investment

is anything over 100 dollars. Big bills haven't been printed for over 50 years, and, as a rule, a ten-thousand dollar bill can be sold for more than four times its face value.

The reverse side of a dollar bill shows both sides of the Great Seal of the United States. The bald eagle is our national symbol and the thirteen stars, the thirteen arrows and the thirteen bars on the shield all represent the thirteen original colonies that declared America independent from Britain. On the other side of the seal, at the bottom of the pyramid, you can read the date 1776 in Roman numerals. 1776 – the year of the Declaration of Independence.

George Washington, whose portrait stares out at you from the middle of the bill, was, of course, the commander-in-chief of the revolutionary army that won the War of Independence and later became the country's first president.

It's easy to understand what these symbols are doing on our bills, but what is this broken pyramid and the strange eye in a triangle? It has been suggested that the pyramid and the eye are both symbols of the secret society of Freemasons. Others identify the all-seeing eye as a symbol of the Illuminati – another secret society of powerful men who are waiting for the opportunity to take control of the entire world. How did these secret societies manage to get their symbols on the Great Seal of the United States? Well, the Declaration of Independence was written by a committee of five men, but for the most part, the work was done by Thomas Jefferson. Thomas Jefferson, who became the third president of the United States, has his own portrait on the rare two-dollar bill. Jefferson, generally accepted to have been the most brilliant president this country has ever seen, was also accused of being a member of the Illuminati.

By and large, the stories that connect the symbols on the dollar bill to secret societies are more entertaining than probable. A simpler explanation for the pyramid is that it shows that the work of the country is not complete. The all-seeing eye is the Eye of Providence, or the Eye of Fortune, a symbol from ancient Egypt, and it simply means that fortune is smiling on the country. The Latin inscription *Novus Ordo Seclorum* means 'New order of the ages' and *E Pluribus Unum* above the eagle could be translated as 'From many, one'.

Whatever these things mean, just check that what you're holding in your hand is the real thing. The Treasury estimates there to be 70 million counterfeit dollars in circulation. If your bill turns out to be a fake, you can always burn it. Burning a counterfeit bill is not a crime, but check the Secret Service aren't watching you, just to be on the safe side.

1 | Review

1 Complete the text with appropriate auxiliary verbs.

Mushroom hunting (1) _____ been popular in some countries for a long time, but more and more people (2) _____ taking it up everywhere. Enthusiasts (3) _____ not need any special equipment, but care needs to (4) _____ taken with mushroom species that have not (5) _____ identified. Last year in the US, three people (6) _____ killed by eating poisonous mushrooms which they (7) _____ not correctly identified. In most cases, however, mushroom poisoning (8) _____ not lead to anything more than an upset stomach.

2 Match the openers 1–7 to the responses a–g.

1 Do you think it matters?
2 Everything was ready on time, I trust.
3 Had it all finished when you got there?
4 Has it been decided yet?
5 I expect it'll be an interesting day.
6 It took you a long time, I imagine?
7 It's going to be good fun, I think.

a Are you kidding? No, it won't.
b No, it doesn't. Of course not.
c No, it didn't. Not really.
d No, it hadn't. Not exactly, anyway.
e No, it hasn't. I'm afraid not.
f No, it isn't. No way.
g No, it wasn't. Not quite.

3 Choose the correct form to complete the questions.

1 How many people *belong / do belong* to a club of some sort?
2 What *do most people / most people* think of collecting football stickers?
3 What *does make / makes* the other people in your class laugh?
4 What sort of things *do people / do people do* on Sunday afternoons?
5 Which football team *does have / has* the most supporters?
6 Who *does have / has* the most original leisure interest in your class?
7 Who *would your class / your class would* vote for as 'Person of the Year'?

4 Speak to other students in your class. Find out the answers to the questions in exercise 3.

5 Insert *is* in the sentences.

1 What he should do take up something active like running.
2 What he's really crazy about golf.
3 What I can't understand how anyone could be interested in celebrity gossip.
4 What I enjoy most the passion of the supporters.
5 What really worries me the fact that she'll give anything a try.
6 What she will get into next anybody's guess.

6 Complete the text with expressions from the box. More than one answer is possible.

> after a while   afterwards   at first
> eventually   finally   later on   to begin with

When Gonzalo said he believed in ghosts, I thought he was joking (1) _____. But he talked about them so much that, (2) _____, I realized he was serious. (3) _____, he even asked me if I would like him to introduce me to a ghost. I laughed and said 'No way!' but he was so persuasive that I (4) _____ agreed. He took me to a room at the top of his house. (5) _____, it was completely dark, but (6) _____ I could see a weird white shape in one corner. We waited in silence for ages and (7) _____ the ghost spoke. 'I am the ghost they call 'La Llorona',' she cried, 'and I have come to warn you.'

2 | Review

1 Complete the text using *will, won't, keep* and *forever.*

Every spring, hundreds of frogs (1) _____ march through our back garden at any time of day or night. And there's no way of stopping them, they just (2) _____ coming. Their final destination is a pond in the field behind us. The problem is that there's a road at the end of our garden and, of course, they're (3) _____ getting run over. So we go out and carry them across to the other side. We've tried building bridges and tunnels but we know they (4)_____ use them. They're (5) _____ hopping onto the road and we just (6) _____ helping them across!

2 Replace *used to* with *would* where possible in the text.

My great aunt Hilda (1) **used to** have a pet Chihuahua. The two of them (2) **used to** go everywhere together. They (3) **used to** be completely inseparable. My aunt Hilda (4) **used to** dress her up in doll's clothes. The dog didn't seem to mind, in fact she seemed quite (5) **used to** it. She (6) **used to** take it to expensive restaurants where the dog (7) **used to** eat from the same plate as her. The waiters didn't like it at first, but then they soon got (8) **used to** it – and the big tips my great aunt Hilda (9) **used to** leave behind!

3 Rearrange the words to make phrases.

1 think   personally   I
2 me   ask   if   you
3 be   honest   to   perfectly
4 convinced   am   absolutely   I
5 but   may   wrong   be   I
6 as   concerned   as   I'm   far

4 Work in pairs. React to the statement in six different ways using the six expressions in exercise 3.

> *Wildlife documentaries bore me –*
> *I never watch them.*

5 Complete the sentences with a word from the box.

aggressive	cold-blooded	cuddly
obedient	inquisitive	tame

1 Everybody loves puppies, they're so cute and _____.
2 Cats are very _____ and sometimes their curiosity can get them into trouble.
3 Crocodiles are ferocious, _____ killers.
4 Whether a dog is docile or _____ depends completely on its training.
5 Pigs are not difficult to train and can be very _____, even more so than dogs.
6 The squirrels in our garden are very _____ and will even eat food from our hands.

6 Put the lines in the correct order to make a paragraph.

☐ a point of trying to clear things
☐ in when I'm talking and don't want to face
☐ add up. That can be incredibly infuriating.
☐ When I have an argument I always make
☐ up as quickly as possible. But I draw the
☐ the fact that what they say just doesn't
☐ line with people who insist on butting

7 Cross out the incorrect option in the sentences below.

1 He *gets angry / gets mad / gets around* when the dog chews his shoes.
2 More people need to *get on with / get involved in / get interested* in local charities.
3 If we need to *get around / get along / get somewhere* fast, we use a taxi.
4 The two of them *get on / get along / get in touch* really well despite the difference in age.
5 He *gets somewhere / gets there / gets to the* door before I've even put the key in the lock.
6 Anger therapy can help you learn how not to *get really worked up / get aggressive / get interested.*

3 | Review

1 Complete the advertisement with the relative clauses a–g.

a that has been well-chosen
b that is right for you
c that will never happen to us
d that you can get
e that you ever spend
f that you wear
g who can defend your case

LLC

We all hope that an appearance in court is something (1)_____. But if it does, you need the best advice (2)_____. Your first priority will be a lawyer (3)_____, but sometimes a good lawyer is not enough.

Judges and juries are only human and you will be judged, in part, by the clothes (4)_____. An outfit (5)_____ can make all the difference between a small fine and a prison sentence.

At Legal Look Consultants, we will help you to find the appearance (6)_____. Our small consultation fee may be the best money (7)_____!

Call 0800 911911 now!

2 In which relative clauses in exercise 1 can you omit the relative pronoun?

3 Complete the quotations with a relative pronoun where necessary.

1 … an individual _____ appearance was so repulsive I had to have my mirrors insured. (*Miss Piggy*)
2 Her hat is a creation _____ will never go out of style. It will look just as ridiculous year after year. (*Fred Allen*)
3 I wish I had invented blue jeans. They have expression, modesty, sex appeal, simplicity – all _____ I hope for in my clothes. (*Yves Saint Laurent*)
4 My philosophy has always been to help women and men feel comfortable and confident through the clothes _____ they wear. (*Giorgio Armani*)
5 Only men _____ are not interested in women are interested in women's clothes. (*Anatole France*)
6 Women's clothes: never wear anything _____ panics the cat. (*PJ O'Rourke*)

4 Choose the correct participle to complete the sentences.

1 Anyone *acted / acting* as dumb as him deserves what he gets.
2 His style consultant, *blamed / blaming* for a number of mistakes, will probably lose his job.
3 I saw Sue at the party, *looked / looking* her best.
4 She was unhappy about the photograph, *taken / taking* while she was on holiday by the paparazzi.
5 The town was full of fans, *had / having* a look-out for celebrities.
6 Two of the players, *psyched / psyching* up for the big event, were sent off after a fight.

5 Work in pairs. Look at the photo and think of at least five things that these football supporters did to prepare for the match. Write a short description of their preparations using the words in the box.

| as well as | besides | in addition |
| on top of that | what's more | |

Compare your description with other pairs of students.

6 Complete the adjectives in the sentences with the beginnings in the box.

| clean | second | short | well | worn |

1 The internet is the best place to look for _____-hand books and DVDs.
2 You don't have to be _____-off to enjoy yourself on holiday. But it helps!
3 Cheap, high street clothes can look scruffy and _____-out after only a couple of washes.
4 Most catwalk fashions are very _____-lived and only look good on tall, skinny models.
5 Parents are always happier if their daughters' boyfriends are _____-shaven and well-dressed.

4 | Review

1 In the text below, four of the verbs in italics should be in the past simple. Change the incorrect verbs.

Sally (1) *has been* scared of snakes for as long as she can remember. She (2) *has never actually had* any personal contact with snakes. In fact, she (3) *has always avoided* them as much as possible. She (4) *has refused* to go on trips to the zoo when she (5) *has been* at school, preferring to stay in her classroom and get on with her homework. Then, two weeks ago, she (6) *has met* and (7) *fallen* in love with Tim, an avid snake lover. Sally (8) *has now decided* that love is stronger than fear and she (9) *has signed up* for a course to help her overcome her phobia. Maybe, one day, she, Tim and his giant Boa, Barry, can all share a happy home.

2 Work in pairs. Complete the radio reports below with phrases from the box. What record do you think each person is trying to break?

| 2,356 | 3 days non-stop | 32 hours | 36 |
| 42 minutes and 37 seconds | | 1985 | |

1 Jon Brodie has been sitting in a bathtub full of rattlesnakes for more than _____.
2 Stevie Mars has been juggling balls underwater for exactly _____.
3 Dick Green has escaped from _____ handcuffs.
4 Joanna Smith has eaten _____ hotdogs in the last hour.
5 Tina and Mario Di Rossi have been dancing the tango for _____.
6 Sue Townley hasn't cut her nails since _____.

Which record do you think
* requires the greatest skill?
* is the craziest? Why?

3 Rewrite the sentences below using the words in brackets.

1 Bob's going on holiday next week because he wants to spend more time with his family. (*so that*)
2 He's taking a laptop because he thinks he'll have time to do some work. (*in case*)
3 He's doing a lot of extra work because he wants to impress his boss. (*in order to*)
4 He has to impress his boss if he wants to have a chance of promotion. (*otherwise*)
5 His boss says he needs to be more self-assured if he wants to do his job well. (*in order to*)
6 Bob's signed up for an assertiveness course to gain more confidence. (*so that*)
7 He's started looking at the job ads in the paper because he's worried the course won't work. (*in case*)

4 Use the words on the right to form another word that fits the space in the lines.

Are you a (1) _____ lover of adventure, or do you prefer not to take part in (2) _____ sports and pastimes? Either way, exactly how (3) _____ you are is a simple question of chemistry. The most (4) _____ people amongst us – those who love skydiving or think that it is perfectly (5) _____ to climb into the mouth of a volcano – simply have higher levels of dopamine in their blood. People with lower levels are more (6) _____, and even activities which appear to be totally (7) _____ to most people, can make them feel quite (8) _____.

    fear
    risk
    bravery
    courage
    reason
    caution
    harm
    anxiety

5 Correct eight spelling mistakes in the text.

Cape Fear is a classic tail of revenge. Max Cady has just been released from jail. His principle aim is to track down the attorney who put him inside and torment him and his hole family. They all fall pray to his evil plans, from the dog to the attorney's plane teenage daughter. When the family can no longer bare the pressure, they escape from their home, take refuge on their yacht and set coarse for Cape Fear. But Cody is following them and he's going to insure that this is one sailing trip they'll never forget.

5 | Review

1 Choose the best verb forms to complete the story.

British graffiti artist, Banksy, (1) *joined / was joining* the ranks of the world's famous artists last week when he (2) *added / had added* one of his own works to an exhibition at the Metropolitan Museum in New York. He (3) *was entering / had entered* the museum wearing a disguise – photos on the internet show that he (4) *was wearing / had worn* an Inspector Clouseau-type raincoat and a fake beard. He (5) *put / was putting* up the painting and left the museum long before anyone (6) *noticed / was noticing* what (7) *happened / had happened*. In fact the painting formed an unofficial part of the exhibition for three days before curators finally spotted it and (8) *took / had taken* it down.

2 Complete the text using the past perfect simple or continuous. If both are possible, use the past perfect continuous.

Young American art student David Halifax (1) _____ (*arrive*) in Paris just before the outbreak of the Second World War. He (2) _____ (*find*) it difficult to make ends meet when an art dealer offered to sell some of the sketches he (3) _____ (*make*) on his visits to the Paris art galleries. David didn't realize that the dealer (4) _____ (*sell*) the sketches as original works. He soon found himself in the police station on charges of forgery. The master he (5) _____ (*study*) under was there too. He presented him with the most difficult decision he (6) _____ (*ever have to*) make.

3 Work in pairs. Describe the two pieces of art in as much detail as possible. Then answer the questions below.

Which is your favourite? Why?

4 Choose the correct words to complete the dialogue below.

A: Have you seen the new painting in reception?

B: Yes. (1) *Whatever / Whenever* made them want to buy it? It's hideous!

A: (2) *However / Whoever* made the decision certainly hasn't got good taste.

B: And (3) *however / wherever* did they manage to get it in through the door? It's huge!

A: Well, (4) *whenever / whatever* they've had to bring heavy furniture in before, they've brought it through the window.

B: Well, that's exactly where it should go now – out again!

A: What and put it in the street, you mean?

B: (5) *Whoever / Wherever*, so long as I don't have to look at it!

5 Complete the sentences with a word from the box.

away	down	to	up	up	with

1 I didn't take _____ him at all.
2 She'll find it hard to live _____ to the success of her last film.
3 I'm not surprised he turned _____ their offer of £50.
4 They set _____ the company two years ago.
5 We had a backstage pass but they turned us _____ at the door.
6 You'll have to come up _____ something better than this!

6 Choose the best phrase a–f to continue the sentences in exercise 5.

1 It was a masterpiece.
2 It's a load of rubbish!
3 It's worth a lot more than that. It's absolutely priceless.
4 It's worth a fortune now.
5 I thought he had no redeeming features.
6 They said it was worthless.

6 | Review

1 Choose the correct form to complete the questions.

1 How will your country change if global warming _____ (*continue*)?
2 How would your life be different if you _____ (*be born*) the opposite sex?
3 If you _____ (*have*) three magic wishes, how would you change your town?
4 Who can people turn to for help in your country if they _____ (*suffer*) from discrimination?
5 Would the world be a better place if more people _____ (*speak*) your language?

2 Work in pairs. Ask and answer the questions in exercise 1.

3 Combine the pairs of sentences with the words in brackets.

1 I'm happy. But not if you're not happy, too. (*so long as*)
2 We'll ask him to do it. So long as he doesn't find it acutely embarrassing. (*unless*)
3 You can borrow my flat. There's one condition: promise not to mess it up. (*provided that*)
4 I don't know how you did that. Somebody probably helped you. (*unless*)
5 You blushed. That's how I knew. (*if*)
6 He might go bright red. Then we'll know he's not telling the truth. (*if*)

4 Complete the second sentences so that they mean the same as the first. Use two or three words.

1 It's a pity that everybody doesn't have the same opportunities.
 I wish _____ the same opportunities.
2 Why can't she find a boyfriend from her own country?
 I wish _____ a boyfriend from her own country.
3 It's a shame that they allow children in here.
 I wish _____ children in here.
4 I don't like being with so many common people.
 If only there _____ many common people.
5 Why can't we all love each other?
 If only we _____ all love each other!
6 Your problem is that you can't see things as they really are.
 If only _____ things as they really are!
7 I was so unhappy to have a daughter.
 If only she _____ born a boy!

5 Match the sentences in exercise 4 to a word in the box.

ageist	elitist	idealist	socialist
sexist	racist	realist	

6 Put the lines in the correct order to make a paragraph.

Election result

☐ after a landslide victory in the general election.

☐ election because the government could not

☐ guarantee security at the polling stations.

☐ papers have now all been counted. The

☐ president's centre-right party has won 97% of

☐ the constituencies, no candidates stood for

☐ The government has been returned to power

☐ the seats in parliament. In the remaining 3% of

☐ The turnout was the usual 100% and the ballot

7 Insert six missing words in the dialogue.

A: You shouldn't say 'fireman'.
B: I'm sorry. I don't follow.
A: 'Fireman.' You shouldn't said that. I mean, it might have been a woman.
B: I'm sorry. What you saying? I'm not allowed to use the word 'fireman'?
A: No, that not what I saying. My point that if you're not sure it was a man, you should have said 'firefighter'.
B: But it was a man.
A: Fine. But all I meant say was that if you're not sure …
B: … I shouldn't have said 'man'!

I was going to say something but you won't like what I say or the words I use to say it so I'm not going to say it even though it's no big deal but you might think it's a big deal so I'm not gonna say it.

The total failure of language

1 Choose the correct forms to complete the article.

Wet cells

Experts predict that mobile internet access (1) *soon becomes / will soon* become as common as ordinary mobile phones are now. When that (2) *happens / will happen*, we (3) *are needing / will need* new handsets, and with over two billion mobile phones worldwide, we (4) *are having / will have* to find a way of recycling all the old ones.
At a conference which (5) *begins / is going to begin* today at the University of Schaerbeek, researchers from Britain (6) *are presenting / present* their design for a completely recyclable cell phone. In a press release, the team of scientists say that they (7) *are going to sell / sell* their idea to the highest bidder.
The new phone (8) *is dissolving / will dissolve* when you (9) *put / are going to put* it in water. However, the scientists (9) *might probably need / will probably need* another two years of research before the phone (10) *is / won't be* ready for commercial trials.

2 Put the verbs in brackets into the future continuous or the future perfect.

1 In the next twenty-four hours, factories around the world _____ (*produce*) more than (a) 1,500 (b) 15,000 (c) 150,000 cars.
2 In the next twenty four hours, (a) 20,000 (b) 200,000 (c) 2,000,000 more people _____ (*live*) on this planet.
3 In the next five years, the average Japanese family _____ (*eat*) (a) 10 kilos (b) 20 kilos (c) 30 kilos of seaweed.
4 In the next five years, your teacher's brain _____ (*lose*) about (a) 1 gram (b) 5 grams (c) 50 grams in weight.
5 In the next ten years, the world _____ (*make*) (a) 1% (b) 25% (c) 50% of its electricity from wind farms.
6 In the next ten years, (a) 500 million (b) 1 billion (c) 2 billion people _____ (*speak*) English.

3 Work in pairs. Can you guess the correct answers in exercise 2?

4 Insert the missing word in five of the lines below.

Some English people attach a lot of importance to their houses. They like, example, to spend the weekend doing DIY to improve their homes. They will happily spend hours in traffic jams to go to home-furnishing stores such IKEA, where they spend a fortune on kitchen accessories, light fittings and Christmas decorations, among things. Leather sofas, particular, are very popular. They also like to give their houses names like The Cottage, Rose Cottage or The Bungalow, name but the three most popular.

5 Complete the search engine queries with a word from the box.

difference	do	most	sense	time

1 You too can make a _____
   Donate blood with the Woodbury Blood Donation Service – WBDS – just one donation can save lives – you too can make a _____.
   www.wbds.org.uk/appeal.html ·Cached · Save

2 WholeBodySense: make _____ for yourself
   We should all make _____ for those little luxuries in life that can turn an ordinary day into a special one. Explore the range of WholeBodySense products and order online.
   www.wholebodysense.com/ Cached ·Save

3 Making _____ of global warming
   The latest volume in the 'Making _____' series provides a brief introduction to the issues surrounding global warming. Fully illustrated.
   www.cheapboox.com/cata?isbn=0276473-9 Save

4 Make the _____ of your laptop
   Make the _____ of your laptop with six-easy-to-follow steps. Learn more about the capabilities of your laptop or PC. Download free software for improved performance …
   www.laptoppotpal.co.uk/content_page_642.php · Save

5 Why make _____ with second best?
   Don't make _____ with second best when it comes to saving energy. SpeeVak Double Glazing® is the market leader in wood and PVC double glazing …
   www.speevak.com Save

6 Complete the sentences with the correct preposition.

1 We need to make further advances _____ solar technology.
2 Ecologists want us to reduce our consumption _____ fossil fuels.
3 In Europe, there is a growing demand _____ organic food.
4 We should all support the drive _____ cleaner energy.
5 Many countries have seen a recent increase _____ home ownership.

8 | Review

1 Choose the best forms to complete the dialogue.

"There are some things they don't teach you in medical school. I think you've got one of those things."

A: Do you think it could (1) *be / have been* serious?

B: It (2) *couldn't / might be*. I think you (3) *can't / may* be developing 'Chronic Laziness Syndrome'.

A: No, it (4) *can't be / must have been* that. I've been vaccinated against it.

B: When was your last vaccination? You might (5) *have needed / need* another injection.

A: Oh, I don't know. Recently. It (6) *can't / must* have been a month or two ago, I guess.

B: Hmm, so if it (7) *can't / might* be that, I think you (8) *may not / must* be suffering from 'Stress Avoidance Disease'.

A: Do you think I (9) *might need / must have needed* an operation?

2 Read the text and complete the sentences with a word or phrase from the box.

The work of OSHA

Most workplaces in the US have to follow the regulations of the OSHA – the Occupational Safety and Health Administration. These regulations are intended to protect people from dangers at work. Companies cannot ask their staff to work without appropriate clothing and equipment, and guards must be fitted to dangerous machines. Before the OSHA regulations, companies did not have to take any special measures, and there were more serious accidents. However, health and safety protection is expensive, and business leaders say that it is difficult to compete against other countries where employers do not have to worry about their staff's safety. These leaders believe that it is better to have safety guidelines (rather than regulations) which can be ignored when necessary. Trade unions, on the other hand, think that the regulations must be updated and strengthened.

not necessary	necessary/obligatory	prohibited

1 Following OSHA regulations is _____.
2 Asking staff to work without special equipment is _____.
3 Fitting guards to dangerous machines is _____.
4 Special protective measures were _____ before the OSHA regulations.
5 In some countries, it is _____ to adopt health and safety measures.
6 It is _____ to follow guidelines all of the time.
7 The unions think that it is _____ to have more regulations.

3 Complete the sentences with a word from the box.

drop	get	look	put	put	sort	talk

1 We'll _____ back to you as soon as we can.
2 I'm sure you'll be able to _____ something out.
3 I don't know how you _____ up with him.
4 I don't think it's a good idea to _____ it off for much longer.
5 Could you _____ me off over there by the corner?
6 Now, you must make sure that you _____ after it.
7 If you find it difficult, I'll _____ you through it.

4 Work in pairs. Look at the sentences in exercise 3 and decide …

- who might be talking to who.
- what they might be talking about.
- how the other person might respond.

5 Put the lines in the correct order to make a paragraph.

☐ high temperature. She says the migraines are
☐ hope it's not the same as my sister. She looks as
☑ I think I'm probably going down with
☐ if she is at death's door and she's got a really
☐ killing her and the doctor's told her to take a
☐ muscles are aching. I know there's a bug going
☐ round at college, so I may have caught that. I
☐ something. I'm feeling a bit run-down and my
☐ week in bed.

9 | Review

1 Complete the descriptions with the adjectives on the right.

AMERICA'S TOP MOVIE HEROES

1 Atticus Finch: the ____ lawyer who fights racism in the novel and film *To Kill a Mockingbird*

Alabaman
middle-aged

2 Clarice Starling: the FBI investigator who has to work with a cannibal with ____ teeth in the thriller *Silence of the Lambs*

metallic
pointed

3 Rick Blaine: the cynical bar-owner who is in love with a ____ freedom fighter in war-time *Casablanca*

beautiful
Swedish

4 Will Kane: the sheriff of a ____ town in the western *High Noon*, who faces the bad guys alone

dangerous
small

5 Ellen Ripley: the all-action ship's officer who fights the monster with a ____ head and no eyes in the spine-chilling *Alien*

black
long

---

2 Work in pairs. Make a list of five more heroes from films or TV programmes. Write short descriptions of them as in the examples above, but do not write the name.

Exchange your descriptions with other students. Can you identify the heroes?

3 Underline the correct modifying adverb.

1 I thought it was *absolutely / very* brilliant!
2 There are one or two moments that are *a bit / totally* terrifying.
3 It was *slightly / totally* long, maybe.
4 The script was *a little / completely* awful.
5 His voice was *absolutely / very* strange.
6 Even adults found it *completely / quite* frightening.
7 Some of the jokes were *absolutely / extremely* funny.
8 The ending was *pretty / totally* weak.

4 Complete the text with appropriate expressions of contrast.

In the last twelve months, car drivers in the town of Ellesmere Port have received nearly 20,000 parking tickets, (1) _____ only three traffic wardens work in the town.
Residents are unhappy about paying £750,000 in parking tickets every year, (2) _____ the money is spent on providing useful services. (3) _____ protests by local residents, the town council insists that the parking fines are not excessive. (4) _____ the fact that £750,000 sounds like a lot of money, it is much less than the money made in neighbouring towns.
The traffic metres and traffic wardens are expected to stay (5) _____ their unpopularity.

5 Complete sentences 1–8 with a phrase a–h.

1 The rescue workers weren't aware
2 She works as a sales rep and is devoted
3 Motorcycle couriers are very familiar
4 The estate agent was intent
5 The traffic warden became involved
6 The bouncer is responsible
7 Work as a firefighter is not restricted
8 The tax inspector was sympathetic

a for security outside the club.
b in a dangerous argument.
c of all the dangers.
d on selling us his own home.
e to her company.
f to men only.
g to my problems filling in the forms.
h with all the short-cuts in their city.

6 Match the crimes to the newspaper headlines.

armed robbery   hijack   kidnapping
murder   smuggling   vandalism

1   Terrorists release two passengers from plane

2   **Man killed in shoot-out**

3   **12-year-old girl smashed school windows**

4   Sixty thousand cigarettes found in lorry

5   Gang demands $5 million for release of businessman

6   Police seek masked man after bank raid

10 | Review

1 Report the telephone conversation.

1 **John:** Liz! It's John. Something amazing is happening here.
John called Liz and told her that something amazing was happening there.

2 **Liz:** Are you all right? Where are you?

_____.

3 **John:** Yes, I'm fine. I'm in the town centre. Be quick. Get here as fast as you can.

_____.

4 **Liz:** Why? What's up?

_____.

5 **John:** You'll never believe it. A guy has just thrown hundreds of bank notes all over the place.

_____.

6 **Liz:** You're joking!

_____.

7 **John:** It's true. People are going crazy trying to pick them up.

_____.

8 **Liz:** I'll be there in about two minutes! Bye!

_____.

2 Choose the correct forms to complete the article.

Raining cash

Lucky shoppers in Aberystwyth couldn't believe their ears and eyes yesterday when a man in the town centre asked (1) *the crowd / to the crowd* who (2) *did want / wanted* 'free money'. He then began to throw handfuls of banknotes into the air. One witness, who asked (3) *not naming / not to be named*, said that the man (4) *had probably thrown / was probably throwing* away between £5,000 and £20,000. Joining in the crowd, the witness admitted (5) *picking / to pick* up £80 himself, but added that some shoppers (6) *are / had been* much luckier than him.
At a press conference later in the day, a police spokesperson explained (7) *that / to* the man (8) *drinking / had drunk* too much and needed medical attention. The spokesperson asked members of the public (9) *if they / to* return the money. Incredibly, most of them did. The town mayor praised the city's shoppers for their honesty.

3 Rearrange the phrases to complete the report.

Confidential: report on John S

John had been working on various projects before being asked to coordinate the

☐ away with his own ideas and this has led to problems in meeting some deadlines.

☐ he needs to develop his skills in certain key areas. Attending more conferences will give

☐ him the chance to extend his professional knowledge. He has a tendency to get carried

☐ members of his team. John has taken pride in his achievements and rightly so, but

☐ Task Force. His new job involves recruiting new agents and setting priorities for the

4 Rearrange the words to complete the sentences.

endanger   for   other   yourself
1 Never _____ people.

about   careful   deceive   not   to   yourself
2 Be _____ your true personality.

a   expressing   of   point   yourself
3 Make _____ clearly.

content   learn   should   to   with   yourself
4 You _____ what you have.

at   distinguish   in   least   one   to   yourself
5 Try _____ area of your life.

are   are   people   remind   that   there   who   yourself
6 Always _____ worse-off than you.

5 Work in pairs. Look at the sentences in exercise 4. Which is the best advice for a parent to give to a teenage child? Why?

6 Complete the sentences with a word from the box.

benefit	call	hand	headache
impression	permission		warning

1 Can you stop that noise? You're giving me a _____.
2 I think we should probably give her the _____ of the doubt.
3 Did anyone give you _____ to do that?
4 He gives the _____ that he really doesn't care.
5 I'm going to give you a _____, but don't do it again, OK?
6 Give me a _____ with the washing-up, will you?
7 Why don't you text me or give me a _____?

11 | Review

1 Complete the text with *the* or *Ø*.

(1) _____ laughter began four million years ago according to (2) _____ evolutionary biologists. (3) _____ new study suggests that (4) _____ laughter evolved at (5) _____ same time as (6) _____ ability to walk. (7) _____ scientists who carried out (8) _____ study claim that (9) _____ first laugh happened when (10) _____ early men and women fell over in their attempts to walk. (11) _____ amused spectators found (12) _____ failed attempts funny in much (13) _____ same way as we laugh at slapstick comedy today. It was two million years later before (14) _____ humans learnt to control (15) _____ muscles of their face and use laughter to communicate (16) _____ other emotions, like (17) _____ embarrassment.

2 Complete the lines with *so* or *such*.

1 holiday. We had ___ a marvellous time there

2 islands really are ___ beautiful at this time of

3 prised to find ___ few tourists who can speak

4 ustomers receive ___ good service. Indeed,

5 at they could be ___ slow. The buses are even

6 thought it was ___ a shame that we couldn't

7 never expected ___ much rain while we were

8 really regretted it. ___ a waste of money! I d

3 Work in pairs. How do you think the lines in exercise 2 continued?

… a marvellous time there that we didn't want to leave

4 Work in pairs. Choose the best answer a–c.

Trivial geography
1 How high are the Iguazu Falls in South America?
(a) 72 metres.   (b) 275 metres.   (c) 2.5 kilometres.
2 How wide is the Panama Canal at its narrowest point?
(a) 3 metres.   (b) 33 metres.   (c) 333 metres.
3 How long is the Malay peninsula?
(a) About 12 kilometres.   (b) About 120 kilometres.
(c) About 1,200 kilometres.
4 Where are the Straits of Magellan?
(a) In the east of China.   (b) In the north of Canada.
(c) In the south of South America.
5 In which ocean is the Bay of Biscay?
(a) The Arctic.   (b) The Atlantic.   (c) The Indian.
6 In which country is Mount Cook?
(a) Australia.   (b) Malta.   (c) New Zealand.
7 Where are the Cape Verde islands?
(a) In the Atlantic Ocean.   (b) In the Gulf of Mexico.
(c) In the Pacific Ocean.
8 Which of the following is an ocean?
(a) The Arctic.   (b) The Caribbean.
(c) The Mediterranean.

9 Put the following places in a line from north to south:
the Baltic Sea, the Seychelles, the Kalahari Desert,
the Amazon, Lake Superior, Tibet, Hawaii.

5 Complete the sentences with words from the box.

black	born	forgive	here	long	short	sick
bred	forget	hard	now	sweet	tired	white

1 I want an explanation _____ and _____!
2 I want it written down here in _____ and _____.
3 I was _____ and _____ in the suburbs.
4 I'd be grateful if you could keep things _____ and _____.
5 I'm happy to _____ and _____ if he does the same.
6 I'm _____ and _____ of hearing about your problems.
7 I've thought about it _____ and _____ and my mind is made up.

12 | Review

1 Put the verbs in brackets into the simple past, active or passive.

The *Mary Rose*, the pride of the English navy, (1) _____ (*sink*) in a battle against the French in 1545. More than four hundred lives (2) _____ (*lose*) and the tragedy (3) _____ (*watch*) from the shore by the king. The king, fat and ill, (4) _____ (*die*) soon afterwards. About four hundred years later, the wreck of the *Mary Rose* (5) _____ (*find*) by divers. After ten years of fundraising, the wreck (6) _____ (*lift*) from the seabed and (7) _____ (*place*) in a museum. The ship's treasures (8) _____ (*include*) many personal possessions of the crew: gambling dice, a complete first-aid kit and clothes that (9) _____ (*wear*) by the sailors. A small number of gold coins (10) _____ (*find*), but the *Mary Rose* was not a treasure ship.

2 Choose the best way to complete the sentences.

1 It is believed *that / to be* some survivors may be living hand-to-mouth in the jungle.
2 The bride's family is rumoured *that / to be* worth a fortune.
3 *He / It* is known that he died without a penny to his name.
4 *It was / She was* thought to be very hard-up, but she lived a secret jetset life.
5 *It's / They're* said they have money to burn.
5 The company is thought *that / to be* in the red.

3 Rearrange the words to make questions.

1 had have often photo taken this year you your
How _____?
2 ever fortune had told you your
Have _____?
3 cut did hair have last you your
When _____?
4 a ever for friend get lie to you you
Would _____?
5 changed have home in like to would you your
What _____?
6 ever got help someone to with work you you your
Have _____?
7 have next passport renewed will you your
When _____?

4 Work in pairs. Ask and answer the questions in exercise 3.

5 Put the phrases in the correct order to make a paragraph.

☐ found on ships with skull-and-crossbones flags. As a
☐ families with young children but mothers and fathers can also find something to enjoy. Pirates are *generally*
☑ Generally speaking, pirate movies do fairly well at the box office. The audience is mostly
☐ *and large*, will buy the DVD when it comes out and enjoy the hokem all over again.
☐ *whole*, the audience knows exactly what will happen, but this doesn't spoil the entertainment. Six months later, all these families, *by*
☐ *rule*, they also have a black patch over one eye. They hunt for treasure and kidnap beautiful girls, but end up at the bottom of the ocean or in the jaws of a crocodile. On the

6 Find the American equivalents of the UK words (in the box) in the word square.

| aubergine | biscuit | bill | football | lift | lorry |
| petrol | tap | taxi | toilet | trousers | waistcoat |

T	S	E	V	E	B	A	C
E	G	G	P	L	A	N	T
C	S	D	A	E	T	K	R
U	O	S	N	V	H	C	U
A	C	A	T	A	R	E	C
F	C	G	S	T	O	H	K
A	E	I	K	O	O	C	V
I	R	N	C	R	M	I	L

7 Complete the phrasal verbs in the newspaper headlines.

1 **Schoolchildren fall _ _ _ scammers' promises**
2 **Travel company rips _ _ _ Scottish tourists**
3 Government hands _ _ _ _ disputed territory
4 Disgraced minister made it all _ _!
5 Angry wife gets her own back _ _ cheating husband
6 **Rap star turned _ _ _ at immigration control**

Macmillan Education
Between Towns Road, Oxford OX4 3PP
A division of Macmillan Publishers Limited
Companies and representatives throughout the world

ISBN: 978-1-4050-1089-4
ISBN: 978-0-230-02080-1 (with CD-ROM)

Designed by Oliver Design

Illustrated by Rowan Barnes Murphy pp 20; Fred Blunt pp 60, 76, 79, 165,167; Jonny Boatfield pp 43, 168, 174; Mark Duffin pp 8, 12, 36, 72, 82, 108, 116, 148; Anna Hymas pp 139, 167; Philip Pepper pp 43, 139, 147, 149
Cover design by Macmillan Publishers Limited

Cover photography by: (from left to right)
Alamy/ Arco Images, Panos Pictures/ Mark Henley, Lonely Planet/ Eric L. Wheater, Science Photo Library/ Damien Lovegrove, Corbis/ Jose Fuste Raga/ Zefa, Dean Ryan 2006, Corbis/ Royalty Free, Alamy/ Arch White, Corbis/ Chris Collins, Photolibrary/ Jon Arnold Images, Corbis/ John-Francis Bourke/ Zefa, Corbis/ Matthias Kulka/ Zefa.

Picture research by Sally Cole.

Authors' acknowledgements
The authors would like to thank: Julie Seddon Jones, Des O'Sullivan, Anne Pontegnie and Neil Ewart of the Royal National Institute for the Blind for their contributions to this book. The authors would also like to thank Nicola Gardner, Andrew Oliver, Jim Scrivener, Celia Bingham, James Richardson, Shona Rodger, Karen White, Sally Cole, Candice Renault, Katie Stephens, Barbara Mercer, Sarah Douglas, Deborah Hughes, Hazel Barrett, Tim Bowen, Tamas Lorincz, Peter Bendall, Nick Sheard and Rafael Alarcon-Gaeta for all their hard work. Grateful thanks are also extended to the Macmillan staff around the world, too numerous to name, who have so warmly looked after us on our visits.

The authors and publishers would like to thank the following people for their help and contribution to the course:
Carolina Mussons, Mari-Carmen Lafuente, Eliseo Picó Mas, Carmen Roig-Papiol and Lourdes Montoro, EOI Sta Coloma de Gramanet, Barcelona. Maggie Hawes, Tony Isaac, Tom Radman and Anita Roberts, British Council, Barcelona. Rosie Dickson and Sarah Hartley, Merit School, Barcelona. Christina Anastasiadis, Andrew Graydon, Steven McGuire, Alan Hammans, Heather Shortland and Roger Edwards, International House Zurbano, Madrid. Guy Heath, British Council, Madrid. Ramón Silles, EOI Majadahonda. Javier Martinez Maestro, EOI Parla. Rosa Melgar, EOI Valdezarza. Susana Galan, The English Centre, Madrid. Yolanda Scott-Tennent Basallote, EOI Tarragona. Marzenna Raczkowska. Yaffite Mor, Alicja Fialek and Ricky Krzyzewski, UEC-Bell School of English, Warsaw. Steve Allen, Joanna Zymelka, Marek Kazmierski, Przemek Skrzyniarz, Colin Hinde, Mireille Szepaniak, Gabriela Pawlikowska and Simon Over, English First, Warsaw. Fiona Harrison-Rees, British Council, Warsaw. Karina Davies and Katarzyna Wywial, Szkola Jezykow Obcych 'Bakalarz', Warsaw. Peter Moran and Joanna Trojanowska, International House, Krakow. Walter Nowlan, British Council, Krakow. Agnieszka Bieniek, Anna Galus, Malgorzata Paprota and Joanna Berej, U Metodystow, Lublin. Mr Paudyna, Alicja Grajek, Eliza Trojanowska and Monika Bochyn'ska, Studium Jezykow Obcych, Minsk Mazowiecki. Paola Randali. Paola Povesi. Roberta Giugni. Mirella Fantin. Rossella Salmoiraghi. Marco Nervegna and Rebecca Kirby, Linguaviva, Milan. Peter Sheekey, Oxford Group, Milan. Irina Kuznetsova, Elena Ivanova, Olga Kekshoeva and Yulia Mukoseeva, Tom's House, Moscow. Asya Zakirova, Tatyana Tsukanova, Natalia Brynzynyuk, Anna Karazhas, Anastasia Karazhas and Nadya Shishkina, Mr English Club, Moscow. Inna Turchin, English First Zhulebino, Moscow. Tatiana Shepelenko, Ljuba Sicheva and Tatiana Brjushkova, Higher School of Economics, Moscow.
Amanda Jeffries, David Willis, Susan Hutchison, Kirsten Holt, Kate Pickering, Cathy Poole, Jenny Roden, Michael West, Howard Smith, Clare Dunlop, Clare Waring and Andrew Mitchell, Oxford House, London. Garth Cadden, Lefteris Panteli and Vicky McWilliam, St Giles College, London. Sarah James, Sarah Lurie, Karen Mathewman, Katherine Griggs, Chris Wroth, Olivia Smith, Sue Clark, Alan Greenslade-Hibbert, King's School of English, Oxford.
Sara Fiorini, CEFETI Centro de Linguas, São Paulo. Neide Silva and Maria Helena Iema, Cultura Inglesa Pinheiros, São Paulo. José Olavo de Amorim and Amini Rassoul, Colégio Bandeirantes, São Paulo. Maria Antonieta and Sabrina Teixeira, Centro Britânico, Perdizes, São Paulo. Loreliz Kessler, Unilínguas, São Leopoldo. Marli Zim, Acele, Porto Alegre. Luciane Duarte Calcara, Britannia, Porto Alegre. Magali Mente, Lingua Lindóia, Porto Alegre. Maria Higina, Cultura Inglesa Savassi, Belo Horizonte. Eliane Peixoto, Green System, Belo Horizonte. Adriana Bozzolla Vieira, Britain English School, Belo Horizonte. Roberto Amorin, ICBEU Centro, Belo Horizonte. Patrícia Brasileiro, Cultura Inglesa Casa Forte, Recife. Eleonor Benício, British Council, Recife. Roseli Serra, Cultura Inglesa Madalena, Recife. Alberto Costa, Cultura Inglesa Olinda, Recife. Glória Luchsinger, English Learning Centre, Recife. Angela Pougy

Azevedo and Márcia Porenstein Toy Centro, Rio de Janeiro. Julian Wing, British Council, Rio de Janeiro. Karla Koppe, Colegio Tereziano, Rio de Janeiro. Márcia Martins. Ricardo Sili and Janine Barbosa, Cultura Inglesa, Rio de Janeiro.
Ágnes Tisza, Ring Nyelvstúdió, Budapest. Katalin Nemeth and Edina Varga, Novoschool, Budapest. Szilvia Hegyi, Mack Alasdair, Eva Lukacsi and Katalin Jonas-Horvath, Babilon Language Studio, Budapest. Nikolett Pozsgai, Európai Nyelvek Stúdiója, Budapest. Krisztina Csiba and Anett Godó, Oxford Hungária Nyelviskola, Budapest. Zsuzsanna Tóth and Szilvia Fülöp, H-Net, Budapest. Judit Csepela, TIT Globe, Budapest. Judit Volner and Rita Erdos, Dover Nyelvi Centrum, Budapest. Ildikó Tóth and Piroska Sugár, Katedra, Budapest. Katalin Terescsik Szieglné and Magdolna Zivnovszki, London Stúdió, Budapest. Agota Kiss and Gabriella Varga, KOTK, Budapest. Rita Lendvai and Judit Szarka, Atalanta, Budapest. Péter Gelléri, Tudomány Nyelviskola, Budapest.

The authors and publishers would like to thank the following for permission to reproduce their material:
Extract from The Guinness Book Of Oddities by Geoff Tibballs (Guinness Publishing, 1995), copyright © Geoff Tibballs 1995, reprinted by permission of the author.
Extract from Macmillan English Dictionary for Advanced Learners (Macmillan Publishers Limited, 2002), Text copyright © Bloomsbury Publishing Plc 2002, reprinted by permission of the publisher.
Extract from 'Imagined Ugly Syndrome' first published in Heat Magazine 14.04.01.
Extract from Girl with a Pearl Earring by Tracy Chevalier (HarperCollins, 1999), copyright © Tracy Chevalier 1999, reprinted by permission of the publisher and Curtis Brown Ltd for audio rights.
Extract from 'Notebook' by Sam Leith taken from Opinion Telegraph 16.05.05, reprinted by permission of the publisher.
Extract from 'How to Have a Heavy Cold' taken from Never Hit a Jelly Fish with a Spade by Guy Browning (Atlantic Books, on behalf of Guardian Newspapers Ltd, 2004), copyright © Guy Browning 2004, reprinted by permission of the author.
Extract from The Year China Discovered the World by Gavin Menzies (Bantam Press, 2002), reprinted by permission of The Random House Group Ltd.
Extract from The Usborne Book of Treasure Hunting by Anna Claybourne and Caroline Young (Usborne Publishing Ltd, 83-85 Saffron Hill, London, EC1N 8RT, 1998), copyright © Usborne Publishing Limited 1998, reprinted by permission of the publishers (www.usborne.com).

Although we have tried to trace and contact copyright holders before publication, in some cases this has not been possible. If contacted we will be pleased to rectify any errors or omissions at the earliest opportunity.

The authors and publishers would like to thank the following for permission to reproduce their photographs: 1421/M.Boss p107(t); AKG Images pp50, 107(b); Alamy/A.White p6(b), National Motor Museum p9, Popperfoto pp11, 27(D), Arco Images p12, C.Magnon p18(b), D.Hoffman p19, D.Crausby p29, Pictorial Press p48-49, A.Copson p67(mb), Picturesby Rob p67(mt), R.Gleed p67(t), P.Horree p67 (tm), R.Harding p68(b), image100 RF p98, F.Kletschkus p100, J. Kase p112(br), S.Lancaster p123, W.Bibikow p128(b), C.Ballentine p132(l); Axiom/I.Cumming p136; Cartoonstock pp7, 63, 92,103, 143,169,171; Comstock/ Royalty-Free p126Courier Newspapers p88(r); Corbis pp27(goth), 52, 166(l), 166(r), 168(b), J.Rinaldi p6(a),A.Fox p23, N.Wier p138, C.Collins p140(b), H.Diltz p27(E),J.Arbogast p27(A), J.Bourke p27(B), Corbis W.Grubitzsch p26, F.Trapper p31, C.Rehder p30(t), O.Graf p33, Bettman Archive p41(l), Reuters pp52(t), 73(r),140(t), R.Galbraith p57, A.Wiegmann p58, T.Graham p140(m), D.Ramazani p70, J.Feingersh p71, S.Wenig p87(b), C.Pringle p96(r), J.Springer Collection p97, T.Page p99, R.Landau p113, J.Raga p116(tr), New Line Cinema p118, B.McDermid p134(b); Focus New Zealand Picture Library p59; H. Dixon p38; Getty Images/D. Greedy p6(c), S.Murphy p6(d), D.Teuma p10(b), J.Rotman p14, D. Bennett p30(b), F.Calfat p32, Hulton Archive pp39, 47, 56(t), J.Fishkin p48, Time & Life Pictures p56(b), B.Willis p62, O.Mazzatenta p81(br), S. Potter p81(l), B.Gotfryd p89, A.Thornton p93, S.Sin/AFP p96(bl), J.Robbins p101, DCA Productions p102, J. Lawrence pp112(l), 112(r), DAJ p112(m), S. Marks p119, A. Walker p132(m), B.Simmons p132(r), R. Clare p137; Kobal/Universal/B.Jasin p90(b); Lonely Planet/E.Wheater p111(ml), M. Daffey p111(l), R.L'Anson p111(mr), S.Victor p111(r); NIH Government p96(tl); Panos Pictures/M.Henley p128(tl), J.Horner p128(tr); Photolibrary/J.Arnold p128(tm); Reuters/J.Rinaldi p42(l), 42(r), S.Hird p53; Rex Features pp27(G), 61(b), K.Schoendorfer p12, A.Pietrangeli p27(F), Everett Collection p41(r), Sipa Press p46, R.Austin p61(t); Ronald Grant Archive/Pathe Pictures pp51, 130, Eon p90(t), New Line Cinema p90(m), Morgan Creek Productions p91(t), Warner Bros p91(b), British Lion Film Corporation/TNT (Turner Network Television), Columbia Pictures/Universal Pictures/Revolution Studios ; Sally & Richard Greenhill p27(c); Science Photo Library/D.Lovegrove p81(tr); Still Pictures/J.Boethling p67(m), P. Hays p67(b); The Granger Collection p40; Topfoto pp10(tr), 13(b), PA p 22, R.Viollet p10(tl), C.Walker p80; J.Zuber p134(l); The Bridgeman Art Library/ Self Portrait with Bandaged Ear, 1889, Gogh, Vincent van (1853-90) / © Samuel Courtauld Trust, Courtauld Institute of Art Gallery, Page 49(br), Glass of Wine, Watermelon and Bread (oil on canvas), Melendez, Luis Egidio (1716-80) / Prado, Madrid, Spain, Giraudon p168(t).
P49(tl) Hanging Spirit by Stephen Knapp reproduced with kind permission of Stephen Knapp.

Commissioned photography by: Rob Judges p98, Dean Ryan pp 12, 28, 145, 147.

Printed in Thailand

2013 2012 2011 2010 2009
9 8 7 6 5